Rabbi Abraham Ibn Ezra's

Commentary On The Book of Psalms

The Reference Library of Jewish Intellectual History

Abraham Ibn Ezra's

COMMENTARY

On The Second Book of Psalms:

CHAPTER 42-72

Translated and Annotated by
H. Norman Strickman

Boston
2009

Library of Congress Cataloging-in-Publication Data
Ibn Ezra, Abraham ben Meïr, 1092-1167.
Rabbi Abraham Ibn Ezra's commentary on the first two books of Psalms / translated and annotated by H. Norman Strickman.
p. cm. -- (The reference library of Jewish intellectual history)
Includes bibliographical references and index.
ISBN 978-1-934843-31-4
1. Bible. O.T. Psalms--Commentaries--Early works to 1800. I. Strickman, H. Norman, 1940- II. Title.

BS1429.I24 2009
223'.2077--dc22

2009008078

Book design by Olga Grabovsky

Published by Academic Studies Press in 2009

28 Montfern Avenue
Brighton, MA 02135, USA
press@academicstudiespress.com
www.academicstudiespress.com

CONTENTS

BOOK 2

CHAPTER 42

1. FOR THE LEADER; MASCHIL OF THE SONS OF KORAH.

FOR THE LEADER... OF THE SONS OF KORAH. *Of the sons of Korah* refers to one of the sons of Heman the grandson of Samuel the prophet.[1]

Rabbi Moses says that this psalm was composed in Babylonia.[2] Others say that it speaks on behalf of the people of this exile.[3]

The word *maskil* (maschil) is lacking the object.[4] Others say that *maskil* is a noun. It is like the word *mashchit* (into corruption)[5] in *for my comeliness was turned in me into corruption* (Dan. 10:8). However, in my opinion the reference[6] is to a poem beginning with the word *maskil*.[7]

1. The prophet Samuel was descended from Korah. See 1 Chron. 6:1-18.

2. For it speaks of the exile. See I.E.'s introduction to psalms.

3. The reference is to the Babylonian exile.

4. Reading *pa'ul* rather then *kaful*. See Filwarg and *Ha- Keter.* According to this interpretation the word *maskil* is a verb. This explanation renders our verse: "For the leader; A psalm which enlightens [people], of the sons of Korah."

5. *Mashchit* looks like a verb but is in reality a noun. According to this interpretation, our verse reads: For the leader; A psalm of enlightenment of the sons of Korah.

6. The meaning of *maschil.*

7. See I.E. on Ps. 4:1. According to this interpretation, our verse reads: For the leader; to be chanted according to the tune of a poem beginning with the word *maschil.*

2. AS THE HART PANTETH AFTER THE WATER BROOKS, SO PANTETH MY SOUL AFTER THEE, O GOD.

THE HART. It is a known fact that the hart eats snakes and its innards grow hot. The hart then seeks brooks of mighty water.[8] *Ayyal* (hart) is employed as a feminine.[9] It is similar to *ez*[10] (she-goat) in *a she goat of the first year* (bat shenatah)[11] (Num. 15:27).

3. MY SOUL THIRSTETH FOR GOD, FOR THE LIVING GOD: WHEN SHALL I COME AND APPEAR BEFORE GOD?

THIRSTETH. Water satiates a person in a moment. He lives and his soul is revived. Not so bread.[12] The psalmist therefore compares his longing for God's house to a thirsty person's longing for water. He compares his desire for the living God to his desire for water, because human life is dependent on water.

WHEN SHALL I COME? He[13] desires the coming of the redeemer.[14]

AND APPEAR BEFORE GOD. The reference is to [*Three times in the year] all thy males shall appear before the Lord God* (Ex. 23:17).[15]

4. MY TEARS HAVE BEEN MY FOOD DAY AND NIGHT, WHILE THEY SAY UNTO ME ALL THE DAY: WHERE IS THY GOD?

HAVE BEEN. Some say that he[16] is thirsty. His tears which consist of water have been like bread to him.[17] The tears are a result of the length of the exile. He no longer goes up

8 I.E.'s rendition of *afike mayim.* Pools formed by gushing water, that is, pools of cold water.

9. Even though its form is that of a masculine. Our verse reads: *ke-ayyal ta'arog* (as the hart panteth). *Ta'arog* is a feminine. Hence I.E.'s comment.

10. *Ez* is a masculine form.

11. *Bat shenatah* is a feminine.

12. It takes a while for bread to satisfy hunger.

13. The exiled Israelite.

14 The messiah.

15 In other words, the reference is to the pilgrimages to Jerusalem.

16. The exiled Israelite.

17. The Psalmist, when thirsty, drinks his tears as a hungry person eats bread.

on pilgrimage[18] to rejoice. [19] Others say that the psalmist cries and sheds tears as [often as] he eats.[20, 21]

DAY AND NIGHT. Constantly. In private and in public.[22]
Where is thy God means, where is the God to whom you made three pilgrimages a year to see His face? [23]

5. THESE THINGS I REMEMBER, AND POUR OUT MY SOUL WITHIN ME, HOW I PASSED ON WITH THE THRONG, AND LED THEM TO THE HOUSE OF GOD, WITH THE VOICE OF JOY AND PRAISE, A MULTITUDE KEEPING HOLYDAY.

THESE THINGS. He[24] remembers the former days when he went up to the temple on the festivals.
Ba-sakh [25](with the throng) is similar in meaning to *mosakh* (covering) [26] in *mosakh ha-shabbat* (the covered place for the Sabbath) (2 Kings 16:18). The "covering" was located on the temple mount (2 Kings 16:18). Others say that the word *ba-sakh* means with all the celebrants. Compare the phrase *sakh cheshbon* (sum of the numbers). [27]
Ben Labrat[28] says that the *dalet* in *eddaddem* (and led them) is doubled. He maintains that *eddaddem* is a variant of *eddom*[29] (I will be silent) (Job 31:34).[30] O that Ben Labrat would

18. To rejoice.

19. In the house of God. The exile prevents the Israelite from making his pilgrimage to the temple and enjoying himself there. See Deut. 12:18.

20. People in Biblical times used to eat two meals a day, one in the morning and one in the evening. *My tears have been my food day and night* means, I cried as often as I ate. I cried daily. See Radak.

21. Before the Lord.

22. Day means in public. Night means in private. This is a second interpretation.

23. See Deut. 16:16.

24. The exiled Israelite.

25. From the root *samekh, kaf, kaf.*

26. According to this interpretation our verse reads: These things I remember, and pour out my soul within me, how I passed under the covering which was on the Temple Mount.

27. According to this interpretation the word, *sakh* means the sum, the totality. *Ba-sakh* means with the sum of the celebrants, that is, with all of the celebrants. See Rashi.

28. Dunash Ha-Levi ben Labrat (920-990). A noted Bible commentator, poet, and grammarian.

29. Spelled *alef, dalet, mem.*

30. From the root *dalet, mem, mem.* According to this interpretation our clause reads: These things I remember, and pour out my soul within me, how I was silent (till I came) to the house of God

be silent (yiddom), for the first root letter is never doubled.[31] [Furthermore,] what reason is there for Scripture to say, I was silent...and then say, *with the voice of joy and praise*? It appears to me that *eddaddem* (I led them) is a *mishnaic* term.[32] Its meaning is, I will move.[33] Scripture, as it were, says I moved with them to the house of God. It is like *eddaddeh* (I shall go softly) in I *shall go softly all my years* (Is. 38:15). *Eddaddem* is in the *nifal*.[34] It is like *va-yillachamuni*[35] (and fought against me) in, *And fought against me without a cause* (Ps. 109:3).

6. WHY ART THOU CAST DOWN, O MY SOUL? AND WHY MOANEST THOU WITHIN ME? HOPE THOU IN GOD; FOR I SHALL YET PRAISE HIM FOR THE SALVATION OF HIS COUNTENANCE.

WHY ? The Psalmist consoles himself.

Yeshu'ot panav (the salvation of his countenance) is similar in meaning to the clause: *His right hand...hath wrought salvation for Him* (Ps. 98:1).[36] It is a metaphor.[37] On the other hand *yeshu'ot* (salvation) might be passive. *Panav* (His face) should be rendered with His face. *Yeshu'ot panav* is similar[38] to *pene Adonai* (the face of the Lord) in *the face of the Lord*[39] *hath divided them* (Lam. 4:16). The word *im* or *et* is missing.[40]

7. O MY GOD, MY SOUL IS CAST DOWN WITHIN ME; THEREFORE DO I REMEMBER THEE FROM THE LAND OF JORDAN, AND THE HEREMONS, FROM THE HILL MIZAR.

31. *Eddaddem* is spelled with two *dalets.*

32. From the root *dalet, dalet, heh.* Compare *ve-ha'ishah medaddah et benah* (Sabbath 18b). By *mishnaic term* Ibn Ezra means, is similar to a *mishnaic* term, for the *Mishnah* was not was not in existence in Biblical times.

33. Or walk.

34. It is in reality a *hitpa'el* with the *tav* missing. If not an oversight then I.E. must mean that *eddaddem* is intransitive. I.E.'s point is that is that *eddaddem* is irregular in that it has an objective pronominal suffix. Intransitive verbs do not usually come with objective pronominal suffixes. Hence I.E.'s comment. Filwarg.

35. A *nifal* with an objective pronominal suffix. It too is an intransitive passive with an objective pronominal suffix.

36. *Yeshu'ot panav* (the salvation of his countenance) means, the salvation which his countenance has wrought for Him.

37. God has no countenance.

38. In that Scripture speaks of God's face as being a source of help.

39. Translated literally.

40. According to this interpretation, *Yeshu'ot panav* is to be read as if written, *yeshu'ot im panav* or *yeshu'ot et panav* (salvation is with His face).

O MY GOD. This (verse) is the answer to:[41] *Why are you cast down, O My soul:* (v. 6).[42] Scripture reads, *from the land of Jordan* because pilgrims used to come [to Jerusalem] from the eastern side of the Jordan to celebrate the festivals.
The *Hermons* are mountains.[43] *Mizar,* too is the name of a mountain.

8. DEEP CALLETH UNTO DEEP AT THE VOICE OF THY CATARACTS; ALL THY WAVES AND THY BILLOWS ARE GONE OVER ME.

DEEP. Our verse is to be interpreted in keeping with the meaning of our chapter.[44] The exiled Israelite[45] recalls the cataracts. He notes that the water flowed down from the high mountains. *Deep calleth unto deep* means; the waters of the cataracts were joined down below. *Deep calleth unto deep* is similar to *And the satyr shall cry to his fellow* (Is. 34:14).[46] Our verse indicates that the exiled Israelite [47] took pleasure when he passed by the mountains [in the Land of Israel]. The waters came down like the billows and waves of the ocean and covered him in the summer. One who explains the verse as referring to the exile errs,[48] for then the verse is not tied to what comes before or what follows.

9. BY DAY THE LORD WILL COMMAND HIS LOVINGKINDNESS, AND IN THE NIGHT HIS SONG SHALL BE WITH ME, EVEN A PRAYER UNTO THE GOD OF MY LIFE.

BY DAY. The exiled Israelite[49] speaks of his, thanks to God's loving kindness, walking with the celebrants during the day in security. At night they would sing like a band of prophets.[50] He notes that the songs were songs of prayer and not love songs.

41. So *Ha-keter.*

42. The psalmist's soul is cast down because he recalls the land of Israel.

43. The mountains forming the Hermon Mountain range.

44. Our verse is to be taken literally and not metaphorically. The psalmist speaks of the exiles recalling the Land of Israel. I.E. comments thus, because he later quotes an opinion that interprets this verse metaphorically.

45. Literally, he.

46. The meaning of *And the satyr shall cry to his fellow* is, each satyr calls to the other satyr to join it. Similarly, *Deep calleth unto deep* means, one pool of water calls to the other to join it.

47. Literally, he.

48. Rashi does. Rashi explains the verse as referring to the troubles experienced in exile. He interprets *Deep calleth unto deep* as follows: One trouble calls to another.

49. Literally, he.

50. 1 Sam.10:5.

UNTO THE GOD OF MY LIFE. The God who will keep the exiled Israelite alive, so that he will see the house of God.

10. I WILL SAY UNTO GOD MY ROCK: WHY HAST THOU FORGOTTEN ME? WHY GO I MOURNING UNDER THE OPPRESSION OF THE ENEMY?

I WILL SAY. The meaning of *God my Rock* is, God who was my rock in the olden days.

WHY HAST THOU FORGOTTEN ME? This was said because of the length of the exile.

WHY GO I MOURNING? [51] Like a mourner who dresses in black.

11. AS WITH A CRUSHING IN MY BONES,[52] MINE ADVERSARIES TAUNT ME; WHILE THEY SAY UNTO ME ALL THE DAY: WHERE IS THY GOD.

AS WITH A CRUSHING IN MY BONES. My bones feel crushed[53] when they say to me "where is thy God?"[54] This is the way I react[55] to this taunt.

12. WHY ART THOU CAST DOWN, O MY SOUL? AND WHY MOANEST THOU WITHIN ME? HOPE THOU IN GOD; FOR I SHALL YET PRAISE HIM, THE SALVATION OF MY COUNTENANCE, AND MY GOD.

WHY… The meaning of *the salvation of my countenance [and my God]* is, for He is the salvation of my countenance and He is *my God* from the days of old. *My God is* in response to *where is thy God*? (v. 11).

51. Literally, why go I in black? Hence I.E.'s comment.

52. Lit. With a murder in my bones.

53. Lit. There is as it were a crushing in my bones.

54. I feel that they are killing me when they to me, "Where is your God?"

55. Lit. I think.

CHAPTER 43.

1. BE THOU MY JUDGE, O GOD, AND PLEAD MY CAUSE AGAINST AN UNGODLY NATION; O DELIVER ME FROM THE DECEITFUL AND UNJUST MAN.

BE THOU MY JUDGE. Exact judgment on my behalf from those who curse me.[1] The latter are many. Scripture therefore reads *against an ungodly nation.*
The import of *an ungodly* is, because I am better then they.
Scripture reads *from... man* [because the psalmist asks God to deliver him] from the many [who are wicked][2] and from the individual [who is evil].[3] The *unjust man* may also allude to the one who is king over the [ungodly] nation.

2. FOR THOU ART THE GOD OF MY STRENGTH; WHY HAST THOU CAST ME OFF? WHY GO I MOURNING UNDER THE OPPRESSION OF THE ENEMY?

FOR THOU ART. *The God of my strength* means, I have no strength to exact judgment from the enemy. I rely on upon You.

3. O SEND OUT THY LIGHT AND THY TRUTH; LET THEM LEAD ME; LET THEM BRING ME UNTO THY HOLY MOUNTAIN, AND TO THY DWELLING-PLACES.

O SEND OUT THY LIGHT. *O send out Thy light* is in contrast to *go I mourning* (v. 2).[4]

1. Punish those who curse me.

2. *An ungodly nation.*

3. *The deceitful and unjust man.*

4. The word *koder* (mourning) means black. I.E. renders the last clause of verse 2: "Why go I in darkness under the oppression of the enemy."

AND THY TRUTH. *And Thy truth* is in contrast to *the deceitful...man* (v. 1). *Lead me* is in contrast to *go I* (v. 2).

THY HOLY MOUNTAIN. Mt. Moriah. *Thy dwelling places* refers to the courtyards that will be built when the third temple is erected.

4. THEN WILL I GO UNTO THE ALTAR OF GOD, UNTO GOD, MY EXCEEDING JOY; AND PRAISE THEE UPON THE HARP, O GOD, MY GOD.

THEN WILL I GO UNTO THE ALTAR OF GOD, UNTO GOD. Who is my exceeding joy.
O God, my God implies,[5] let the ungodly nation see that you are my God.

5. WHY ARE THOU CAST DOWN, O MY SOUL? AND WHY MOANEST THOU WITHIN ME? HOPE THOU IN GOD; FOR I SHALL YET PRAISE HIM, THE SALVATION OF MY COUNTENANCE AND MY GOD.

WHY. The Psalmist said that Israel should hope in God.[6] He uttered the latter while under Divine inspiration.[7]

5. Literally, means.

6. And that Israel will yet praise him for being their salvation. The psalmist prophesied that God would hearken to Israel and redeem them.

7. For the psalmist prophesied: *I shall yet praise him.*

CHAPTER 44.

1. FOR THE LEADER; [A PSALM] OF THE SONS OF KORAH. MASCHIL.

2. O GOD, WE HAVE HEARD WITH OUR EARS, OUR FATHERS HAVE TOLD US; A WORK THOU DIDST IN THEIR DAYS, IN THE DAYS OF OLD.

O GOD, WE HAVE HEARD WITH OUR EARS, OUR FATHERS HAVE TOLD US. Those who told us [what you did in the past] were our fathers. They were righteous [men]. They are faithful witnesses.[1] Another meaning for *our fathers* [*told us*] is, every father loves his son and he will always teach him only the truth.[2]

3. THOU WITH THY HAND DIDST DRIVE OUT THE NATIONS, AND DIDST PLANT THEM IN; THOU DIDST BREAK THE PEOPLES, AND DIDST SPREAD THEM ABROAD.

THOU. I have already noted[3] that it is customary for the Hebrews to omit a *bet*.[4] Compare, *I have found...in the house of the Lord* (bet Adonai) (11 Kings 22:8).[5] *Attah yadekhah* (Thou Thy hand) should be interpreted as if written, *attah be-yadekhah* (Thou with Thy

1. Hence we believe what they told us.

2. A father will only transmit the truth to his son.

3. See I.E. on Ps. 3:8.

4. A *bet* prefix, an inseparable preposition.

5. *Bet Adonai* (house of the Lord) should be read as if written *be-vet Adonai*. The problem is that our texts of 11 Kings 22:8 have *be-vet Adonai*. I.E. either had a different reading of 11 Kings 22:8 or he erred in quoting the text. He possibly had 11 Kings 12:11 in mind. The latter reads *bet Adonai* rather than *be-vet Adonai*. See I.E. on Ps. 3:8 and the notes thereto.

hand).[6] The meaning of *Thou with Thy hand* is You with your power, or You with Your blow.[7]

The *mem*[8] of the word *va-tita'em* (and didst plant them) refers back to *our fathers* (v. 2).[9] The *lamed* of *le-ummim* (peoples) is a preposition.[10] Compare the word *ummim* (peoples) in *Laud Him, all the peoples* (*ha-ummim*) (Ps.117: 1).[11] The *mem* of *va-teshal-lechem* (and didst spread them abroad)[12] refers to the peoples. *Va-teshallechem* means, You expelled them. [13]

4. FOR NOT BY THEIR OWN SWORD DID THEY GET THE LAND IN POSSESSION, NEITHER DID THEIR OWN ARM SAVE THEM; BUT THY RIGHT HAND, AND THINE ARM, AND THE LIGHT OF THY COUNTENANCE, BECAUSE THOU WAST FAVORABLE UNTO THEM.

FOR NOT BY THEIR OWN SWORD. The *mem*[14] of *ve-charbam* (by their own sword) refers back to *our fathers* (v. 2).[15]

BUT THEY RIGHT HAND, AND THINE ARM, AND THE LIGHT OF THY COUNTENANCE, BECAUSE THOU WAST FAVORABLE UNTO THEM. This alone saved them.

---

6. Our verse literally reads: "Thou Thy hand didst drive out the nations." Hence I.E.' comment.

7. I.E. comments thus to avoid any anthropomorphism.

8. The *mem* suffixed to a verb is a pronoun meaning "them."

9. In other words the term *them* in *and didst plant them* refers to our fathers.

10. I.E. renders *le-ummim.* To the nations. He renders *tara le-ummim* (Thou didst break the peoples): You brought evil upon the nations.

11. We thus see that the word *ummim* means, nations. There is a similar word for nations viz. *le'ummim.* Hence I.E.'s comment. See I.E. on verse 15.

12. In contrast to the *mem* of *va-titta'em* .

13. *Va-teshallechem* lit. means, and you sent them away. The latter can also have a positive connotation, that is, it may mean, and you accompanied them. See I.E. on Gen. 24:59. Hence I.E.'s comment. I.E. renders our verse: You with Your hand drove out the nations; You planted our fathers [in their place]; You did evil to the peoples, and sent them away, that is, You expelled them from the land.

14. Which is a pronominal suffix meaning their.

15. *Their* refers to the fathers.

5. THOU ART MY KING, O GOD; COMMAND THE SALVATION OF JACOB.

THOU. The poet speaks on behalf of Israel. He mentions Jacob in his psalm [because Jacob prayed:] *the angel who hath redeemed me from evil* (Gen. 48:16).[16]

6. THROUGH THEE DO WE PUSH DOWN OUR ADVERSARIES; THROUGH THY NAME DO WE TREAD THEM UNDER THAT RISE UP AGAINST US.

THROUGH THEE. With Your help we are able to push down our adversaries so that they do no harm to us. Furthermore, through your name we tread them down.

7. I TRUST NOT IN MY BOW, NEITHER CAN MY SWORD SAVE ME.

FOR. *For I trust not in my bow* are the words of an archer,[17] one of the [18] masses.[19] [*Neither can*] *my sword [save me]* was said by one of the warriors.[20] Our verse is therefore in the singular.[21]

8. BUT THOU HAST SAVED US FROM OUR ADVERSARIES, AND HAST PUT THEM TO SHAME THAT HATE US.

BUT. We have also seen that You save us from our enemies. This has verified what our fathers told us.[22]

---

16. *Command the salvation of Jacob* means, command the angel, who redeemed our father Jacob from all evil, to redeem us.

17. Lit. One who treads the bow.

18. Lit., our masses.

19. In medieval armies commoners served as bowmen and the nobility carried swords. I.E. assumes that the same was the case in the armies of Israel.

20. Lit. A warrior among us.

21. The psalmist quoted an archer and a warrior.

22. See verse2.

9. IN GOD HAVE WE GLORIFIED ALL THE DAY, AND WE WILL GIVE THANKS UNTO THY NAME FOREVER. SELAH.

IN GOD HAVE WE GLORIFIED ALL THE DAY. We will compose psalms. The meaning of *In God have we glorified all the day* is, we praised ourselves[23] by saying that You are our king.

10. YET THOU HAST CAST OFF,[24] AND BROUGHT US TO CONFUSION; AND GOEST NOT FORTH WITH OUR HOSTS.

YET. The Jerusalemite[25] says that a *bet* has been omitted from the word *af* (yet).[26] Our verse should read *be-af zanachta*[27] (You have cast us off in anger).[28] However, his interpretation is incorrect, for if he was right, then the word *af* would not be joined to *zanachta.*[29] Compare, *af Adonai* (the anger of the Lord) (Ex. 4:14).[30] If the Jerusalemite was correct[31] then the *alef* would be vocalized with a *kametz.*[32] On the contrary *af-zanachta* (yet Thou hast cast us off) is similar to *gam bi-sechok* (even in laughter) (Prov. 14:13).[33]
[The psalmist complains:] You saved us in the earlier days and you put our enemies to shame (v. 8). However, now not only do you not save us, but You have also cast us off.[34]

AND BROUGHT US TO CONFUSION. In contrast to[35] *and hast put them to shame* [*that hate us* v. 8].

---

23. The object of *glorified* is missing. I.E. assumes that the object is "ourselves."

24. Hebrew, *af- zanachta.*

25. The reference is possibly to Chayyim al- Makamas. So *Ha-Keter.*

26. The word *af* can mean yet, also, or anger. I.E. believes that the latter is its meaning here. Hence His comment.

27. Our verse reads: *af - zanachta.*

28. Rather than *Yet Thou has cast us off.*

29. By a hyphen. It would read: *af zanachta*, rather than *af- zanachta.*

30. Wherein *af* is not joined to *Adonai* by a hyphen.

31. That *af* is short for *be-af.*

32. To indicate that the word *af* means anger. This comment present a problem. When the word *af* means anger it is always vocalized with a *pattach* unless it comes at the end of a verse or at an *etnachta*. This is not the case here. See Fillwarg.

33. *Gam* means also. So too *af.*

34. In other words the meaning of *af* (yet) is also, even.

35. In contrast to the days of old when You *put to shame* them *that hate us.*

11. THOU MAKEST US TO TURN BACK FROM THE ADVERSARY; AND THEY THAT HATE US SPOIL AT THEIR WILL.

THOU MAKEST US TO TURN BACK. Not only do You not help us but[36] you make us turn back, that is, you put fear into our hearts so that we flee [from before our enemies].

AND THEY THAT HATE US SPOIL AT THEIR WILL. The word *lamo* (at their will) means, for themselves.[37] They take for themselves spoil from our money.

12. THOU HAST GIVEN US LIKE SHEEP TO BE EATEN; AND HAST SCATTERED US AMONG THE NATIONS.

THOU HAST GIVEN US. Some of us were killed.[38] Some of us have escaped and are scattered among the nations.

13. THOU SELLEST THY PEOPLE FOR SMALL GAIN, AND HAST NOT SET THEIR PRICES HIGH.

THOU SELLEST. Some of us were sold into servitude for very little gain, or were given away for free.

AND HAST NOT SET THEIR PRICES HIGH. Scripture repeats itself.[39]

14. THOU MAKEST US A TAUNT TO OUR NEIGHBORS, A SCORN AND DERISION TO THEM THAT ARE ROUND ABOUT.

THOU MAKEST US. Our remnants are an object of taunt to those who recognized us when we were in our country.

15. THOU MAKEST US A BYWORD AMONG THE NATIONS, A SHAKING OF THE HEAD AMONG THE PEOPLES.

THOU MAKEST US A BYWORD AMONG THE NATIONS. Who are far from the land of Israel.

---

36. Reading *rak. Ha-Keter.* The printed texts read *she-lo*. This is an error. The texts should read *ela*.

37. I.E. renders our clause: And they that hate us take for themselves.

38. I.E.'s interpretation of the first part of our verse.

39. The second part of the verse repeats the ideas expressed in the first part.

A SHAKING OF THE HEAD AMONG THE PEOPLES. A *shaking of the head* is parallel to *They...wag their head* (Lam. 2:15). The *lamed* in *le'ummim* (nations) is a root letter.[40] Compare *u-le'om mi-le'om ye'ematz* (and the one people shall be stronger than the other people) (Gen. 25:23).

16. ALL THE DAY IS MY CONFUSION BEFORE ME, AND THE SHAME OF MY FACE HATH COVERED ME.

ALL THE DAY. Even if one Jew lives among the nations, they taunt him.[41]

17. FOR THE VOICE OF HIM THAT TAUNTETH AND BLASPHEMETH; BY REASON OF THE ENEMY AND THE REVENGEFUL.

FOR THE VOICE OF HIM THAT TAUNTETH AND BLASPHEMETH. Wickedly and publicly.

18. ALL THIS IS COME UPON US; YET HAVE WE NOT FORGOTTEN THEE, NEITHER HAVE WE BEEN FALSE TO THY COVENANT.

ALL THIS IS COME UPON US. The word *ba'atnu* means, is come upon us. [I note this] because the word is an intransitive verb.[42]

19. OUR HEART IS NOT TURNED BACK, NEITHER HAVE OUR STEPS DECLINED FROM THY PATH.

OUR HEART IS NOT TURNED BACK. The word *nasog* (turned back) is a *nifal.*[43] The word *lo* (not) is to be read as if written twice. Our verse is to be read as if written *ve-lo tet ashurenu* (neither have our steps declined).[44]

---

40. The root of *le'om* is, *lamed, alef, mem.* So too, our word.

41. I.E.'s comment probably reflects personal experience.

42. *Ba* (comes) is an intransitive verb. An intransitive verb cannot be combined with the direct object. However it is in *ba'atnu.* Hence I.E. notes that *ba* is to be treated as a transitive verb and translated as, come upon us.

43. Its *nun* is not a root letter.

44. The second part of our verse lit. reads: our steps declined from Thy path. Hence I.E.'s comments.

20. THOUGH THOU HAST CRUSHED US INTO A PLACE OF JACKELS, AND COVERED US WITH THE SHADOW OF DEATH.

THOUGH THOU HAST CRUSHED US INTO A PLACE OF JACKELS.[45] The *mem* of *tannim* (jackels) is in place of a *nun.*[46] Compare, *be-chayyyin*[47] (their lives) (Dan. 7:12) and *le-ketz ha-yamin*[48] (at the end of days) (Ibid. 12:13).
The meaning of our verse is, [You cast us into] the bottom of the sea, the place of *tannim*[49] and dark water, which is what The *shadow of death* refers to. It[50] is a metaphor.[51] The term *dikkitanu* (Thou hast crushed us) which is similar to the word *dokhyam* (their waves) (Ps. 93:3) is proof of this.[52] Others say that our verse refers to a place where people do not live.[53] Only jackals (tannim) and ostriches [live there]. [54]

21. IF WE HAD FORGOTTEN THE NAME OF OUR GOD, OR SPREAD FORTH OUR HANDS TO A STRANGE GOD.

IF WE HAD FORGOTTEN. *If we had forgotten the name of our God* is parallel to *yet have we not forgotten Thee* (v. 18).

OR SPREAD FORTH OUR HANDS TO A STRANGE GOD. This is parallel to *Neither have our steps declined from Thy path* (v. 19).

45. Hebrew, *tannim.*

46. *Tannim* is a variation of *tannin. Tannin* refers a sea serpent or a large sea creature. See Gen. 1:21; and Ps. 74: 14.

47. *Chayyin* is the Aramaic version of the Heb. word *chayyim.* In *chayyin* a *nun* has been substituted for a *mem.* The reverse is the cases with *tannim.* I.E.'s point is that the *nun* and *mem* sometimes interchange. He does not see any problem that his proof is from Aramaic rather than Hebrew, for these languages are related.

48. *Yamin* is the Aramaic form of *yamim.*

49. See note 45 .

50. The shadow of death.

51. For the deep waters.

52. That our verse speaks of the deep waters. I.E. renders *dikkitanu* as, "you waved us" i.e. you caused waves to pass over us. He relates *dikkitanu* to the word *dokhi,* which means a wave. Compare *dokhyam* in Ps. 93:4. According to this interpretation our verse reads: Though You caused waves to pass over us at the bottom of the sea and covered us with the shadow of death.

53. A desert.

54. According to this interpretation *tannim* means jackals. If so, then a nun has not been substituted for a *mem* in the word *tannim.*

22. WOULD NOT GOD SEARCH THIS OUT? FOR HE KNOWETH THE SECRETS OF THE HEART.

WOULD NOT GOD SEARCH THIS OUT? If God had to,[55] then He could search this[56] out. He certainly knows this, for He knows the secrets of the heart.

23. NAY, BUT FOR THY SAKE ARE WE KILLED ALL THE DAY; WE ARE ACOUNTED AS SHEEP FOR THE SLAUGHTER.

NAY, BUT FOR THY SAKE. The fact that we willingly offer our lives for the glory of Your name and that we willingly offer our selves to be considered as sheep for the slaughter, though we are better men than those who kill us, is proof that what we say is true. The word *tivchah* (slaughter) is similar to *ha-tabbachim* (of the slaughterers) of the slaughterers[57] in *rav ha-tabbachim* (captain of the slaughterers). [58]

24. AWAKE, WHY SLEEPEST THOU, O LORD? AROUSE THYSELF, CAST NOT OFF FOR EVER.

AWAKE, WHY SLEEPEST THOU, O LORD? You do nothing.[59] You are like one who sleeps, for You did not save us. Or, the psalmist speaks on behalf of the enemy. The enemy speaks of You and says; *peradventure He sleepeth, and must be awaked* (1 Kings 18:27).

25. WHEREFORE HIDEST THOU THY FACE, AND FORGETTEST OUR AFFLICTION AND OUR OPPRESSION?

WHEREFORE. On the other hand, You act like a person who hides his face so that he doesn't see what his enemies do? Or,[60] You saw and You forgot. You therefore forget our affliction and our oppression.

Scripture reads *forgettest* because it wants to contrast God' forgetfulness with *we have not forgotten Thee* (V. 18).

55. Which He doesn't, for He is omniscient.

56. What the psalmist mentions in the earlier verses.

57. Translated according to I.E.

58. Cf. Jer. 52:12. However, there and elsewhere in Scripture the reading is *rav tabbachim.* It should be noted that Gen. 39:1 reads *sar ha-tabbachim.* If not a scribal error then I.E. quoted from memory and conflated the two readings.

59. Lit. He does nothing.

60. I.E.'s interpretation of and *forgettest our affliction and our oppression.*

26. FOR OUR SOUL IS BOWED DOWN TO THE DUST; OUR BELLY CLEAVETH UNTO THE EARTH.

FOR. What hope can there be for us when our soul which comes from the high heavens *is bowed down to the dust* and cleaves unto the earth, that is, the grave?
Our belly refers to the body.

27. ARISE FOR OUR HELP, AND REDEEM US FOR THY MERCY'S SAKE.

ARISE FOR OUR HELP. Arise to help us. Or, Arise You who were our help in the past.

CHAPTER 45

1. FOR THE LEADER; UPON SHOSHANIM; [A PSALM] OF THE SONS OF KORAH. MASCHIL. A SONG OF LOVES.

FOR THE LEADER; UPON SHOSHANIM. A poem beginning with the word *shoshanim.*[1]

LOVES. The word *yedidot* means, loves.

2. MY HEART OVERFLOWETH WITH A GOODLY MATTER; I SAY: 'MY WORK IS CONCERNING A KING'; MY TONGUE IS THE PEN OF A READY WRITER.

MY HEART OVERFLOWETH. The psalmist's heart speaks his words.[2] Some say that the psalmist's mouth speaks the thoughts of his heart.
This psalm refers to David or the messiah his son,[3] for the messiah is called David. Compare, *And David My servant*[4] *shall be their prince for ever* (Ezek. 37:25).

MY WORK. This psalm, which was composed by the poet.

1. This psalm was to be performed to the tune of a song which began with the word *shoshanim.* See I.E. on Ps. 4:1.

2. The psalmist speaks in his heart.

3. The messiah who will be a descendent of David.

4. The reference is to the messiah.

3. THOU ART FAIRER THEN THE CHILDREN OF MEN; GRACE IS POURED UPON THY LIPS; THEREFORE GOD HATH BLESSED THEE FOR EVER.

THOU ART FAIRER. Some say that the word *yafyafita* (thou art fairer) consists of two doubled root letters.[5] It is like *shecharchoret*[6] (blackish) (Songs 1:6), *secharchar*[7] (palpitation) (Ps. 38:11); and *adamdemet*[8] (reddish) (Lev. 13:24). *Shecharchoret* refers to a color lacking white. *Adamdemet* refers to a color not totally red. This being so, how can the psalmist employ the term *yafyafita* which means lacking in beauty?[9] The answer is as follows: When the second and third letters of the root are doubled it indicates a diminution.[10] However, when the first and second letters of the root are doubled[11] it indicates an addition. The word *tesagsegi*[12] (thou didst make it grow) (Is. 17:11) which refers to a greater growth than *tisgi* (you will make it grow) is proof of this.[13] *Yafyafita* means you are fairer [than other men] in appearance and form.[14]

GRACE IS POURED UPON THY LIPS. The word *hutzak* (is poured) is related to the word *ve-yitzku*[15] (and pour it) in *and pour it on the burnt offering* (1 Kings 18:34). Grace, so to speak, is poured in his mouth. [16] Now according to the surface meaning of the text the psalmist describes the form of the king's[17] body and of his speech. He notes that the latter are beautiful. If we take the verse metaphorically then the psalmists speaks of the king's[18] soul. He says that the king's soul is firmly established[19] and his wisdom very broad. Scripture says *Grace is poured upon thy lips* because man's inner speech[20] is found in his soul.

5. That is, it comes from the root *yod, peh, heh*. The *heh* is dropped and the *yod* and *peh* doubled.

6. From the root, *shin, chet, resh*. The *chet* and *resh* are doubled in *shecharchoret*.

7. From the root *samekh, chet, resh*. The *chet* and *resh* are doubled in *secharchar*.

8. From the root *alef, dalet, mem*. The *dalet* and *mem* are doubled in *adamdemet*.

9. A root which has been doubled indicates a diminution. Thus *yayafita* means less than beautiful. The psalmist would hardly have used such a word here.

10. As in *shecharchoret* and *adamdemet*.

11. As in *yafyafita*.

12. From the root *sin, gimel, heh*.

13. *Tesagsegi* means, you made it to grow quickly (I.E on Is. 17:11). *Tisgi* refers to normal growth.

14. Literally, in his appearance and his form.

15. From the root *yod, tzadi, kof*.

16. Beautiful speech pours out of his mouth.

17. King David or King Messiah. Literally, his.

18. See note 17.

19. Fully developed.

20. Man's thoughts.

4. GIRD THY SWORD UPON THY THIGH, O MIGHTY ONE, THY GLORY AND THY MAJESTY.

GIRD. The psalmist also speaks of the king's[21] might. He tells the king to gird his sword on his thigh, for this is the manner of a truly mighty man.
The word *gibbor* (mighty one) should be interpreted as if written *attah ha- gibbor* (you the mighty one).[22] On the other hand it might me missing a *kaf.* [23] It is like *va-yikra aryeh* (and called a lion)[24] (Is. 21:8), which is to be read as if written *va-yikra ke-aryeh* (and he called as a lion). The word *aryeh* is clearly [25] missing a *kaf.*[26]

[THY GLORY AND THY MAJESTY] This[27] is your glory.

5. AND IN THY MAJESTY PROSPER, RIDE ON, IN BEHALF OF TRUTH AND MEEKNESS AND RIGHTEOUSNESS; AND LET THY RIGHT HAND TEACH THEE TREMENDOUS THINGS.

AND THY MAJESTY. The word *va-hadorekhah* (and Thy majesty) is missing a *bet.*[28] It is similar to *for six days* [29] *the Lord made heaven and earth*[30] (Ex. 20:11). Our verse should be interpreted as if written *u-va-hadarekhah tzelach* (and in thy majesty prosper). The word *tzelach* (prosper) is similar to *tzelach* (prosper) in *For no man of his seed shall prosper* (Jer. 22:30). The meaning of *tzelach rekhav* (prosper ride on) is, prosper when you ride. Others say that the word *tzelach* (prosper) is related to the word *yitzlach* (he break out) in *Lest He break out like a fire in the house of Joseph* (Amos 5:6).[31]

---

21. See note 17.

22. Our text literally reads, "Gird thy sword upon thy thigh, mighty one."

23. An inseparable preposition meaning, like. In this case our clause reads, "Gird thy sword upon thy thigh like a mighty one."

24. Translated lit.

25. For otherwise the verse reads, *And a lion called upon the watchtower*...See I.E. on Ps. 11:1.

26. Reading *ve-yiheyeh chaser kaf* rather than, *o yiheyah chaser kaf.* See Filwarg. *Ha- Keter* omits the phrase *ve-yiheyeh chaser kaf* (or, *o yiheyah chaser kaf).*

27. To appear with a sword upon his thigh.

28. *Va-hadorekhah* (lit. and thy majesty) should be read as if written *u-va-hadorekhah* (and in thy majesty). Our clause lit. reads, "and thy majesty prosper." Hence I.E.'s comment.

29. Hebrew, *sheshet yamim.*

30. Translated lit. *For six days the Lord made heaven and earth* is to be interpreted as if written, *for in six days* (be-sheshet yamim) *the Lord made heaven and earth.*

31. In this case our verse reads, and in thy majesty break forth i.e. destroy your enemies.

Note: In addition telling us of the king's might the psalmist also speaks of the king's honesty, meekness and righteousness.
The meaning of *ve-anvah tzedek*[32] is meekness and[33] righteousness. *Ve-anvah tzedek* is to be so interpreted whether the word *anvah* (meekness) in *ve-anvah tzedek* is in the absolute[34] or in the construct.[35]

TEACH. *Yeminekha* (thy right hand) is the subject.[36] The object is missing.[37] Our verse should be interpreted as if written, and let your right hand teach you to do mighty deeds.[38] *Ve- nora'ot* (tremendous deeds) means, wars.[39] Our verse is similar to *Glorious things are spoken of Thee* (Ps. 87:3).[40]
Rabbi Joseph says that *ve-torekha* (and...teach thee) is related to the word *va-yorem* (but... doth shoot at them) in *But God doth shoot at them* (Ps. 64:8).[41] *Thy arrows are sharp* (v. 6) which follows is proof. This would be correct were it not for the fact that *va-yorem* is used in a negative sense,[42] that is, it means, he shot at them. However, the word *ve-torekha* is used in a positive sense.[43]

6. THINE ARROWS ARE SHARP – THE PEOPLES FALL UNDER THEE – [THEY SINK] INTO THE HEART OF THE KING'S ENEMIES.

THINE ARROWS. The psalmist first said *thy sword* (v. 4). He now says, also *thine arrows are sharp* when the peoples [fall] under thee.[44]

---

32. Literally, a*nd meekness righteousness.*

33. Lit. With.

34. In this case our phrase literally reads*: and meekness righteousness.*

35. In this case our phrase literally reads: *and meekness of righteousness.*

36. Our verse literally reads: *And teach thee tremendous deeds thy right hand.*

37. Our verse literally reads, And teach thee thy right hand tremendous things. Hence I.E.'s comment.

38. Hebrew *gevurot.*

39. Our verse thus reads: *And let thy right hand teach thee to do mighty deeds and tremendous deeds,* that is, to wage war.

40. Ps. 87:3 lit. reads: *Glorious spoken of Thee. Glorious* is short for glorious praises. See I.E. on Ps. 87:3. Similarly here, *teach thee* is short for *teach thee to do.*

41 According to this interpretation *And let thy right hand teach thee tremendous things* is to be interpreted, And let thy right hand shoot in war.

42. It refers to inflicting harm.

43. The suffix *kha* in *ve-torekhah* is directed to the king. Thus if we connect *ve-torekhah* to *va-yorem* then our verse means, and your right hand will shoot at you. This is hardly the meaning of our verse.

44. In other words, our verse is in keeping with the theme of verse 4.

FALL. Your arrows fall into the heart of your enemies. The word *yippelu* (fall) is therefore vocalized at an *etnachta*[45] as if it were connected to the following word.[46] It is so vocalized because it serves two words.[47]

7. THY THRONE GIVEN OF GOD IS FOR EVER AND EVER; A SCEPTRE OF EQUITY IS THE SCEPTRE OF THY KINGDOM.

THY THRONE. Some say that the term *Elohim* (God) is similar to *Elohim* (God) in *Thou shalt not revile God* (Ex. 22:27).[48] The Gaon[49] says that *kisakha Elohim*[50] (Thy throne given of God) means; God will establish your throne. In my opinion the word *kisakha* (thy throne) is to be read as if written twice. It is similar to *even the prophecy Oded the prophet* (11 Chron. 15:8)[51] which is to be read as if written, "even the prophecy, the prophecy of Oded the prophet." Our verse is similarly to be read, *your throne*,[52] *God's throne*. It is comparable to[53] *Then Solomon sat on the throne of the Lord* (11 Chron. 29:23). Those who say that *Thy throne* was addressed to God are contradicted by the verse which follows.

8. THOU HAST LOVED RIGHTEOUSNESS, AND HATED WICKEDNESS; THEREFORE GOD, THY GOD, HATH ANOINTED THEE WITH THE OIL OF GLADNESS ABOVE THY FELLOWS.

THOU HAST LOVED. If our psalm speaks of David then *above thy fellows* refers to Saul. If it speaks of the messiah then it refers to other pious people in the messiah's generation.

---

45. A note which breaks the verse in half. In such cases *yippelu* (fall) is vocalized *yippolu*.

46. As if there were no *etnachta* beneath it.

47. *Yippelu* is connected to that which comes before it, and what follows it. Our verse is to be read as follows: *Your arrows are sharp, the nations fall* (yippelu), *they fall* i.e. thy sink (yippellu*) into the heart of the king's enemies.*

48. According to the Talmud, the term *Elohim* does not only mean God. It can also refer to a Judge or a king. Indeed the Talmud interprets the term *Elohim* in Ex 22:7 as referring to a judge. See *Sanhedrin* 66a and I.E. on Ex. 22:27. Our verse reads *kisakha Elohim* (Thy throne given of God). This literally means, Thy Throne God. Now up to now the king is being addressed. Thus "Thy throne God "seems out of place. Hence these commentators interpret *kisakha Elohim* to mean," your throne O king."

49. Rabbi Saadiah Gaon.

50. Lit. Thy throne God.

51. Translated lit.

52. This is addressed to the king.

53. God's throne.

9. MYRRH, AND ALOES, AND CASSIA ARE ALL THY GARMENTS; OUT OF IVORY PALACES STRINGED INSTRUMENTS HAVE MADE THEE GLAD.

MYRRH. There is a difference of opinion regarding the word *mor* (myrrh).[54] Those who say that *ahalot* (aloes) is found among the fish of the sea are in error, for Scripture states, *As aloes* (ahalim) *planted of the Lord* (Num. 24:6).[55] Others say that also *ketzi'ot* (cassia)[56] is a separate kind[57] that has a pleasant odor.[58] It is the style of the holy tongue to place a *vav* before the last noun.[59] Compare, *odem pitedah u-vareket* (a row of carnelian, topaz, and smargd) (Ex. 28:17). At other times the *vav* is omitted.[60] Compare, *adam, shet, enosh* (1 Chron. 1:1). This being the case our verse should have read *mor ahalot ketzi'ot* (myrrh, aloes, cassia) or *mor ahalot u-ketzi'ot* (myrrh, aloes, and cassia).[61] Perhaps *ketzi'ot*[62] is irregular.[63] In reality the word *ketzi'ot* (cassia) is related to the word *ha-miktzo'ot* (corners)[64](Ezk. 46:22). The word is connected *to all thy garments.*[65] The reason why *thy garments* is connected to *ivory palaces* is that the garments are kept in chests in ivory palaces. *Out of ivory palaces* means, when they are taken out of ivory palaces. The word *asher* (that which) has been omitted [from the last clause in our verse]. Our text should be read as if written, *out of ivory palaces*, out of that which made you glad.[66] On the other hand *have made thee glad* might refer to *out of ivory palaces*[67] because the garments were brought from there.

54. Some identify it with musk. Others believe that it is made from the sap of a tree. Radak.

55. It is thus a type of plant.

56. Like myrrh and aloes.

57. The Hebrew reads *va-ahalot ketzi'ot*, aloes cassia. The latter seems to be referring to one kind. Hence this opinion points out that *va-ahalot ketzi'ot* is to be read as if written *va-ahalot u-ketzi'ot*. See Radak.

58. It is a spice.

59. When Scripture lists a number of items, it places a connective *vav* before the last item.

60. From before the last of the nouns.

61. *Mor ve-ahalot ketzi'ot* (myrrh, aloes, cassia). Hence it appears that *ahalot ketzi'ot* refers to one item.

62. Lit. This word.

63. For a *vav* should have been placed before it.

64. Or cut. The garments are perfectly cut or shaped.

65. According to I.E., our clause reads: Myrrh and aloes, your garments are (finely) shaped.

66. The garments chosen from the palaces are garments which made David (or the messiah) glad. See I.E. on v. 2. Our verse reads*: minni simmechukha (stringed instruments have made thee glad).* I.E. renders *minni* (instruments), from. Thus according to I.E. *minni simmechukha* literally reads: from they made you glad. He explains the latter as meaning, from that which made you glad.

67. Not to the garments.

The one who says that *minni* (instruments)[68] is the name of a people or a state errs, for the word *shen* (ivory)[69] is vocalized with a *tzere*[70] like all terms in the absolute.[71] It is not vocalized with a vowel that connects it to another word.

10. KINGS' DAUGHTERS ARE AMONG THY FAVORITES; AT THY RIGHT HAND DOTH STAND THE QUEEN IN GOLD OF OPHIR.

KINGS' DAUGHTERS ARE AMONG THY FAVORITES. The word *biy-kerotekha* (are among thy favorites) is related to the word *yakar* (precious). The meaning of *benot melakhim biy-kerotekha* (kings daughters are among thy favorites) is, among your precious maid servants are the daughters of kings. The one who says that *biy-kerotekha* is connected to the word *bikkoret* (inquisition) in *there shall be inquisition* (Lev. 19:20)[72] does not speak correctly, for no one disputes that the word *biy-kerotekha* is spelled with a *yod*.[73] The difference of opinion between the Masoretes and the "reading"[74] only pertains to the following: One opinion reads the word *biy-kerotekha*.[75] It compares it to the word *biy-mino* (in his right hand) (Gen. 48:13).[76] The other opinion reads it like *mi-yeshene* (of them that sleep) in *of them that sleep in the dust* (Dan. 12:2).[77]

The word *shagel* (queen) refers to the woman who is prepared and designated for sex.[78] The word *yishgelennah* (shall lie with her) (Deut. 28: 30) proves this.

According to the opinion that maintains that our Psalm refers to David, this verse is to be taken according to its plain meaning. According to the opinion that asserts that this

---

68. I.E. renders *minni* (instruments) from .

69. Our verse reads: *min hekhle shen minni* (ivory stringed instruments). These commentators render this as, out of palaces made out of ivory from *minni.*

70. Lit. A small *kametz.*

71. If *sheni* were connected to *minni* then it should have been vocalized with *segol.* However, *shen* is vocalized with a *tzere.* It thus must conclude a phrase and is not connected to what follows it. Our verse should thus be read *min hekhele shen, min ni simmechukha.*

72. This is the opinion of Rashi. He renders our clause, the daughter of kings inquire after you.

73. Its root is therefore *yod, kof, resh* whereas the root of *bikkoret* is *bet, kof, resh.*

74. The way the text is read.

75. According to the "reading" the *yod* is swallowed by the *chirik* which precedes it. I.E.'s point is that no one disputes that the word is spelled with a yod. They only differ as to whether the *yod* is to be sounded.

76. They sound the *yod.*

77. This opinion pronounces the word *bi-yekorekhah.*

78. *Shagel* refers to a woman that one has sexual intercourse with. Here it refers to the queen.

psalm speaks of the messiah the daughters of the king[79] is a metaphor for the cities[80] and the queen (the shagel) is a metaphor for the messiah's city.[81]

11. HEARKEN, O DAUGHTER, AND CONSIDER, AND INCLINE THINE EAR; FORGET ALSO THINE OWN PEOPLE, AND THY FATHERS'S HOUSE.

HEARKEN O DAUGHTER. If this psalm speaks of David then the poet spoke to the *shagel* (queen).[82] The meaning of *forget also thine own people* is similar to *thy people shall be my people* (Ruth 1:16).[83] Its meaning is, convert and accept the religion of David. If the verse speaks of the messiah then the meaning of *O daughter* is, O congregation [of peoples]. Compare, *daughter of Judah* (Lam. 1:15).[84] The concept conveyed by our verse[85] is similar to, *to serve him with one consent* (Zeph. 3:9).

12. SO SHALL THE KING DESIRE THY BEAUTY; FOR HE IS THY LORD; AND DO HOMAGE UNTO HIM.

SO SHALL THE KING DESIRE. If this psalm speaks of David then this verse is to be taken according to its plain meaning. If it speaks of the messiah then the king refers to God or to the messiah.

13. AND, O DAUGHTER OF TYRE, THE RICHEST OF THE PEOPLE SHALL ENTREAT THY FAVOR WITH A GIFT.

AND O DAUGHTER OF TYRE. If this psalm deals with David then a *bet* is missing in the word *u-vat* (and O daughter). Our text is to be read as if written *u-ve-vat tzor*. The meaning of the latter is, and with the daughter of Tyre.[86] *All glorious [is the kings daugh-*

79. The *shagel.*

80. Reading, *ha-kerayot,* rather than *ha-yekarot.* See *Ha-Keter*

81. The capitol of his kingdom. The term employed by I.E. is *medinato. Medinah* is usually rendered state. However, it also has the meaning of city.

82. The *shagel.*

83. Its meaning is, forsake the religion of your people, for the meaning of *people* in the Book of Ruth is, the faith of your people.

84. The meaning of which is, congregation of Judah.

85. According to the latter interpretation.

86. The daughter of the king of Tyre. The rich men of Tyre will join the daughter of Tyre in offering a gift to David's new wife or the rich men of Tyre shall offer the daughter of Tyre herself as a maidservant to David's new wife. Filwarg.

ter] (v. 14) is the object.[87] If our psalm speaks of the messiah then our verse is be taken as a metaphor.[88]

14. ALL GLORIOUS IS THE KINGS DAUGHTER WITHIN THE PALACE; HER RAIMENT IS OF CHECKER WORK INWROUGHT WITH GOLD.

ALL GLORIOUS. Scripture reads *within the palace* because the kings daughter stayed inside of her palace and was unseen by the public.

ALL. We find that David married[89] the daughter of Talmai king of Geshur (11 Sam. 2:3).

15. SHE SHALL BE LED UNTO THE KING ON RICHLY WOVEN STUFF; THE VIRGINS HER COMPANIONS IN HER TRAIN BEING BROUGHT UNTO THEE.

ON RICHLY WOVEN STUFF. The *lamed* in *li-rekamot* [90] (on richly woven stuff) is in place of a *bet.*[91]

SHE SHALL BE LED. The reference is to the daughter of the king.

16. THEY SHALL BE LED WITH GLADNESS AND REJOICING; THEY SHALL ENTER INTO THE KING'S PALACE.

THEY SHALL BE LED. If the psalm speaks of the messiah its meaning is, the nations shall come by themselves. They shall not be forced to come.[92] The daughter of the king with her companions who are in the king's citadel will enter the king's palace. The king refers to David or to the messiah.

87. The king's daughter spoken of in the next verse is the recipient of the gift spoken of in our verse.

88. According to Radak, the king represents the messiah, the king's daughter stands for Israel and the maidservants symbolize the nations of the world.

89. Maacah. According to this note the king's daughter refers to Maacah daughter of Talmai.

90. The literal meaning of *li-rekamot* is, to richly woven stuff.

91. Our text literally reads; she shall be led to woven stuff (*li-rekamot*) to the king. According to I.E. our verse is to be interpreted, she shall be led in woven stuff (*bi-rekamot*) to the king.

92. To the messiah.

17. INSTEAD OF THY FATHERS SHALL BE THY SONS, WHOM THOU SHALT MAKE PRINCES IN ALL THE LAND.

INSTEAD. In place of the generations that passed another generation shall come, for your generation is intermediary.[93] This interpretation is correct whether the psalm speaks of David or whether it speaks of the messiah.

18. I WILL MAKE THY NAME TO BE REMEMBERED IN ALL GENERATIONS; THEREFORE SHALL THE PEOPLES PRAISE THEE FOR EVER AND EVER.

I WILL MAKE THY NAME TO BE REMEMBERED. Some say that this verse is directed to David, for since David's children were princes, the memory of David's name will endure and generation to generation will speak of David's glory. Others say that *thy name* is directed to God the revered, for the poet praises God for the greatness of David and his seed.

93. Your generation is the bridge between the past and the future.

CHAPTER 46.

1. FOR THE LEADER; [A PSALM] OF THE SONS OF KORAH, UPON ALAMOTH. A SONG.

FOR THE LEADER; [A PSALM] OF THE SONS OF KORAH, UPON ALAMOTH. *Alamoth* is the name of a song.[1] Some say that this poet was of the seed of the son's of Korah.[2] He lived in the days of King Hezekiah when Sennacherib was turned back.[3] In my opinion the poet speaks of Jerusalem, of the wars.[4]

2. GOD IS OUR REFUGE AND STRENGTH, A VERY PRESENT HELP IN TROUBLE.

GOD. The following is the meaning of our verse: If any trouble from an enemy should befall us, then God will save us.

3. THEREFORE WILL WE NOT FEAR, THOUGH THE EARTH DO CHANGE, AND THOUGH THE MOUNTAINS BE MOVED INTO THE HEART OF THE SEAS.

THEREFORE. Those who have mastered the natural sciences say: since the height of the sun moves higher and higher from constellation to constellation, a time will come when

1. This psalm was to be performed to the tune of a song called *Alamot.* See I.E. on Ps. 4:1.

2. See Num.16.

3. See 11 Kings 18-19.

4. Wars pertaining to Jerusalem. In other words, the psalm is not limited to the period of Hezekiah. Perhaps what I.E. means by "the poet speaks of Jerusalem, of the wars" is; the poet speaks of Jerusalem and of the wars that will be waged in the messianic era. See Verse 10. Also see Rashi and Radak.

the dry land turns into a sea and the sea become dry land. [5] Others say[6] that the meaning of our verse is, if it were so,[7] even though it will not be so, for God has set a boundary to the sea so that it does not return to cover the land.

4. THOUGH THE WATERS THEREOF ROAR AND FOAM[8], THOUGH THE MOUNTAINS SHAKE AT THE SWELLING THEREOF. SELAH.

ROAR. The following is the meaning of our verse: When the sea roars its waters become muddy. They resemble clay. The mountains also shake. They quake because of the winds that are beneath the earth, which are brought forth by God.[9]

AT THE SWELLING THEREOF. SELAH. The word *selah* means, as I have previously explained, it is truthfully so.[10]

5. THERE IS A RIVER, THE STREAMS WHEREOF MAKE GLAD THE CITY OF GOD, THE HOLIEST DWELLING-PLACE OF THE MOST HIGH.

THERE IS A RIVER. Its meaning is as follows: If the waters of the sea[11] become muddy (v. 4), the river of Jerusalem, which was [called] the Gichon,[12] [will gladden the city of God].

THE STREAMS WHEREOF MAKE GLAD. All the inhabitants of the city of God,[13] which is holy, for it is the dwelling-place of the Most High.

5. Our verse lit. reads: Therefore will we not fear when the earth changes and when the mountains are moved into the heart of the seas. Hence I.E.'s interpretation.

6. Reading, *va-acherim ameru* (others say) in place of *ve-achar ken ameru* (they then said). Filwarg.

7. Our verse should be interpreted: Therefore will we not fear even if the earth changes and even if the mountains are moved into the heart of the seas.

8. Hebrew. *Yechmeru.* I.E. renders *yechmeru,* they will clay, that is, they become like clay. The root of the Hebrew word for clay is, is *chet, mem, resh.* Hence his interpretation.

9. I.E. renders *yirashu harim be-ga'avato* (the mountains shake at the swelling thereof), the mountains shake by His might, that is, by God's might.

10. See I.E. on Ps. 3:3.

11. Literally, their waters.

12. Perhaps we should read *she-hu gichon* rather than *she-hayah gichon.* In this case I.E, reads: the river of Jerusalem, that is, the Gichon. The Gichon is a spring in the Kidron Valley, east of Jerusalem. See I Kings 1:33. I.E identified it with the Gichon, a river which issued from the Garden of Eden. See I.E. on Gen. 2:11.

13. In other words *The city of God* means the inhabitants of the city of God,

6. GOD IS IN THE MIDST OF HER, SHE SHALL NOT BE MOVED; GOD SHALL HELP HER, AT THE APPROACH OF MORNING.

GOD. Even if the mountains shall be moved, mount Zion will not be moved. *At the approach of morning* means, close to morning.[14] It might also mean every day.[15]

7. NATIONS WERE IN TUMULT, KINGDOMS WERE MOVED; HE UTTERED HIS VOICE, THE EARTH MELTED.

TUMULT. It is possible that everything mentioned by the psalmist[16] is a metaphor regarding the enemies of Israel. It is like *the waters had overwhelmed us* (Ps. 124:4).[17] It might also mean, then[18] the sea will storm[19] and the mountains melt by the might of God.[20] The same will happen to the nations. Scripture therefore reads *Nations were in tumult, kingdoms were moved.*

MELTED. Opposite its nature,[21] which is very dry.[22]

8. THE LORD OF HOSTS IS WITH US; THE GOD OF JACOB IS OUR HIGH TOWER. SELAH

THE LORD. The nations will then see that God is with us, for unlike them, we will not be moved.

9. COME, BEHOLD THE WORKS OF THE LORD, WHO HATH MADE DESOLATIONS IN THE EARTH.

COME. One nation shall say to another: *Come, behold the works of the Lord...*

14. To the morning of the day of salvation. Filwarg.
15. The morning of each and every day. Filwarg.
16. The changing of the earth, the quaking of the mountains, the storming of the sea.
17. Which is a metaphor for Israel's enemies. See I.E. on Ps. 124:4.
18. Reading *az ha-yam* rather than *o ha-yam. Ha-Keter.*
19. See v. 4.
20. See verses 3-4.
21. Reading, *toledotah. Ha-Keter.*
22. Earth is dry. Dry things do not melt.

The word *shammot* means desolations. The reference is to the desolation of the lands of the kingdoms,[23] when they will quake.

10. HE MAKETH WARS TO CEASE UNTO THE END OF THE EARTH; HE BREAKETH THE BOW, AND CUTTETH THE SPEAR IN SUNDER; HE BURNETH THE CHARIOTS IN THE FIRE.

HE MAKETH WARS TO CEASE. From Jerusalem. It is possible that the psalmist spoke under the influence of the Holy Spirit,[24] regarding Gog.[25]

HE BURNETH THE CHARIOTS IN THE FIRE. In his anger.[26]

[CHARIOTS.][27] Wagons which are used to transport weapons or food to those waging war.

11. LET BE, AND KNOW THAT I AM GOD; I WILL BE EXALTED AMONG THE NATIONS, I WILL BE EXALTED IN THE EARTH.

LET BE. The aforementioned are the words of God to the nations of the world prior to the breaking of their bows.

12. THE LORD OF HOSTS IS WITH US; THE GOD OF JACOB IS OUR HIGH TOWER. SELAH.

THE LORD OF HOSTS IS WITH US. After this there is no fear of wars, for they ceased.

23. The pagan kingdoms.

24. The psalmist prophesied.

25. A nation that will wage war against Israel in the messianic era.

26. Lit. The meaning [is,] in his anger.

27. Hebrew, *agalot* (wagons). Hence I.E.'s comment.

CHAPTER 47

1. FOR THE LEADER; A PSALM OF THE SONS OF KORAH.

FOR THE LEADER. This psalm speaks of the days of messiah. Rabbi Moses says that it was composed in Babylonia.[1] There is a commentator who says that this psalm was composed in the days of David, when they brought the ark up to Jerusalem. He says that *God is gone up amidst shouting* (v. 6) is proof of this.[2] However, this interpretation is incorrect, for the psalm reads *He chooseth* [3]*our inheritance for us* (v. 5).[4] The commentator who asserts that our psalm was composed in the days of David answers: *He chooseth*[5] *our inheritance for us* alludes to mount Moriah, which was unknown[6] when this psalm was composed.[7]

1. During the first exile.

2. This interpretation takes *God is gone up amidst shouting* to mean, God's ark has ascended to Jerusalem amidst shouting.

3. Hebrew, *yivchar*. He will choose.

4. For the psalm literally reads: *He will choose our inheritance for us.* However, in the days of David, Israel's inheritance was already chosen.

5. Hebrew, *yivchar*, he will choose.

6. As the place where the temple was to be built.

7. When the ark was brought to Jerusalem they did not know where it would be ultimately placed. Hence our verse reads: *He will choose our inheritance for us*, that is, God will one day choose a place for us to build a temple to house the ark.

2. O CLAP YOUR HANDS, ALL YE PEOPLES; SHOUT UNTO GOD WITH THE VOICE OF TRIUMPH.[8]

ALL. If this psalm relates to the days of David then *all ye peoples* refers to the nations who were subservient to David.[9]

If the psalm speaks of the days of the messiah then *all ye people* is to be taken according to its plain meaning.[10] The latter is the correct interpretation.

3. FOR THE LORD IS MOST HIGH, AWFUL; A GREAT KING OVER ALL THE EARTH.

FOR. This[11] is what the voice of *triumph* (rinnah), that is, the voice of the herald shall proclaim; [for] *rinnah* means, a herald. Compare, *And there went a cry* (ha-rinnah) *throughout the host* (1 Kings 22:36).[12]

4. HE SUBDUETH PEOPLES UNDER US, AND NATIONS UNDER OUR FEET.

HE SUBDUETH PEOPLES UNDER US. The word *yadber* (subdueth) means, he will lead. Compare the word *ha-davero* (their pasture)[13] in *As a flock in the midst of their pasture* (ha-davero) (Micah 2:12).

God is king over all the earth (v. 3) and all people are in his hands.[14]

5. HE CHOOSETH[15] OUR INHERITANCE FOR US, THE PRIDE OF JACOB WHOM HE LOVETH. SELAH.

HE CHOOSETH. Whether the psalm was written in Babylonia or whether it speaks of the days of the messiah its meaning is: Israel will return to its inheritance.

8. Hebrew, *rinnah*. See I.E. on the next verse.

9. Literally, under David's hand.

10. It refers to the nations of the world.

11. *For the Lord is most high, awful; a great King over all the earth.*

12. I.E. renders this as, *And the voice of the herald went throughout the host.* He renders the end of verse 2: *Shout unto God with the voice of a herald.*

13. That is, the place where the sheep are led.

14. Hence He was able to "subdue peoples under us, and nations under our feet."

15. Lit. He will choose.

6. GOD IS GONE UP AMIDST SHOUTING, THE LORD AMIDST THE SOUND OF THE HORN.

GOD IS GONE UP. The reference is to the Holy Ark[16] which was hidden.[17] The ark shall go up[18] and be seen. Others say that its meaning is as follows: God will place the nations under us.[19] When we will shout upon the nations[20] with trumpets and the sound of the *shofar* God will be exalted thereby.[21] Hence, God is referred to *as Most High* (v. 3).[22]

7. SING PRAISES TO GOD, SING PRAISES; SING PRAISES UNTO OUR KING, SING PRAISES.

SING. Its meaning is as follows: Sing praises to God, who is known by His deeds through the agency of the rational mind. *Sing praises unto our King*, who is known to us alone,[23] when His glory dwells among us.

8. FOR GOD IS THE KING OF ALL THE EARTH; SING YE PRAISES IN A SKILLFUL SONG.

FOR. Since the psalmist said[24] *unto our King* he goes on to say *For God is the King of all the earth.*

SING YE PRAISES IN A SKILLFUL SONG.[25] All who are intelligent sing this praise.[26]

---

16. "God's throne, that is the ark, is called by God's name. It is so called in the Book of Chronicles (1 Chron. 13:6). [It is so called] because *the name of the Lord of Hosts that sitteth upon the cherubim is upon it* (2 Sam. 6:2)." *Yesod Mora* Chap. 12. The Secret of the Torah, p 176.

17. According to Rabbinic tradition the Holy Ark was hidden in a cave by the prophet Jeremiah.

18. From its hiding place.

19. Verse 4.

20. The nations which God placed under Israel.

21. *God has gone up* thus means, God is exalted.

22. God is referred to as *Most High* because He will be exalted by Israel's sounding of the trumpets and the shofar.

23. I.E.'s interpretation of *our King.*

24. In the previous verse.

25. Hebrew, *zammeru maskil* is short for *zammeru zeh, kol maskil.*

26.They will sing: *God is the King of all the earth.*

9. GOD REIGNETH OVER THE NATIONS; GOD SITTETH UPON HIS HOLY THRONE.

GOD REIGNETH. God showed His kingship many times in passed generations, when He executed justice and vengeance upon the nations.[27] This is the meaning of *God sitteth upon His holy throne.*[28] Or its meaning is, thus[29] shall it be said in the days of the messiah. Therefore *the princes of the peoples are gathered* (10). [30]

10. THE PRINCES OF THE PEOPLES ARE GATHERED TOGETHER, THE PEOPLE OF THE GOD OF ABRAHAM; FOR UNTO GOD BELONG THE SHIELDS OF THE EARTH; HE IS GREATLY EXALTED.

THE PRINCES OF THE PEOPLES. *Nedive ammim* (the princes of the people) means, the revered of the nations. The meaning of the *people of the God of Abraham* is, to be the people of the God of Abraham.[31] Abraham is mentioned because of the souls which he acquired in Haran[32] and because he called God's name in every place.[33]

THE SHIELDS OF THE EARTH. The reference is to the kings. Compare, *For the Lord is our shield* (Ps. 99:19). God will then be very exalted in the eyes of all.

27. I.E.'s interpretation of *God reigneth over the nations.*

28. Scripture goes on to explain itself.

29. *God reigneth over the nations.*

30. *The princes of the peoples are gather*ed to accept God as their King.

31. I.E. renders the first part of our verse, as follows: The revered of the nations gather to be the people of the God of Abraham.

32. According to Rabbinic tradition, *and the souls that they had gotten in Haran* (Gen. 12:5) refers to the people that Abraham and Sarah converted. See *Tanchumah* on Gen.12:5.

33. See Gen. 12:8 and I.E.'s comment thereto.

CHAPTER 48

1. A SONG; A PSALM OF THE SONS OF KORAH.

A SONG; A PSALM. We are not able to distinguish between *shir mizmor* (a song; a psalm)[1] and *mizmor shir* (a psalm; a song) (Ps. 30:1).[2] It is like, *mi-tzur ha-challamish* (out of the rock of flint) (Deut. 8:15) and *me-chalmish tzur* (out of the flinty rock) (ibid. 32:13).

2. GREAT IS THE LORD, AND HIGHLY TO BE PRAISED, IN THE CITY OF OUR GOD, HIS HOLY MOUNTAIN.

GREAT IS THE LORD, AND HIGHLY TO BE PRAISED. This is a very lofty psalm, for it mentions the praise of Jerusalem.

3. FAIR IN SITUATION,[3] THE JOY OF THE WHOLE EARTH; EVEN MOUNT ZION, THE UTTERMOST PARTS OF THE NORTH, THE CITY OF THE GREAT KING.

FAIR IN SITUATION. The word *nof* (situation) means a region.[4] Compare *sheloshet ha-nafet* (the three regions) (Josh. 17:11). The word *ha-nafet*[5] follows the paradigm of *rachat*[6]

1. Which is the way our Psalm opens.

2. Which is the way Psalm 30:1 opens.

3. Hebrew, *yefeh nof.*

4. According to I.E. the opening of our Psalm reads: Beautiful region. See Radak.

5. Which comes from the root *nun, vav, peh.*

6. Which comes from the root *resh, vav, chet.* However, *rachat* is vocalized with a *pattach* because the *chet* is a vowel letter.

(shovel) in *Which hath been winnowed with the shovel* (Is. 30:24). It makes no sense to render *nof* a branch[7] or to connect it to the word *tenufah* (offering).[8]

EVEN MOUNT ZION. In northern Jerusalem.[9]

THE GREAT KING. The word *rav* means great. Compare *rav*[10] (officers) in *to all the officers of his house* (Est. 1:8). The reference is to David.[11] Compare, *the city where David encamped* (Ps. 29:1).[12]

4. GOD IN HER PALACES HATH MADE HIMSELF KNOWN FOR A STRONGHOLD.

GOD. The meaning of our verse is as follows: Even though Jerusalem has[13] many palaces,[14] God is her fortress. This has already been known by the mighty acts which God has demonstrated.[15]

5. FOR, LO, THE KINGS ASSEMBLED THEMSELVES, THEY CAME ONWARD TOGETHER.

FOR, LO, THE KINGS ASSEMBLED. The kings that assembled and came upon her.[16]

6. THEY SAW, STRAIGHTWAY THEY WERE AMAZED; THEY WERE AFFRIGHTED, THEY HASTED AWAY.

THEY SAW, When they saw the might of God they were affrighted.

---

7. As the first interpretation of Rashi does. Rashi renders *yefeh nof* as, the beautiful branch.

8. See Ex. 29:26; Lev. 7:30. According to this interpretation, our verse opens: Beautiful wave offering. According to I.E., it makes no sense to compare Jerusalem to a beautiful branch or a beautiful wave offering.

9. Which is situated in northern Jerusalem.

10. Lit. The great one.

11. Not to God.

12. Our verse reads: *kiryat melekh rav*. Ps. 29:1 reads: *kiryat chanah david.* According to I.E. *chanah david* is interchangeable with *melekh rav* and thus explains it.

13. Reading *lah* rather than *lo. Ha-Keter.*

14. Fortified palaces.

15. I.E.'s interpretation of *hath made himself known.*

16. This is how our verse should be interpreted, for our verse leads into the next verse. Our verse should be interpreted as follows: The kings that assembled and came upon her...they saw...they were amazed etc.

7. TREMBLING TOOK HOLD OF THE THEM THERE, PANGS, AS A WOMEN IN TRAVAIL.

TREMBLING. They therefore fled. This is the meaning of *nechpazu* (they hasted away)[17] (v. 6).

8. WITH THE EAST WIND THOU BREAKEST THE SHIPS OF TARSHISH.

WITH THE EAST WIND. The psalmist compares the trembling, which seized the kings, to an east wind which, when on the sea breaks the ships.

9. AS WE HAVE HEARD, SO HAVE WE SEEN IN THE CITY OF THE LORD OF HOSTS, IN THE CITY OF OUR GOD - GOD ESTABLISH IT FOR EVER. SELAH.

AS WE HAVE HEARD. Our verse prophesies that when Israel returns to Jerusalem they will say [*As we heard, so have we seen ....*]

10. WE HAVE THOUGHT ON THY LOVINGKINDNESS, O GOD, IN THE MIDST OF THY TEMPLE.

WE HAVE THOUGHT. Israel will then say: We used to[18] contemplate in our hearts and visualize Your loving-kindness which fills Your temple. Or, its interpretation is as follows: [We used to contemplate in our hearts and think of Your loving-kindness which was manifest] when you were in the midst of Your temple.

11. AS IS THY NAME, O GOD, SO IS THY PRAISE UNTO THE ENDS OF THE EARTH; THY RIGHT HAND IS FULL OF RIGHTEOUSNESS.

AS IS THY NAME. In Your temple.

[SO IS THY PRAISE] Your praise is: *Thy right hand is full of righteousness.*

17. They fled, because trembling took hold of them.

18. Before the coming of the messiah.

12. LET MOUNT ZION BE GLAD, LET THE DAUGHTER OF JUDAH REJOICE, BECAUSE OF THY JUDGMENTS.

LET MOUNT ZION BE GLAD. *The daughter of Judah* refers to those who dwell in the cities around Zion, for Jerusalem is like a mother.
The meaning of *because of Thy judgments* is; because You do judgments as you did to the kings who gathered.[19]

13. WALK ABOUT ZION, AND GO ROUND ABOUT HER; COUNT THE TOWERS THEREOF.

WALK ABOUT ZION. The aforementioned are words of Jerusalem to the nations. Rabbi Moses says that this[20] occurred in the days of David. Many say that this refers to the days of the messiah.

14. MARK YE WELL HER RAMPARTS,[21] TRAVERSE HER PALACES; THAT YE MAY TELL IT TO THE GENERATION FOLLOWING.

MARK YE WELL HER RAMPARTS .The word *chelah* (its ramparts) is similar to *chel* (bulwarks) in *Walls and bulwarks* (Is. 26:1).

TRAVERSE.[22] Look upon her palaces which are her peaks.[23]

15. FOR SUCH IS GOD, OUR GOD, FOR EVER AND EVER; HE WILL GUIDE US ETERNALLY.[24]

FOR… ETERNALLY. *Al-mut* means eternally. The poet says this[25] because God exists eternally and He will be the eternal Guide. According to the master of the Masorah[26] *al-*

19. Verses 6-8.

20. What is described in our verse.

21. Hebrew, *chelah.*

22. Hebrew, *passegu.*

23. Our text reads *passegu armenoteha* (traverse her palaces). The word *passegu* is related to the word *pisgah* (a peak). Thus *passegu armenoteha* literally means, peak her palaces. Hence I.E.'s interpretation.

24. Hebrew, *al-mut.*

25. *He will guide us eternally.*

26. Those who transmitted the tradition as to how the words in Scripture are to be read.

mut consists of two words.[27] It means, until our death. Rabbi Moses says that the word *al-mut* is related to the word *elem* (youth).[28] Its meaning is: He will always lead us like young people, that is, He will lead us as He did in our youth.[29] Others say that *al-mut* is related to the word *ve-ne'elam* (being hid)[30] in *the thing being hid* (Lev. 4:13). Its meaning is: God will lead us in a good manner which is hidden from those who are created.[31]

27. Whereas according to I.E., the word is to be read as one word *almut* (eternally).

28. He too reads *al-mut* as one word, *almut.*

29. In the days of old. See Radak.

30. This interpretation reads *al-mut* as one word, *almut.*

31. God's ways are hidden from man.

CHAPTER 49

1. FOR THE LEADER; A PSALM OF THE SONS OF KORAH.

2. HEAR THIS, ALL YE PEOPLES; GIVE EAR, ALL YE INHABITANTS OF THE WORLD.

HEAR THIS, ALL YE PEOPLES. This is a very important psalm, for it explicitly speaks of the light of the world to come and of the rational soul which is immortal.

HEAR. This thing which the psalmist will make known applies to all those who live, all those in whom God breathed the breath of life. The Psalmist therefore states: *Give ear, all ye inhabitants of the world.*

3. BOTH LOW AND HIGH, RICH AND POOR TOGETHER.

BOTH LOW AND HIGH. People who have no status are called *bene adam* (low). Scripture also addresses those who have status. Those who are known. This is the meaning of *bene ish* (and high). [The psalmist speaks to] the rich and the poor.[1]

4. MY MOUTH SHALL SPEAK WISDOM, AND THE MEDITATION OF MY HEART SHALL BE UNDERSTANDING.

MY MOUTH. The psalmist wishes to teach [the high and the low] all the wisdom that is hidden from them. Those who are "wise of heart" mention these things by employing parables.[2]

1. Reading *ve-ha-evyonim*. Our psalm is addressed both to the poor and the rich.

2. The *wise of heart* employ parables when they speak of esoteric subjects. Hence the psalmist goes on to say: *I will incline my ear to a parable.*

The meaning of *ve-hagut libbi tevunot* (and the meditation of my heart shall be understanding) is, the understanding which my heart meditated upon.[3]

5. I WILL INCLINE MINE EAR TO A PARABLE; I WILL OPEN MY DARK SAYING UPON THE HARP.

I WILL INCLINE. I will speak concerning this wisdom by means of a parable. Compare, *they shall never see the light* (v. 20); *Like sheep they are appointed for the nether world* (v. 15). [4] The psalmist says *I will open* because the "dark saying" is closed.[5] It is also shut.[6] Scripture reads *upon the harp* because this psalm was to be played upon the harp. It is possible that the meaning of *I will incline* is, I too will incline my ear to the parable. The meaning of the latter is; I too will chastise myself.

6. WHEREFORE SHOULD I FEAR IN THE DAYS OF EVIL, WHEN THE INIQUITY OF MY SUPPLANTERS COMPASSETH ME ABOUT.

WHEREFORE SHOULD I FEAR IN THE DAYS OF EVIL. Its meaning is as follows: Why should I toil [in my youth] to acquire wealth because I fear for the days of my old age.[7] Old age is referred to as the days of evil. Compare, *Before the evil days come* (Ecc. 12:1). The latter refers to old age, for the verse earlier speaks[8] *of the days of thy youth* (ibid).

WHEN THE INIQUITY OF MY SUPPLANTERS.[9] This is connected to *Wherefore should I fear*. Our verse should be understood as follows: The psalmist fears, that when he acquires his wealth, he may need to do so in a manner that entails sinning. *Avon akevai yesubbeni* (when the iniquity of my supplanters compasseth me about) means, I will go in a way that is not straight, and the latter sin[10] will always surround me.[11] The psalmist,

3. The insights which my heart contemplated.

4. Both quotes are parables.

5. Its meaning is not apparent.

6. The music will help one to unravel the "dark saying." *Metzudat David.*

7. I.E. renders *bi-yeme ra* (in the days of evil), because of the days of evil.

8. Lit., begins.

9. Hebrew, *ekev*. Literally, heel. I.E. renders our clause, when the iniquity of my foot compasseth me about.

10. The sin of walking in a path that is not straight.

11. The sin will always be with me.

as it were, says: Wherefore should I fear because of the days of evil[12] and be concerned that the sin of my foot[13] should encompass me about?[14]

7. OF THEM THAT TRUST IN THEIR WEALTH, AND BOAST THEMSELVES IN THE MULTITUDE OF THEIR RICHES.

THEM THAT TRUST IN THEIR WEALTH. Rabbi Moses says that *ha-botechim* (of them that trust) is the object of *ira* (I fear) (v. 6).[15] However, this interpretation makes no sense.[16] In reality *ha-botechim* (them that trust) is the beginning of a new statement. The meaning of *ha-botechim al chelam* is: Behold, those who trust in their wealth. *Chelam* means their wealth. Compare, *chayil* (wealth) in *my hand hath gotten me this wealth* (Deut. 8:17).

8. NO MAN CAN BY ANY MEANS REDEEM HIS BROTHER, NOR GIVE TO GOD A RANSOM FOR HIM.

BROTHER . Rabbi Jonah says that the word *ach* (brother) means one.[17] Others say that the meaning of *ach* (brother) is similar to *ach* (alas) in *and say: Alas* (Ezek. 6: 11). [18]
In my opinion the word *ach* is the object and *ish* (man) is the subject. Scripture is, at it were, saying: Look, the rich can not ransom their brothers; neither can they ransom themselves from death.[19] Now what good does a person derive from all of his money? A man can not ransom his brother from death. Furthermore, one can not ransom his own life from death, Therefore [Scripture states:] *For too costly is the redemption of their soul*

12. Old age.

13. Walking in a path that is not straight.

14. The Psalmist says: Wherefore should I sin by gathering wealth illegally in my youth, because of my fear of old age.

15. Reading *pa'ul* rather then *po'el. Ha-Keter.* Rabbi Moses reads our verse as follows: "Wherefore should I fear in the days of evil... them that trust in their wealth, and boast themselves in the multitude of their riches."

16. For there is no reason to connect *Wherefore should I fear* which opens verse 6 to *Of them that trust in their wealth* which opens verse 7.

17. Our verse reads: *Ach lo fado yifdeh ish.* According to Rabbi Jonah, *ach* is short for *echad.* He interprets our verse as follows: One, that is, one man, can not by any means redeem another man.

18. According to this interpretation our verse reads: Alas, No man can by any means redeem.

19. I.E. interprets *nor give ...a ransom for him* as meaning, "nor give ...a ransom for himself."

[v. 9].[20] The meaning of *ve-chadal le-olam* (and must be let alone for ever) (v. 9) is, this[21] cannot ever be.

10. THAT HE SHOULD STILL LIVE ALWAY, THAT HE SHOULD NOT SEE THE PIT.

THAT HE SHOULD STILL LIVE ALWAY. How can the one who gathers wealth think [*that he should still live alway...*?]

11. FOR HE SEETH THAT WISE MEN DIE, THE FOOL[22] AND THE BRUTISH[23] TOGETHER PERISH, AND LEAVE THEIR WEALTH TO OTHERS.

FOR HE SEETH THAT WISE MEN DIE. Does he not see that men wiser than he die in every generation. The psalmist mentions death with regards to the wise, and perish with regard to the fool and the brutish, because the fool and the brutish will be annihilated.[24] The *kesil* (fool) walks on a perverse path.[25] The *ba'ar* (brutish), like a beast, lacks understanding. Both of them shall perish.[26]

THEIR WEALTH. This corresponds to *of them that trust in their wealth* (v. 7).

12. THEIR INWARD THOUGHT IS, THAT THEIR HOUSES SHALL CONTINUE FOR EVER, AND THEIR DWELLING-PLACES TO ALL GENERATIONS; THEY CALL THEIR LANDS AFTER THEIR OWN NAMES.

THEIR INWARD THOUGHT. Some say that the word *kirbam* (their inward thought) is the word *kivram* (their grave) with some of the letters[27] reversed.[28] It refers to the house

20. The meaning of which is, a man is not able to redeem himself from death.

21. For man to be able to redeem himself or his brother from death.

22. Heb. *Kesil.*

23. Heb. *Ba'ar.*

24. They will perish upon dieing.

25. The term *kesil* refers to one who behaves perversely.

26. After they die.

27. The *bet* and *resh*.

28. Lit. "Some say that it (kirbam) is the opposite of the word *kivram* (their grave)."

which is called man's eternal home (Ecc: 12:5).[29] *They call their lands after their names* means; they erect structures on their graves.[30]

Others say that the word *kirbam* (their inward thought) is related to the word *kerev* (inward thought) in *the inward thought of every one* (Ps. 64:7). Our clause means, they think in their inner thoughts that their houses will last.

According to my opinion the word *kirbam* is missing a *bet. Kirbam* should be interpreted as if written *be-kirbam* (amidst them).[31] It means in amidst of those to whom they left their wealth. Its import is, they are not remembered, save that people say, this is the house of so and so and this tower was built by so and so. This is the meaning of *they call.* Now all of this is of no avail.[32]

13. BUT MAN ABIDETH NOT IN HONOR; HE IS LIKE THE BEASTS THAT PERISH.

BUT MAN. Some say that *bi-yekar* (in honor) means, that which is dear[33] to him. It refers to man's wealth. A person's holdings shall not abide with him when he dies. On the contrary he shall leave it behind.[34] The meaning of *abideth (*yalin) in *abideth not* is similar to *yalin* (abide) in *His soul shall abide in prosperity* (Ps. 25:13). Man is thus like the beasts. They too will perish[35] when they die.[36]

THAT PERISH. *Nidmu* means that perish.[37]

The Jerusalemite[38] says that *nimshal* (he is like) refers to the individual, who is one of the group,[39] and *nidmu* (that perish) to the group.[40]

---

29. Lit. "His eternal home." This interpretation reads our verse as follows: Their graves are their eternal homes and their dwelling places to all generations, they call the monuments which are over their graves after themselves."

30. They erect structures over their graves to memorialize their names.

31. *Bi-kirbam* is the proper Hebrew way of saying amidst them.

32. To the person who built the house or tower.

33. The word *yakar* means precious.

34. I.E. renders *adam bi-yekar bal yalin* (man abideth not in honor), man with that which is dear to him shall not abide.

35. Literally, "die."

36. Man, like the beasts, will perish at their deaths.

37. Lit., that are cut off.

38. Possibly Rabbi Chayyim of Jerusalem. So *Ha-Keter.*

39. *Nimshal* is a singular.

40. *Nidmu* is a plural.

14. THIS IS THE WAY OF THEM THAT ARE FOOLISH, AND THOSE AFTER THEM APPROVE THEIR SAYINGS. SELAH.

THIS IS THE WAY. *Ve-acharehem* (those after them) refers to their children. Their offspring want to follow in their path.[41]
The meaning of *their sayings* is; they charged their children in this manner.[42] Others say their children will pay for their sins.[43]

15. LIKE SHEEP THEY ARE APPOINTED FOR THE NETHER-WORLD; DEATH SHALL BE THEIR SHEPHERD; AND THE UPRIGHT SHALL HAVE DOMINION OVER THEM IN THE MORNING; AND THEIR FORM SHALL BE FOR THE NETHER-WORLD TO WEAR AWAY, THAT THERE BE NO HABITATION FOR IT.

LIKE SHEEP. The word *shattu* (they are appointed) is similar to *shattu* (they have set) in *They have set their mouth against the heavens* (Ps. 73:9). *Ka-tzon li-she'ol shattu* (like sheep they are appointed) means, they put into their minds the thought that they are like sheep.[44]

DEATH SHALL BE THEIR SHEPHERD. For their end is to be slaughtered.

AND THE UPRIGHT SHALL HAVE DOMINION OVER THEM. After their death. The upright refers to the four elements[45] that do not consist of compounds. That part of man which is compounded from fire returns to fire. The part of man which consists of wind returns to wind. That part of man which comes from water returns to water. The bones which are made out of dust return to dust.
In the morning is in contrast to *abideth* (v. 13).[46] Its meaning is that they will become sick after a half a day.[47]

41. I.E. renders *yirtzu* (approve) as, want.

42. I.E. renders *be-fihem* (their sayings) as, with their mouths. He explains ve-*acharehem be-fihem yirtzu* (and those after them approve their sayings) as meaning: Those who come after them want to walk in the ways that their parents told them to take.

43. See Lev. 26:4. This interpretations renders, *ve-acharehem be-fihem yirtzu* (and those after them approve their sayings) as meaning: Those who come after them and follow their ways, shall pay for the sins of their parents.

44. They are not aware that they have a soul which is potentially immortal. See I.E.'s comment on verse 21.

45. Fire, water, wind (air) and earth (dust).

46. Heb., *yalin.* Literally, pass the night. Since Scripture earlier used the metaphor of night it now employs the image of day.

47. After the morning has passed.

Ve-tzuram (and their form) is a variant of *ve-tzuratam* (and their form).[48] Compare *ki-tevunam* (according to their own understanding) in *according to their own understanding, even idols* (Hos. 13:2) which is a variant of *ki-tevunatam.*

[AND THEIR FORM SHALL BE FOR THE NETHER-WORLD TO WEAR AWAY.] Its meaning is that the grave which is below, wherein the body is placed, shall consume the form of the body.

[THAT THERE BE NO HABITATION FOR IT.] The meaning of *mi-zevul* [*lo*] (that there be no habitation [for it]) is, from the habitation[49] in which he dwells. Destruction shall come to each and every one from there.[50]
Rabbi Moses says that the word *ha-rodim* (the rulers) has been omitted [from our clause].[51]
Scripture reads *upright* because no man shall be able to escape.[52]
Rabbi Jonah says that *mi-zevul lo* (that there be no habitation for it) refers to the judgment from heaven upon each one.[53]

16. BUT GOD WILL REDEEM MY SOUL FROM THE POWER OF THE NETHER-WORLD; FOR HE SHALL RECEIVE ME. SELAH.

BUT. I have previously noted in my book[54] that the terms *nefesh* (life), *neshahamah* (soul) and *ru'ach* (spirit) are all terms for man's highest soul[55] which is everlasting and is im-

48. In other words *ve-tzuram* means and their form. *Ve-tzuratam* is the proper grammatical form for the word. *Ve-tzuram* might be taken to mean and their rock. Hence I.E.'s comment.

49. The grave wherein the body is placed. The literal meaning of *mi-zevul,* is from the habitation. Hence I.E.'s interpretation.

50. Destruction shall come to each and every one from the grave (his habitation).

51. According to Rabbi Moses our clause should read *va-yirdu vam ha- rodim ha- yesharim* and the upright rulers have dominion over them. The "upright rulers" refers to the judgments meted out to the wicked. Filwarg.

52. From the upright rulers.

53. Rabbi Jonah renders *mi-zevul lo* as, from the dwelling place (that is, heaven) to him. Hence his interpretation.

54. Literally, the book. See *Yesod Mora* 7:4.

55. According to I.E., there are three souls in the body. *Neshamah* (rational soul), *ru'ach* (spirit) and *nefesh* (life). Only the rational soul is immortal. *The Secret of the Torah,* pp. 96-97.

mortal. It is called *nefesh* (life)[56] and also *ru'ach* (spirit)[57] because it[58] is not visible to the eye but with the aforementioned.[59] Now because the psalmist was filled with the spirit of wisdom and God's writing[60] was engraved on his soul he said *But God will redeem my soul from the power of the nether-world.* It is impossible for him to have meant[61] that he will not die as other people do, for *What man is he that liveth and shall not see death* (Ps. 89:49).[62] The meaning of *for He shall receive me* is that the soul of the psalmist will cleave to the upper soul which is the soul of heaven.[63] The same is the case with *for God took him*[64] (Gen.5:24) and, *And afterward receive me with glory* (Ps. 73:24).

17. BE NOT THOU NOT AFRAID WHEN ONE WAXETH RICH, WHEN THE WEALTH OF HIS HOUSE IS INCREASED.

BE NOT THOU NOT AFRAID. The poet backtracks to what he mentioned earlier namely, *I will incline mine ear to a parable* (v. 5). He once again chastises himself.[65] On the other hand he might be chastising the intelligent. He says, *Be not afraid* if you lack wealth and you envy the rich.

18. FOR WHEN HE DIETH HE SHALL CARRY NOTHING AWAY; HIS WEALTH SHALL NOT DESCEND AFTER HIM.

FOR WHEN HE DIETH HE SHALL CARRY NOTHING AWAY. [*Ha-kol*[66] (nothing) means] even a portion of it.

56. The *neshamah* is referred to as *nefesh* even though the *nefesh* "is the power of growth...It is located in the liver...It is that part of the psyche that desires food and sex." *The Secret of the Torah*, p. 96.

57. *Ru'ach* refers to the soul that "animates man and governs movement." "It is located in the heart...It is that part of the psyche that waxes angry." *The Secret of the Torah*, p. 96. Nevertheless it is also used as a synonym for "man's highest soul." Ibid. P. 96.

58. Man's rational soul.

59. The *nefesh* and the *ru'ach*. The rational soul expresses itself via the *nefesh* and the *ru'ach*.

60. I.E. defines God's writing as the knowledge of the sciences and of philosophy. See next note.

61. Literally, said.

62. "When God's writing, which consists of the categorical knowledge of the things made out of the four elements, the knowledge of the spheres, the throne of glory, the secret of the chariot, and the knowledge of the Most High is inscribed [upon the soul,] the soul cleaves to God the Glorious while it is yet in man and also afterward when its power is removed from the body." *The Secret of the Torah* p. 143; *Yesod Mora*, Chap. 10.

63. In line with other medieval thinkers I.E. believed in the existence of a world soul from which individual souls emanated. Upon death, if worthy, the individual soul returns to the world soul.

64. Enoch. Enoch's soul was united with the world soul.

65. In other words, the psalmist addresses himself.

66. *Ha-kol* literally means everything. Hence I.E.'s comment.

Compare *kol*[67] (nothing) in *Our soul is dried away; there is nothing at all* (Num.11:6).[68] The psalmist first mentioned that riches will not save a man from death. He now notes that riches will not avail him after his death. The following is the meaning of our verse: If man[69] acquires wisdom, then the wisdom will avail him after his death. Wealth only avails during one's lifetime for it provides food and drink. Otherwise it has no value.[70] This is the meaning of *Though while he lived he blessed his soul.* (V. 19). [71]

19. THOUGH WHILE HE LIVED HE BLESSED HIS SOUL: 'MEN WILL PRAISE THEE, WHEN THOU SHALT DO WELL TO THYSELF.

MEN WILL PRAISE THEE. The poor and the wealthy.[72]

WHEN THOU SHALT DO WELL TO THYSELF. The Psalmists tells the intelligent that he should seek that which will be good for him at the end.[73] Hence Scripture afterward states [*It shall go to the generations ...*]

20. IT SHALL GO TO THE GENERATION OF HIS FATHERS; THEY SHALL NEVER SEE THE LIGHT.

IT SHALL GO. The reference is, as is stated above, to the souls of the wealthy.[74]

TO THE GENERATION OF HIS FATHERS. Who like him had no wisdom.

THEY SHALL NEVER SEE THE LIGHT. The reference is to the reward and pleasure of the soul when it is illuminated by the light of its Master who gave it and took it. The light of the world to come is similarly called, in the book *Ben Gurian,* the great light.[75] I have previously mentioned why.

---

67 Literally, everything.

68. Here too *kol* means a portion.

69. Literally, he.

70. Lit. For there is no value in wealth, except in his life, so that he eats and drinks.

71. Its meaning is; wealth has no ultimate value even though one enjoys it while alive.

72. The poor and the wealthy will praise you.

73. After his death.

74. V. 19.

75. Josiphon.

21. MAN THAT IS IN HONOR UNDERSTANDETH NOT; HE IS LIKE THE BEASTS THAT PERISH.

MAN. Rabbi Judah Ha-Levi who rests in glory says that *ve- adam bi-yekar bal yalin* (But man abideth not in honor) (v. 13) means there is something glorious in man that that does not go to sleep[76] that is, something that does not lie down and die. [77] The thing referred to is, the glory of the soul.[78] Similarly [here].[79] A person who does not learn will not understand this.[80] He is therefore like the beasts that perish.[81]

76. Literally, that does not spend the night.

77. *Ve-adam bi-yekar bal yalin* can be rendered, And man, in glorious, does not spend the night. Rabbi Judah Ha-Levi renders this, and man, in him is a glorious thing, it does not go to sleep.

78. Man's rational soul.

79. *Yakar* has a similar meaning here. It refers to the soul.

80. That man has a soul which is potentially immortal.

81. According to Rabbi Judah *adam bi-yekar ve-lo yavin nimshal la-behemot nidmu* (man that is in honor understandeth not; He is like the beasts that perish) means, if man who has a glorious thing in him does not know this and live accordingly, then he is like the beasts that perish.

CHAPTER 50.

1. A PSALM OF ASAPH. GOD, GOD, THE LORD, HATH SPOKEN, AND CALLED THE EARTH FROM THE RISING OF THE SUN UNTO THE GOING DOWN THEREOF.

A PSALM OF ASAPH. GOD. *El Elohim* (God, God) means, God who has the power[1] to execute judgment.[2] The term *Elohim* (God) therefore [follows El]. The term *YHVH* (Lord) means, the One who exists forever without any change.[3]

AND CALLED THE EARTH. He called the inhabitants of the earth, who dwell from the rising of the sun unto the going down thereof.[4] This[5] is where the inhabitants of the earth dwell.[6] [Scripture reads *called the earth*[7]] even thou the entire earth is not settled, for there is definite proof that less than one quarter of the earth is inhabited.

2. OUT OF ZION, THE PERFECTION OF BEAUTY, GOD HATH SHINNED FORTH.

OUT OF ZION. Which is in the center of the inhabited world, in the length and in the breadth.

1. *El* means the powerful one.
2. *Elohim* signifies a judge.
3. Thus *El Elohim YHVH* means, the unchanging God who has the power to execute judgment.
4. *And called the earth* means, and called the inhabitants of the earth.
5. From the rising of the sun till its setting.
6. In other words, *the earth* is short for the inhabitants of the earth.
7. *Called the earth* implies that the entire earth is inhabited.

A PSLAM OF ASAPH. GOD, GOD, THE LORD HATH SPOKEN

GOD HATH SHINNED FORTH. God's glory has shinned forth.[8]

3. OUR GOD COMETH, AND DOTH NOT KEEP SILENCE; A FIRE DEVOURETH BEFORE HIM, AND ROUND ABOUT HIM IT STORMETH MIGHTILY.

OUR GOD COMETH. These are the words of the righteous who hope that God will destroy those who sin against Him. This is the meaning of *a fire devoureth before Him.*

STORMETH. *Nisarah* (stormeth) is similar to the word *se'arah* (stormy) in *stormy wind* (Ps. 148:8).This is so even though *nisarah* is spelled with a *sin.*[9]

4. HE CALLETH TO THE HEAVENS ABOVE, AND TO THE EARTH, THAT HE MAY JUDGE HIS PEOPLE.

HE CALLETH TO THE HEAVENS. To the Angels.[10]

AND TO THE EARTH. To its inhabitants.

5. GATHER MY SAINTS[11] TOGETHER UNTO ME; THOSE THAT HAVE MADE A COVENANT WITH ME BY SACRIFICE.

GATHER. Gather, for reproof, the saints of Israel who made a covenant with Me.[12] The meaning of *ali zevach* (by sacrifice) is, because of sacrifice,[13] that is, because of the sacrifice.[14]

Ali zevach is another way of saying *al devar zevach* (because of sacrifice).

8. I.E. interprets thus to avoid anthropomorphism.

9. And *se'arah* with a *samekh.*

10. *He calleth to the heavens* means, He calls to the angels.

11. Heb. *Chasidai.*

12. God's response to the request of the righteous (v. 2-4).

13. The word *al* means, on. Thus *ali zevach* would ordinarily be translated, upon the sacrifice. Hence I.E.'s comment.

14. In other words, the reference is to specific sacrifices viz. the sacrifices offered when God made a covenant with Israel at Sinai. See Ex. 24:4-8.

6. AND THE HEAVENS DECLARE HIS RIGHTEOUSNESS; FOR GOD, HE IS JUDGE. SELAH.

DECLARE. The reference is to the angels. [15] They are perpetual witnesses that God is eternally a righteous judge. This[16] is the reproof.

7. HEAR, O MY PEOPLE, AND I WILL SPEAK; O ISRAEL, AND I WILL TESTIFY AGAINST THEE; GOD, THY GOD, AM I.

HEAR. The meaning of our verse is as follows: I made a covenant with you for only one reason, namely, so that I would be your God. This is the import of, *God, thy God, am I.*

8. I WILL NOT REPROVE THEE FOR THY SACRIFICES; AND THY BURNT-OFFERING ARE CONTINUALLY BEFORE ME.

I WILL NOT. I will not now reprove you if you do not offer your sacrifices before me. Compare the words of Jeremiah, *Add your burnt-offerings unto your sacrifices* (Jer. 7:21). *Thy sacrifices* refer to sin and guilt offerings. I will similarly not reprove you and tell you that your burnt-offering should always be before me.[17]

9. I WILL TAKE NO BULLOCK OUT OF THY HOUSE, NOR HE-GOATS OUT OF THY FOLDS.

NO BULLOCK. I have no need to take a bullock out of your house. The psalmist mentions the largest animal[18] offered on the altar.

OUT OF THY FOLDS. *Mi-mikhle'otekha* (out of thy folds) is similar to *mi-mikhlah* (from the fold) in *The flock shall be cut off from the fold* (Hab. 3:17). The *alef* and the *heh* interchange.[19]

15. I.E. renders *And the heavens declare,* and the angels declare.

16. What follows.

17. I.E.'s interpretation of *And thy burnt-offerings are continually before Me.*

18. A bullock.

19. Hence the words are related. *Mikhlah* in *mikhle'otekha* is spelled with an *alef.* However, *mikhlah* in Hab. is spelled with a *heh.* Hence I.E.'s comment.

10. FOR EVERY BEAST OF THE FOREST IS MINE, AND THE CATTLE UPON A THOUSAND HILLS.

FOR. The *vav* of *chayto* (beast of) is superfluous.[20] It is like the *vav* in *beno* (son of)[21] in *the son of Beor* (Num. 24:3).

UPON A THOUSAND HILLS. *Harere elef* (a thousand hills)[22] means either a thousand hills;[23] a thousand Persian miles,[24] or mountains which have a thousand bullocks.[25] Rabbi Moses says that *elef* (a thousand) is similar to *alafekha* (thy kine) in *the increase of thy kine* (Deut. 7:13). The meaning of *harere elef* is mountains full of cattle.[26] Our verse is to be so interpreted, because Scripture earlier (v. 9) speaks of a bullock.

11. I KNOW ALL THE FOWLS OF THE MOUNTAINS; AND THE WILD BEASTS OF THE FIELD ARE MINE.

I KNOW. Scripture says *I*[27] *know all the fowls of the mountains,* because it is beyond the ken of man to know all of the fowl, for they are numerous.

AND THE WILD BEASTS OF THE FIELD. The wild beasts that are in the field. People do not dominate them, because these beasts are far from settled areas.

12. IF I WERE HUNGRY, I WOULD NOT TELL THEE; FOR THE WORLD IS MINE, AND THE FULLNESS THEREOF.

IF I WERE HUNGRY. Rabbi Moses says that its meaning is as follows: If I were a human being in need, I would not ask anyone to give me from what he has, when he only has a little. How much more so is the case, when in reality all is in My hand and I am not in need.

---

20. It is not a pronominal suffix. In other words *chayto* has the same meaning as the more commonly used form *chayyat.*

21. Here too the *vav* has no meaning. It is not a pronominal suffix. In other words *beno* has the same meaning as the more commonly used form *ben.*

22. *Harare elef* (a thousand hills) literally means, hills of a thousand. Hence the interpretations that follows.

23. This interpretation interprets *hills of a thousand* as meaning, a thousand hills.

24. This interpretation interprets *hills of a thousand* as being short for, hills of a thousand Persian miles.

25. This interpretation explains hills *of a thousand* as being short for, hills of a thousand bullocks.

26. This interpretation renders *harare elef* as, hills of cattle.

27. God.

13. DO I EAT THE FLESH OF BULLS, OR DRINK THE BLOOD OF GOATS?

DO I EAT THE FLESH OF BULLS. *Abbirim* means bulls. Our verse is in keeping with *I will take no bullock out of thy house* (v. 9).

14. OFFER UNTO GOD THE SACRIFICE OF THANKSGIVING; AND PAY THY VOWS UNTO THE MOST HIGH.

THE SACRIFICE. The psalmist mentions all of this[28] because [God says,] the sacrifices which I commanded to be offered before Me do not benefit Me, but on the contrary are for your own good.
Scripture mentions the Thanksgiving offering[29] because the burnt offering is entirely consumed by fire. The sin offering and the guilt offering belong to the *kohen.*[30] The meaning of our verse is: It is better to be Torah observant and offer a Thanksgiving offering, of which only certain designated inner organs are burnt on the altar, than to offer a burnt offering without being Torah[31] observant.

15. AND CALL UPON ME IN THE DAY OF TROUBLE; I WILL DELIVER THEE AND THOU SHALT HONOR ME.

AND CALL UPON ME. Its meaning is as follows: If you brought a vow offering or a free will offering in keeping with the utterance of your lips (V. 15), then if you call upon me another time, in a day of trouble, I will deliver you. You will also honor Me[32] by fulfilling your vows.

16. BUT UNTO THE WICKED GOD SAITH: WHAT HAST THOU TO DO TO DECLARE MY STATUTES, AND THAT THOU HAST TAKEN MY COVENANT IN THY MOUTH.

BUT UNTO THE WICKED. Scripture states this because the psalmist earlier said that *He (God) may judge His people* (v. 4). God, up to this point, reasoned with the pious. He

28. Verses 8-14.

29. In our verse.

30. However, the thanksgiving offering was eaten by the celebrant and his family after certain designated portions were burnt on the altar and the priestly portions given to the *kohen.*

31. Reading *Torah* rather than *todah.* Filwarg; *Ha-Keter.*

32. After I deliver you.

now speaks with a wicked man who is wise, for God hates him. This is the meaning of *What hast thou to declare my statutes* when you do not observe them.

17. SEEING THOU HATEST INSTRUCTION, AND CASTEST MY WORDS BEHIND THEE.

SEEING THOU HATEST. You hate the instruction, which I imparted to you, so that it will be well with you.

18. WHEN THOU SAWEST A THIEF, THOU HADST COMPANY WITH HIM, AND WITH ADULTERERS WAS THY PORTION.

WHEN THOU SAWEST A THIEF, THOU HADST COMPANY WITH HIM. *Va-tiretez* (thou hadst company) is similar to the word *ratzo* (ran) in *ran and returned* (Ezek. 1:14).[33] In this case there are two roots for the word *run*.[34] On the other hand it is possible that *va-tiretz* is related to the word *ratzon* (desire, want). In this case the meaning of *va-tiretz immo* (thou hadst company with him) is, you wanted to join him.

19. THOU HAST LET LOOSE THY MOUTH FOR EVIL, AND THY TONGUE FRAMETH DECEIT.

THY MOUTH. *Thou hast let loose thy mouth* to speak words which are harmful to your fellow man.

FRAMETH DECEIT. *Tatzmid mirmah* (frameth deceit) means, you combine deceitful words.[35]

20. THOU SITTTES AND SPEAKEST AGAINST THY BROTHER; THOU SLANDEREST THY MOTHER'S SON.

THOU SITTTES. In the seat of the scornful. Look, you let loose your mouth against those who are unrelated to you (v. 19).[36]

33. This interpretation renders the first part of our verse. When you saw a thief, you ran with him.

34. *Resh, tzadi, heh* for *va-tiretz*; and *resh, vav, tzadi* for *ratzo.*

35. *Tatzmid* means, you join. Thus *tatzmid mirmah* (frameth deceit) means, you combine deceit. According to I.E. the meaning of "you combine deceit" is, you combine deceitful words.

36. And you do the same to your brother.

21. THESE THINGS HAST THOU DONE , AND SHOULD I HAVE KEPT SILENCE? THOU HADST THOUGHT THAT I WAS ALTOGETHER SUCH A ONE AS THYSELF, BUT I WILL REPROVE THEE, AND SET THE CAUSE BEFORE THINE EYES.

THESE THINGS. *And ...I have kept silence* means; it is as if I kept silence, for I am long suffering.

THOU HADST THOUGHT. That I like you, do not know hidden things. Scripture therefore afterwards reads: *But I will reprove thee, and set the cause before thine eyes.*[37] The word *ve-e'erkhah* (and set) is similar to the word *erkhah* (set...in order) in *set thy words in order before me* (Job 33:5).[38] The psalm reads thus,[39] because the son of his mother does not know what his brother secretly said.[40]
Rabbi Moses says that it is incorrect to say *shemor shamarti* (I have truly kept) or *shemor eshmerah* (I will truly keep). In other words, it is incorrect to vocalize the *shin* of *shamor* with a *sheva.* It has to be vocalized with a long *kametz.*[41] The same applies to *asot e'eseh* (I will truly do).[42] However, what will he do with the phrase *heyot eheyeh* (I was altogether) in *I was altogether such a one as thyself.*[43] There is no other such word.[44]

22. NOW CONSIDER THIS, YE THAT FORGET GOD. LEST I TEAR IN PIECES, AND THERE BE NONE TO DELIVER.

NOW CONSIDER THIS, YE THAT FORGET GOD. The reference is to thieves, adulterers and defamers. The psalmist compares the evil that shall come upon them to an attack by a lion, from whose claws no one can deliver, for a shepherd can save [a sheep or goat] from a bear or a wolf. Or *etrof*[45] (lest I tear) might also be understood as, *etrof trefah*

37. Our clause literally reads, "and set before thine eyes."

38. According to I.E., "and set before thine eyes" means, I will set your deeds before your eyes. The meaning of the aforementioned is; I will show you that I know all that you do.

39. I will set your deeds before your eyes.

40. But God does.

41. When the infinitive is combined with a perfect or imperfect, the infinitive has to be vocalized with a *kametz.*

42. This rule does not only apply to whole roots like *shamar*, it also applies to roots ending in a *heh* like *asah*.

43. *Heyot* is vocalized with a *sheva* (a chataf segol) and not with a *kametz.* However, according to Rabbi Moses it should be vocalized with a *kametz.*

44. There is no other infinitive combined with a perfect or imperfect that is vocalized with a *sheva.*

45. There does not appear to a difference between this interpretation and the one that comes before it.

I will tear, a tear.[46] The meaning of our clause is: I will tear a type of tear that none can deliver from. Scripture says this for a shepherd can deliver from a bear. [What a shepherd is able to save from a bear] is unlike that which he is able to save from a lion.[47]

23. WHOSO OFFERETH THE SACRIFICE OF THANKSGIVING HONORETH ME; AND TO HIM THAT ORDERETH HIS WAY ARIGHT WILL I SHOW THE SALVATION OF GOD.

THE SACRIFICE. The one who *offereth the sacrifice of Thanksgiving* is the one who honors Me.

AND TO HIM THAT ORDERETH HIS WAY. He to whom the right way has become clear. *Ve-sam* (and to him that ordereth) means, and to him that understands. Compare *ve-yasimu ve-yaskilu* (and consider and understand) (Is. 41:20). The meaning of *yasimu*[48] thus is they understand.[49]
The *bet* of *be-yesha* (the salvation) in *the salvation of God* is similar to the *bet* in *bi-yeshuati* (in my salvation)[50] in *And make him to behold My salvation* (Ps. 91:16).

Filwarg suggests emending *etrof* to *ve-amar etrof.* He reads I.E. as follows: The psalmist compares the evil that shall come upon them to an attack by a lion, from whose claws no one can deliver, for a shepherd can save [a sheep or goat] from a bear or a wolf. The word *Etrof* (lest I tear) is to be understood as, *etrof trefah,* I will tear, a tear. The meaning of our clause is: I will tear a tear that there is none to deliver from…

46. In other words the verb *etrof* "includes" in it the noun *terefah.* The Hebrew text reads, *lest I tear. In pieces* is not in the text. Our clause literally reads, lest I tear, and there is non to deliver. I.E. says that the latter is to be interpreted lest, I tear a tear from which none can deliver.

47. The most that a shepherd can save from a lion is a leg or a piece of ear. He can not save the life of the sheep. Compare, *as he rescueth out of the mouth of the lion two legs, or a piece of ear* (Amos 3:12).

48. In Is. 41:20.

49. Similarly, here too *ve-sam* means, and he understands. The usual meaning of *sam* is," puts." Hence I.E.'s comments.

50. It is superfluous. The *bet* usually means in. Here and in Ps. 91, it is not to be translated.

CHAPTER 51.

1. FOR THE LEADER. A PSALM OF DAVID.

2. WHEN THE PROPHET NATHAN CAME UNTO HIM, AFTER HE HAD GONE IN TO BATH-SHEBA.

WHEN THE PROPHET NATHAN CAME UNTO HIM. When Nathan prophesied regarding David and told him, *The Lord also hath put away thy sin; thou shalt not die* (2 Sam. 12:13).[1] The word *also* indicates that David had repented.[2] The prophet therefore told him *The Lord also hath put away thy sin.* I have previously explained the incident of Bath-Sheba.[3] I noted that she was not really a married woman.[4]

3. BE GRACIOUS UNTO ME, O GOD, ACCORDING TO THY MERCY; ACCORDING TO THE MULTITUDE OF THY COMPASSION BLOT OUT MY TRANSGRESSIONS.

---

1. *When Nathan the prophet came before him…* is to be understood as meaning, when Nathan the prophet came before him and said *The Lord also hath put away thy sin; thou shalt not die. When Nathan the prophet came before him…* could be understood as meaning, when Nathan the prophet came before David and castigated him for his sin. However, no castigation of David follows. Hence I.E.'s comment.

2. The full text of 2 Sam. 12:13 reads: *And David said unto Nathan: 'I have sinned against the Lord.' And Nathan said unto David: The Lord also hath put away thy sin; thou shalt not die.* Hence I.E.'s comment

3. The reference is most probably to I.E.'s commentary on Samuel. However, the latter is lost.

4. I.E. apparently accepted the opinion of the Talmud that Uriah had given Bath-Sheba a conditional divorce, that is, a divorce that would take effect from the time that is was presented to Bath-Sheba if Uriah failed to return from the war. Now since Uriah was eventually killed in the war, Bath-Sheba was technically a divorcee when David slept with her. See *Shabbat* 56a; Ketubot 9b and *Kiddushin* 43a.

BE GRACIOUS UNTO ME. For my lust has, as it were, dealt violently with me[5] and has overcome my[6] reason. *Pesha'ai* (my transgressions)[7] refers to the incident of Bat-Sheba[8] and the incident of Uriah.[9]

4. WASH ME THROUGHLY[10] FROM MINE INIQUITY, AND CLEANSE ME FROM MY SIN.

THROUGHLY. *Herev* (thoroughly) is an imperative. *Herev* is similar to *heref* (stay)[11] in *Stay, and I will tell thee* (1 Sam. 15:16). If this is the case then *kabbeseni* (wash me) is an infinitive.[12] It is to be interpreted as if written *le-khabbeseni* (to wash me). On the other hand *herev* (thoroughly) might be a noun. It is like *harbeh* (a lot). [13] In this case *kabbeseni* (wash me) is an imperative.[14]

David compared the soul which has been defiled by doing that which is unseemly, to a dirty object which requires cleansing and purification.

5. FOR I KNOW MY TRANSGRESSIONS; AND MY SIN IS EVER BEFORE ME.

FOR. *My sin* refers to David's intention,[15] for he did not observe God's commandments.[16] *My transgressions* means, my transgressions before men.[17]

---

5. Lit., with him.

6. Lit., his.

7. Prima facae our text should have read *my transgression*, for the psalm deals with the sin that David committed with Bath-Sheba. Hence I.E. explains that the plural *poshe'im* (transgressions) refers to the incidents of Bat-Sheba and Uriah.

8 See 11 Sam. 11:2-4.

9. Ibid. Verses 14-26.

10. Heb. *Herev kabbeseni.*

11. Which is an imperative.

12. For Hebrew does not employ two imperatives back to back. According to this interpretation our Psalm reads, Be thorough in washing me.

13. Which is a noun.

14. In this case our verse reads, a lot wash me i.e. wash me a lot.

15. Literally, thought. I.E. accepts the Rabbinic assertion that David did not actually sin with Bath Sheba, for as things turned out she was technically not a married women when he had intercourse with her. However, he was not aware of this when he slept with her. Thus his intention was to commit adultery. David thus committed adultery in thought, though not in practice. Filwarg.

16. He intended to violate, "Thou shalt not commit adultery."

17. What David did only appeared to people to be a sin. See I.E. on Ps. 32:1.

6. AGAINST THEE, THEE ONLY, HAVE I SINNED, AND DONE THAT WHICH IS EVIL IN THY SIGHT; THAT THOU MAYEST BE JUSTIFIED WHEN THOU SPEAKEST, AND BE IN THE RIGHT WHEN THOU JUDGEST.

AGAINST THEE. The sin which is always before me is the sin which I committed against You alone.[18]

That thou mayest be justified is tied to *I know my transgressions* (v. 5). Its meaning is as follows: I confess my transgressions and there is no need to chastise me. On the other hand it might be connected to *Be gracious unto me* (v. 3). In this case its meaning is as follows: *Be gracious unto me* because I confess my transgressions and You promised[19] that You will forgive those who repent and confess their sins.

7. BEHOLD, I WAS BROUGHT FORTH IN INIQUITY, AND IN SIN DID MY MOTHER CONCEIVE ME.

BEHOLD. *I was,* as it were, *brought forth in iniquity* because the inclination to lust is planted in the heart of man. Scripture says the aforementioned, because the evil inclination is planted in man's heart at the time of birth.[20]

The word *yechematni* (conceive me) is irregular.[21] It is as if Scripture read [and in sin] my mother [was] "pregnant with me."[22] *Yechematni* (conceive me) is similar to *le-yachmennah* (that they might conceive) (Gen. 30:41).[23] There are those who say that our verse alludes to Eve, who did not give birth till after she sinned.[24]

18. Intending to commit adultery.

19. Lit., said.

20 According to I.E. *I was brought forth in iniquity* does not refer to the act of coitus, but rather to the moment of birth. Man is born with a desire to commit acts, which in certain circumstances are sinful.

21. Intransitive verbs do not come with a pronominal suffix. Y*echematni* (conceive me) is an intransitive verb with a pronominal suffix. It is a compound of *yechemeh* (she conceived) and *oti* (from me). It literally means, she was pregnant me. Hence I.E.'s comment.

22. That is *yechematni* is to be interpreted, she was pregnant with me.

23. Y*echematni* and *le-yachmennah* come from the same root. Gen. 30: 41 reads le-*yachmennah ba-maklot* (that they might conceive among the rods). According to I.E. the meaning of *le-yachmennah ba-maklot* is, to conceive from the rods i.e. conceived spotted sheep because of the rods.

24. By eating from the tree of knowledge. It is to be noted that I.E. insists that the sin mentioned in our verse does not refer to the sexual act per se.

8. BEHOLD, THOU DESIREST TRUTH IN THE INWARD PARTS; MAKE ME, THEREFORE, TO KNOW WISDOM IN MINE INMOST HEART.

BEHOLD. The following is the meaning of our verse: Even though I sinned, my heart's faith in Your Divinity was not corrupted. This is what You desire and want from man.

IN THE INWARD PARTS. The word *va-tuchot* (in the inward parts) refers to the hidden parts which are the foundations of the heart.[25] The early sages said that *tuchot* refers to the kidneys which are covered[26] with fat. Compare the word *ba-tuchot* (the inward parts) in *Who hath put wisdom in the inward parts*? (Job 38:36).[27]

IN MINE INMOST HEART.[28] Teach me, and let me know the thing which is hidden from me.[29]

In my opinion the second half of the verse repeats the first part. The *tav* of *todi'eni* (make me...to know) goes back to the word *emet* (truth), for the original form of the word *emet* is *amenet.*[30] The *tav* of *todi'eni* is the sign of the feminine.[31] Compare *titzmach* (springeth out) in *Truth springeth out of the earth* (Ps 85:12). [32] *Emet* is similar to *bat* (daughter).[33] The word *bitto* (his daughter) is another form of the word *benato* (his daughter). The same is the case with the word *amitto* (his truth) (Ps. 91:4).[34] The plural of *emet* is *emunnot* (faithful) (Prov. 28:20) and not *amitim.* Similarly, the plural of *bat* (daughters) is *banot*, not *batim.*[35]

---

25. For our verse goes on to speak of the heart.

26. *Tu'ach* means covered.

27. This is not proof to the sages. I.E. is merely pointing out that the word *tuchot* in our verse has the same meaning as that in Job.

28 Heb. *U-va-satum*. Lit. And that which is hidden.

29. I.E. renders the last part of our verse as follows: Make me to know wisdom concerning that which is hidden from me.

30. The point is, *emet* is a feminine, for it is a variant of a*menet* which is a feminine.

31. According to this interpretation the last half of our verse reads: And truth will make knowledge of hidden things known to me.

32. The *tav* of *titzmach* is a third person feminine imperfect prefix governing *emet.*

33. Both words come from roots which have a *nun* as one of their stem letters, but have dropped the *nun.*

34. It drops the *nun* of *amemet.*

35. For the root of *bat* is *bet, nun, tav.*

9. PURGE ME WITH HYSSOP, AND I SHALL BE CLEAN; WASH ME, AND I SHALL BE WHITER THAN SNOW.

PURGE ME. David compares that which befell his soul to a plague of leprosy on the body. He therefore states, *purge me with hyssop.*[36]
Albin (I shall be clean) is an intransitive verb.[37] Compare the word *hilbinu* [38](are made white) in *The branches thereof are made white* (Joel 1:7).

10. MAKE ME TO HEAR JOY AND GLADNESS; THAT THE BONES WHICH THOU HAST CRUSHED MAY REJOICE.

MAKE ME TO HEAR. David pleaded *Make me to hear joy* because his soul was mourning.[39]

THAT THE BONES...MAY REJOICE. The foundation of the might and power of the body[40] [shall] similarly [rejoice].

11. HIDE THY FACE FROM MY SINS, AND BLOT OUR ALL MINE INIQUITIES.

HIDE THY FACE. This is a metaphor.[41] It means; may God's burning anger not be manifest.

12. CREATE ME A CLEAN HEART, O GOD; AND RENEW A STEADFAST SPIRIT WITHIN ME.

Being that David earlier said that he was *brought forth in iniquity* (v. 7), that is, that the lust which is implanted in the human heart brought him to sin, he now prayed to God and asked Him to help him overcome his impulse, so that he would not commit a similar sin again. This is the meaning of [create me] *a clean heart.*

A STEADFAST SPIRIT. Scripture repeats itself.[42]

36. Which is used in purging a leper. See Lev. 14:1-7.

37. Even though it is in the *hifil.*

38. Which is in the *hifil* and is intransitive.

39. Because of his sin.

40. The bones. See Radak. Also my bones shall rejoice.

41. For God has no face.

42. The second half of the verse repeats the idea of the first half.

13. CAST ME NOT AWAY FROM THY PRESENCE; AND TAKE NOT THY HOLY SPIRIT FROM ME.

CAST ME NOT AWAY. David was afraid that he would fall from the status of being one of the men possessed by the Holy Spirit.[43] We find that in his later says David said: *The spirit of the Lord spoke by me* (11 Sam. 23:2).[44]

14. RESTORE UNTO ME THE JOY OF THY SALVATION; AND LET A WILLING SPIRIT UPHOLD ME.

RESTORE. David was joyful before he sinned, for he had never transgressed. Hence he said: *Restore*. The *tav* of *tismekheni* (uphold me) is connected to *a willing spirit*.[45] Its meaning is: *Let a willing spirit uphold me* so that I will willingly teach [transgressors Your ways].

15. THEN WILL I TEACH TRANSGRESSORS THY WAYS; AND SINNERS SHALL RETURN UNTO THEE.

TRANSGRESSORS. *Poshe'im* (transgressors) is parallel to *for I know my transgressions* (v. 5). *And sinners* is parallel to *and my sin is ever before me* (v.5).

16. DELIVER ME FROM BLOODGUILTINESS, O GOD, THOU GOD OF MY SALVATION; SO SHALL MY TONGUE SING ALOUD OF THY RIGHTEOUSNESS.

DELIVER ME. David prayed *Deliver me from blood guiltiness* because of the killing of Uriah. *So shall my tongue sing loud of Thy righteousness* means, I am not a murderer who deserves to be put to death, for David did not order that Uriah be killed.[46] However, David had evil intentions, for he ordered Uriah to be placed in a dangerous place.[47]

---

43. Because of his sin.

44. David's request was thus granted.

45. *Tismekheni* (uphold me) can be either a third person or a second person. Hence I.E.'s comment that it is a third person.

46. David did not explicitly order that Uriah be killed.

47 2 Sam. 11:15.

17. O LORD, OPEN THOU MY LIPS; AND MY MOUTH SHALL DECLARE THY PRAISE.

O LORD. Help me to declare Your praise.[48]

18. FOR THOU DELIGHTEST NOT IN SACRIFICE, ELSE WOULD I GIVE IT; THOU HAST NO PLEASURE IN BURNT OFFERINGS.

FOR. For You did not request and demand in Your Torah a burnt or a sin offering for a sin such as this.

19. THE SACRIFICES OF GOD ARE A BROKEN SPIRIT; A BROKEN AND A CONTRITE HEART, O GOD, THOU WILT NOT DESPISE.

THE SACRIFICES OF GOD. Repentance is considered as *sacrifices of God*.[49] Repentance consists of a broken and a contrite heart.

20. DO GOOD IN THY FAVOUR UNTO ZION; BUILD THOU THE WALLS OF JERUSALEM.

DO GOOD. One of the wise men of Spain said that these two verses were added [to the original psalm] by one of the pious men who lived in Babylonia, when he fell in prayer before God, and prayed employing this psalm. The earlier mentioned scholar[50] felt compelled to offer this interpretation because Zion was not known as the chosen place till David's old age.[51] It is also correct to interpret *Do good in thy favour unto Zion…*[52] as being said under the influence of the Holy Spirit.[53]

48. By opening my lips.

49. Sacrifices offered to God.

50. Literally, he.

51. See 2 Sam. 24:18-24.

52. Literally, it.

53. Hence David spoke prophetically when he spoke of Zion.

21. THEN WILT THOU DELIGHT IN THE SACRIFICES OF RIGHTEOUSNESS, IN BURNT-OFFERING AND WHOLE OFFERING; THEN WILL THEY OFFER BULLOCKS UPON THINE ALTAR.

THEN WILT THOU DELIGHT IN THE SACRIFICES OF RIGHTEOUSNESS. *Sacrifices of righteousness* refer to peace offerings. The *burnt-offering* refers to the daily burnt-offering and the additional burnt-offering. [54] The *whole offering* refers to the meal offering of the Kohen.[55]

54. Offered on New moon and festivals.

55. This was wholly consumed by the fire on the altar. See Lev. 12:12-16.

CHAPTER 52.

1. FOR THE LEADER. MASCHIL OF DAVID.

FOR THE LEADER. MASCHIL. *Maschil* refers to a poem that opens with the word *maskil.*[1] The purpose of this psalm is to declare that the wicked shall come to an evil end.

2. WHEN DOEG THE EDOMITE CAME AND TOLD SAUL, AND SAID UNTO HIM: DAVID IS COME TO THE HOUSE OF AHIMELELCH.[2]

WHEN DOEG ...CAME. Scripture[3] is brief in relating what happened, [4] for the incident is known.[5]

3. WHY BOASTEST THOU THYSELF OF EVIL. O MIGHTY MAN? THE MERCY OF GOD ENDURETH CONTINUALLY.

WHY. David told Doeg: Why do you, who are mighty when it comes to doing evil, boast of the evil that you do?

The meaning of *The mercy of God endureth continually* is: Rather than boast of evil, you should praise the mercy of God, which includes all of us. On the other hand it might mean:

1. *Maschil* is a psalm to be chanted to the tune of a song that opens with the word *maskil.* See I.E. on Ps. 4: 1.

2. **Achimelech** (Ahimelech) was the **kohen** of **Nob. He** extended hospitality to David, when David fled from Saul.

3. Our psalm.

4. Scripture is brief in relating what happened when Doeg told King Saul that David came to the house of Achimelech.

5. It is reported in full in 1 Sam. 21:1-11; 22:6-18.

Do you not know that God's mercy is with me continually?[6] The fact that David says at the end of the psalm: *I trust in the mercy of God forever and ever* (v. 10) is proof of this.
Some say that the word *chesed* (mercy) is missing a *kaf*.[7] The meaning of *chesed El* [the mercy of God] is, like the mercy of God.[8]

4. THY TONGUE DEVISETH DESTRUCTION; LIKE A SHARP RAZOR, WORKING DECEITFULLY.

DESTRUCTION. David employed the word "deviseth" with regard to the tongue[9] because the tongue is, as it were, an interpreter and through it one's thoughts are revealed. [10]
The meaning of *havvots* (destruction) is things that you imagine to be.[11]
Some say that the word *remiyyah* (deceitfully) comes from the word *ramah* (thrown) in *hath he thrown into the sea* (Ex. 15:1).[12] Others connect *remiyyah* to the word *mirmah* (deceit), [13] for they[14] have one root.[15]

5. THOU LOVEST EVIL MORE THAN GOOD; FALSEHOOD RATHER THAN SPEAKING RIGHTEOUSNESS. SELAH.

THOU LOVEST. *Mi-tov*[16] is to be rendered, *more than good*.[17] Some say *mi-tov* is to be rendered, in place of good. However, we never find the *mem* so used.[18]

---

6. God will prevent you from harming me.

7. The word should be interpreted as if written *ke-chesed*.

8. According to this interpretation our verse reads: "Why boastest thou thyself of evil...like the mercy of God that endures forever." In other words, you boast of your evil as if it were the mercy of God, which endures forever.

9. The tongue is a mere organ. It has no intelligence and cannot devise anything. Hence I.E.'s comment.

10. Hence the tongue appears to devise actions.

11. The evil things that you wish to come about. The word *havvah* means, become. Hence I.E.'s comment.

12. According to this interpretation, our clause reads, Like a sharp razor doing its thrusting i.e. like a sharp razor cutting.

13. In this case our verse reads: *Like a sharp razor, working deceitfully.*

14. *Remiyyah, mirmah* and *ramah.*

15. *Resh, mem, heh.*

16. Lit., from good.

17. The *mem* placed before the word *tov* has the meaning of, more than. The *mem* usually means from. Hence I.E.'s comment.

18. We do not find the *mem* to have the meaning of, in place of.

FALSEHOOD. For Doeg said that Achimelech knew that David was fleeing.[19] Achimelech was therefore killed.[20]
The meaning of *ahavta ra* (thou lovest evil) is, you, you loved evil.[21]

6. THOU LOVEST ALL DEVOURING WORDS, THE DECEITFUL TONGUE.

THOU LOVEST ALL DEVOURING WORDS. You, the deceitful tongue, love all devouring words, that is, words which will devour and destroy you. Scripture therefore after wards reads: [*God will likewise break thee for ever…*]

7. GOD WILL LIKEWISE BREAK THEE FOR EVER, HE WILL TAKE THEE UP, AND PLUCK THEE OUT OF THY TENT, AND ROOT THEE OUT OF THE LAND OF THE LIVING. SELAH.

GOD WILL LIKEWISE. David said to Doeg: "God will take thee up and pluck thee up from His tent,"[22] because Doeg *was detained*[23] *before the Lord*[24] (1 Sam. 21:8).

AND ROOT THEE OUT OF THE LAND OF THE LIVING. As you uprooted the family of Achimelech.[25]

SELAH. In truth.[26] David said this[27] by way of prayer[28] or under the influence of the Holy Spirit.[29]

---

19. Doeg said that Achimelech knew that David was fleeing From King Saul when he gave a weapon and food to David.

20. By King Saul.

21. That is, the meaning of, *ahavta ra* is, you loved evil. According to I.E. verses 5 and 6 are connected to each other: They should be interpreted as follows: *Thou: thou lovest evil more than good; falsehood rather than speaking righteousness,* [thou] *the deceitful tongue lovest all devouring words.*

22. The sanctuary at Nob.

23. Hebrew *ne'etzar.* Literally held back. The term connotes involvement in religious service.

24. Was tarrying in the temple.

25. Doeg destroyed all the inhabitants of Nob. 1 Sam. 22:18-19.

26. See I.E. on Ps.3: 3.

27. That Doeg would ultimately be destroyed.

28. Our verse is to be understood as a prayer that Doeg be destroyed.

29. David prophesied that Doeg would be destroyed.

8. THE RIGHTEOUS ALSO SHALL SEE, AND FEAR AND LAUGH AT HIM:

THE RIGHTEOUS ALSO SHALL SEE. The *righteous* shall continue to fear God.[30]

9. LO, THIS IS THE MAN THAT MADE NOT GOD HIS STRONGHOLD; BUT TRUSTED IN THE ABUNDANCE OF HIS RICHES, AND STRENGTHENED HIMSELF IN HIS WICKEDNESS.

LO. Doeg shall serve as an example. People shall say: Behold the man who put his trust in his wealth.

And strengthened himself in his wickedness (havvato) is in keeping with the earlier statement: *Thy tongue deviseth destruction* (havvot)[31] (v. 4).

10. BUT AS FOR ME, I AM LIKE A LEAFY OLIVE-TREE IN THE HOUSE OF GOD; I TRUST IN THE MERCY OF GOD FOREVER AND EVER.

BUT AS FOR ME. I am planted in the house of God.
David said: "and pluck thee out of the tent (v. 7)"[32] because *Doeg was detained* before the Lord.[33]

Ve-shereshkha (and root thee out) (v. 7) is a piel.[34] Its meaning is, to cut the root. However, it has the reverse meaning in the *hifil.*[35]

30. After Doeg's destruction.

31. According to I.E, the meaning of *havvot* (destruction) is, "things that that you think are", that is, the evil things that Doeg hopes to bring into about.

32. Translated literally. I.E. takes *tent* to mean God's tent. This and what follows belongs in I.E.'s comments on verse 7.

33. He was ensconced in God's tent.

34. Lit., the heavy conjugation.

35. The *hifil* form of the root *shin, resh, shin* means you will be rooted.

11. I WILL GIVE THEE THANKS FOREVER, BECAUSE THOU HAST DONE IT; AND I WILL WAIT FOR THY NAME, FOR IT IS GOOD, IN THE PRESENCE OF THY SAINTS.

I WILL GIVE THEE THANKS. *I will give Thee thanks* because you executed justice on my behalf upon Doeg.

AND I WILL WAIT FOR THY NAME. I will wait for You to do Doeg in accordance to his deeds, namely, that You will execute vengeance on my behalf upon him.

CHAPTER 53.

1. FOR THE LEADER; UPON MAHALATH. MASCHIL OF DAVID.

FOR THE LEADER; UPON MAHALATH. Some say that the word *machalat* is related to the word *chalul*[1] (hollow).[2] It is like the word *mikhsat* (the number of) in *according to the number of the souls* (Ex. 12:4). It comes from a double root.[3] However, this is incorrect, for *be-mikhsat*[4] is in the construct.[5] In reality *upon mahalth* means, according to the tune of a song opening with the word *machalat*.[6]
I have previously explained the meaning of the term *maskil*.[7]

2. THE FOOL HATH SAID IN HIS HEART: 'THERE IS NO GOD'; THEY HAVE DEALT CORRUPTLY, AND HAVE DONE ABOMINABLY INIQUITY; THERE IS NONE THAT DOETH GOOD.

[THE FOOL HATH SAID IN HIS HEART:] Rabbi Moses says that our verse is to be interpreted as follows: The fool, because he has corrupted his way,[8] *hath said in his heart* [*there is no God*]. However, in my opinion the opposite is the case.[9]

1. From the root *chet, lamed, lamed.*

2. *Machalat* refers to a hollow instrument.

3. *Machalat* like *mikhsat* comes from a double root. The root of *mikhsat* is *kaf, samekh, samekh.* Its *mem* is a form letter. Similarly, the *mem* of *machalat*, for (according to this interpretation) *machalat* comes from the root *chet, lamed, lamed*

4. Lit. *Be-mikhsat.*

5. Hence it ends in *tav*. However, *machalat* is an absolute.

6. See I.E. on Ps. 4:1.

7. See I.E. on Ps. 32:1.

8. Reading *she-hischit* (he has corrupted) rather than *she-shishchitu* (they have corrupted).

9. Our verse is to be interpreted: The fool saith in his heart there is no God **therefore** they have dealt corruptly.

Our verse first employs the singular and then the plural,[10] because the wicked sins and causes others to sin.

THEY HAVE DEALT CORRUPTLY.[11] They have corrupted their ways[12]

AND HAVE DONE ABOMINABLY They have abominated[13] by the iniquity which they have done.[14] The word *aval* (abominable) is lacking a *bet*.[15] It is similar to *that was found in the house of the Lord* (11 Kings 12:11). [16]
I have explained the next three verses in my comments on the earlier psalm.[17]

6. THERE ARE THEY IN GREAT FEAR, WHERE NO FEAR WAS; FOR GOD HATH SACTTERED THE BONES OF HIM THAT ENCAMPETH AGAINST THEE; THOU HAST PUT THEM, TO SHAME, BECAUSE GOD HATH REJECTED THEM.

WHERE NO FEAR WAS. *Lo hayah pachad* (where no fear was) means, there was no fear like it.[18] It is similar to *this is the people there was not* (Is. 23:13).[19] The meaning of the aforementioned is; this is the people; there was not a people like it.
The word *chonakh* (that encampeth against thee) is related to the word *chanah* (camped).[20] The *kaf*[21] refers to God or to the messiah. [22] *Chonakh* is an intransitive verb.[23] Therefore

---

10. Our verse opens with the singular viz., *The fool saith...* and then goes on to employ the plural, viz., *They have dealt corruptly ...*

11. Heb., *hishchitu*. Lit., they have corrupted.

12. In other words "they have corrupted" is short for they have corrupted their ways.

13. They have abominated their ways. Radak.

14. *Ve-hitivu avel* (and have done abominably iniquity) is to be interpreted as if written *ve-hitivu be-avel*. Our verse reads: *ve-hitivu avel*. This literally means: they have abominated evil. However, this cannot be the import of our verse, for our text speaks of the wicked. Hence I.E.'s comments.

15. *Avel* is to be interpreted as if written *be-avel*, by the iniquity. Our phrase is to be read: *ve-hitivu be- avel* (and have abominated [their ways] by the evil [which they have done].

16. Here too the word *bet* (house) is to be read as if written *be-vet* (in the house). See I.E. on Ps. 3:8 and the notes thereto.

17. Ps. 14.2-4.

18. *Lo hayah pachad* literally means; there was no fear. Hence I.E.'s interpretation.

19. Translated literally.

20. From the root *chet, nun, heh*.

21. Here it has the meaning of *thee*. The *kaf* suffixed to a verb indicates the second person.

22. In other words *thee* in *that encampeth against thee* refers to God or to the messiah.

23. Thus *chonakh* literally means, encamp you.

chonekh is to be rendered, those that encamp against you.[24] *Chonakh* is similar to *anakh*[25] (he will answer thee) in *When he shall hear, He will answer thee* (Is. 30:19).
The *tav* of *hevishotah*[26] (thou hast put them to shame) pertains to David. Our clause means, you (David) have put them to shame because God has rejected them.

7. OH THAT THE SALVATION OF ISRAEL WERE COME OUT OF ZION! WHEN GOD TURNETH THE CAPTIVITY OF HIS PEOPLE, LET JACOB REJOICE, LET ISRAEL BE GLAD.

OH THAT. I have previously explained this.[27]

24. For "encamp you" makes no sense.

25. It too is an intransitive verb with the *kaf* suffixed to it. Furthermore, it too comes from a root ending in a *heh*, and drops the *heh*.

26. Which indicates that the verb is a second person perfect.

27. See I.E. on Ps. 13:7.

CHAPTER 54.

1. FOR THE LEADER; WITH STRING MUSIC. MASCHIL OF DAVID.

WITH STRING MUSIC. *Neginot* (string music) is a word that opened a poem.[1]

2. WHEN THE ZIPHITES CAME AND SAID TO SAUL: DOTH NOT DAVID HIDE HIMSELF WITH US.[2]

3. O GOD, SAVE ME BY THY NAME, AND RIGHT ME BY THY MIGHT.

BY THY NAME. Which I call. *Be-shimekhah* (by thy name) means, because of your name.[3]

AND... BY THY MIGHT. You have the might to exact my judgment from the Ziphites.[4]

4. O GOD, HEAR MY PRAYER; GIVE EAR TO THE WORDS OF MY MOUTH.

HEAR MY PRAYER. Which I utter in my heart.

TO THE WORDS OF MY MOUTH. Uttered by my tongue.

1. This Psalm was to be chanted to the tune of a song that opened with the word *neginot*. See I.E. on Ps. 4: 1.
2. For a description of this incident see 1 Sam. 23:14-28.
3. The meaning of *O God Save me by Thy name* is, O God Save me because of Your name, which I call.
4. To punish my enemies on my behalf.

[*Hear my prayer* is to be rendered, hear my prayer which I utter in my heart] because the word tefillah (prayer) is basically similar to *va-yefallel*[5] (and wrought judgment) (Ps. 106: 30) and to *pillalti*[6] (I...thought) in, *I had not thought* (Gen. 48:11).[7]

5. FOR STRANGERS ARE RISEN AGAINST ME, AND VIOLENT MEN HAVE SOUGHT AFTER MY SOUL; THEY HAVE NOT SET GOD BEFORE THEM. SELAH.

FOR STRANGERS. Men not of David's nation.[8]
Violent men refer to the Ziphites.

6. BEHOLD, GOD IS MY HELPER; THE LORD IS FOR ME AS THE UPHOLDER OF MY LIFE.[9]

BEHOLD. Rabbi Moses says that *Adonai be-somekhe nafshi*[10] *(the Lord is for me as the upholder of my life)* does not mean, God is one of the upholders of my life.[11] On the contrary its meaning is, in contrast to all those who uphold my life; God alone is the true support of my life.
However, according to my opinion, David prayed that God exact his judgment from those who sought his evil[12] and that God would help those who support him and do not slander him.

7. HE WILL REQUITE THE EVIL UNTO THEM THAT LIE IN WAIT FOR ME; DESTROY THOU THEM IN THY TRUTH.

HE WILL REQUITE THE EVIL UNTO THEM. God will requite them the evil, which they intended to do me.

---

5. Its root is *peh, lamed, lamed.*

6. Its root is *peh, lamed, lamed*

7. Thinking and judgment taker place in the heart. So does prayer.

8. Non-Jews.

9. Hebrew, *nafshi.* J.P.S. renders *nafshi,* my soul. However, the translation *my life* is here more exact.

10. *Adonai be-somekhe nafshi* literally means, "The Lord is among the upholders of my life."

11. This interpretation renders *Adonai be-somekhe nafshi* as, The Lord stands out, among the upholders of my life.

12. I.E.'s paraphrase of the first half of the verse

In Thy truth means, they murder[13] they slander and they desire to kill me without any reason.[14]

8. WITH A FREE WILL- OFFERING WILL I SACRIFICE UNTO THEE; I WILL GIVE THANKS UNTO THY NAME O LORD, FOR IT IS GOOD.

WITH A FREE WILL- OFFERING WILL I SACRIFICE UNTO THEE. When You destroy my enemies.[15] I will give thanks for this [unto Thy name O Lord, for it is good] and say: [*For He hath delivered me out of my trouble; And mine eye hath gazed upon mine enemies.* (v. 9)].

[9. FOR HE HATH DELIVERED ME OUT OF ALL TROUBLE; AND MINE EYE HATH GAZED UPON MINE ENEMIES.]

Hath delivered me[16] refers back to *Thy name* mentioned in the previous verse.[17]

13. Literally, they stand over blood.

14. *Destroy Thou them in Thy truth* means, destroy them because You know the truth, that is, You know that they murder they slander and they desire to kill me without any reason.

15. Lit., them.

16. In verse 9.

17. Verse 8. I. E. interprets v. 9 as reading: *For **it** hath delivered me (hitzilani) out of my trouble.* Hence his interpretation.

CHAPTER 55

1. FOR THE LEADER; WITH STRING MUSIC. MASCHIL OF DAVID.

2. GIVE EAR, O GOD, TO MY PRAYER; AND HIDE NOT THYSELF FROM MY SUPPLICATION.

GIVE EAR, O GOD, TO MY PRAYER. *Give ear...* and *hide not Thyself...* have one meaning.[1] Listen with an ear [2]as people do,[3] and do not turn Your eye[4] from seeing how I[5] supplicate You.[6]

3. ATTEND UNTO ME, AND ANSWER ME; I AM DISTRAUGHT IN MY COMPLAINT, AND I WILL MOAN.

ATTEND UNTO ME... I AM DISTRAUGHT. *Arid* (I am distraught) means, I cry out. The word *tarid* (thou shalt cry out) in *and it shall come to pass when thou shalt cry out.*[7] (Gen. 27:40) is similar.[8] So too *horidehu* (and cry out at them)[9] in *neheh al hamon mitzrayim ve-horidehu* (wail for the multitude of Egypt, and cry out at them) (Ezek. 32:18); for the meaning of *horidehu* is, cry out at them. Similarly and *ve-yaradti* (and wail) in *and*

1. Both parts of the verse say the same. They call upon God not to ignore the prayer of the psalmist.

2. In other words, *Ha'azinah* (give ear) means, give ear, listen.

3. *Ha'azinah* is an anthropomorphism.

4. Hebrew, *titallam*. I.E. renders this, *hide not your eye.*

5. Lit., he.

6. Literally, before You.

7. Translated according to I.E.

8. *Arid* and *tarid* come from the same root, *resh, vav, dalet.*

9. Translated according to I.E.

wail upon the mountains (Judges 11:37).[10] This is so [11] even though *arid*[12] comes from a different root.[13] There are many such cases.[14] The fact that Scripture reads *hakshivah* (attend)[15] is proof that the word *arid* (I am distraught) means, I cry out.

4. BECAUSE OF THE VOICE OF THE ENEMY, BECAUSE OF THE OPPRESSION OF THE WICKED; FOR THEY CAST MISCHIEF UPON ME.

BECAUSE OF THE VOICE OF THE ENEMY. Its meaning is, because the enemy raises his voice against me.

OPPRESSION. *Mi-pene akat rasha* (because of the oppression of the wicked)] is to be understood as rendered by the *Targum*.[16] It means because of the evil that comes upon me from the wicked.[17] Others say that *akat* is related to the word *ta'ik* (creaketh) in *as a cart creaketh*[18] (Amos 2:13).[19]

THEY CAST. *Yamitu* (they cast) is related to the word *matah* (cast down) in *and his hand is cast down with thee*[20] (Lev. 25:35). *Yamitu* is in the *hifil*.[21] The word *aven* (mischief) is the object.[22]

---

10. Translated according to I.E.

11. *Arid is* similar in meaning to ve-*yaradti* and *horidehu.*

12. Literally, it.

13. *Arid* comes from the root *resh vav, dalet. Ve-yaradti* and *horidehu* come from the root *yod, resh, dalet.*

14. Where words with a similar meaning come from different roots.

15. Lit., listen.

16. The Targum renders the word *tzarah* (trouble) by the Aramaic word *aka.* See Targum on our verse.

17. According to this interpretation *mi-pene akat rasha* means, from the trouble of the wicked.

18. I.E. renders this, will press.

19. According to this interpretation *mi-pene akat rasha* means, from the pressure (oppression) of the wicked.

20. Translated according to I.E.

21. It is a causative.

22. *Yamitu* (they cast).

5. MY HEART DOTH WRITHE WITHIN ME; AND THE TERRORS OF DEATH ARE FALLEN UPON ME.

MY HEART. This alludes to the fear that the soul experiences when it hears the voice of the enemy. It is a fear similar to the terror experienced by all those who hear the roar of a lion.

6. FEAR AND TREMBLING COME UPON ME, AND HORROR HATH OVERWHELMED ME.

FEAR AND TREMBLING. Fear in the heart and trembling in the body.

7. AND I SAID: OH THAT I HAD WINGS LIKE A DOVE! THEN I WOULD FLY AWAY AND BE AT REST.

AND I SAID. Some say that *ever* (wings)[23] is Aramaic for a wing.[24] The poet speaks of a dove, for it dwells among people and kings use it to send their letters.[25]

8. LO, THEN I WOULD WANDER FAR OFF; I WOULD LODGE IN THE WILDERNESS. SELAH.

LO. The poet would then distance himself from settled places[26] and would lodge in the wilderness. It would then be truly well with him.

9. I WOULD HASTE ME TO A SHELTER FROM THE STORMY WIND AND TEMPEST.

I WOULD HASTE ME. I would then escape from the enemy.
The word *achishah* (I would haste) is a transitive verb. *Yachishah* (let Him make speed) in *Let Him make speed, let Him hasten His work* (Is. 5:19) is similar to it. [27]

23. The word *ever* means an organ. Hence this interpretation.

24. This interpretation renders our clause: Oh that I had a wing like a dove.

25. Hence the phrase, *and fly away.*

26. In other words *Lo, then would I wander far off* means, I would wander far from inhabited places.

27. It too is transitive.

FROM THE STORMY WIND. The word *so'ah* (stormy)[28] means traveling.[29] *So'ah* is used in the same sense that *si'o*[30] (his journey)[31] is, in *Though his journey goes up to the heavens* (Job 20:6).[32] Rabbi Moses says that the meaning of our verse is as follows: I would hasten to find a shelter for myself from the wind and from the storm that is preventing me from flying.

10. DESTROY, O LORD, AND DIVIDE THEIR TONGUE; FOR I HAVE SEEN VIOLENCE AND STRIFE IN THE CITY.

DESTROY. The *lamed* of *balla* (destroy) has a *dagesh* because of the guttural.[33]

AND DIVIDE THEIR TONGUE. This is a poetic expression.[34] The meaning of *divide* (pallag) is, may what happened to the generation that was divided[35] happen to them, for they all gathered in the city to do violence to me.

11. DAY AND NIGHT THEY[36] GO ABOUT IT[37] UPON THE WALLS THEREOF; INIQUITY ALSO AND MISCHIEF ARE IN THE MIDST OF IT.

DAY. The psalmist compares the city to a circle.[38] He says that *violence* surrounds him in the city. *Violence* forms the line that goes round about the circle.[39] Iniquity and mischief form the dot of the circle. This is the meaning of *in the midst of it.*

28. Spelled *samekh, ayin, heh.*

29. I.E. renders, *me-ru'ach so'ah* (from the stormy wind), from the traveling wind.

30. Spelled *sin, yod, alef.*

31. For the *sin* and *samekh* interchange.

32. Translated according to I.E.

33. The *ayin* that follows the *lamed.*

34. David did not really expect God to confound their language, as he did to the generation that built the tower of Babel.

35. Hebrew, *dor haflagah.* The generation that built the tower of Babel. See Gen. 11:1-9.

36. Violence and strife.

37. Hebrew, *yesovavuha.* Lit., they circle it.

38. I.E explains that in *their midst* refers to the center of a circle.

39. The circumference of the circle.

12. WICKEDNESS IS IN THE MIDST THEREOF; OPPRESSION AND GUILE DEPART NOT FROM HER BROAD PLACE.

WICKEDNESS IS IN THE MIDST THEREOF. Scripture repeats itself.[40]

FROM HER BROAD PLACE. *Me-rechovah* (her bread place) refers to the broad line. It is the line that goes round about the circle. Our verse adds [oppression and guile] *depart not* [from her broad place].[41]

13. FOR IT WAS NOT AN ENEMY THAT TAUNTED ME, THEN I COULD HAVE BORNE IT; NEITHER WAS IT MINE ADVERSARY THAT DID MAGNIFY HIMSELF AGAINST ME, THEN I WOULD HAVE HID MYSELF FROM HIM.

FOR. The psalmist now mentions men who were his friends and are now his enemies.

THEN I COULD HAVE BORNE. His taunt, for he was my enemy.

THAT DID MAGNIFY HIMSELF.[42] *Higdil* (that did magnify) is an intransitive verb.[43] Or its meaning is; he spoke arrogantly. [44]
A person can hid himself from an enemy. [However, he cannot do so from] an enemy[45] who knows his secret.[46]

14. BUT IT WAS THOU, A MAN MINE EQUAL, MY COMPANION, AND MINE FAMILIAR FRIEND.

BUT IT WAS THOU. David speaks with one of his enemies.[47]

40. The first half of verse 12 repeats in different words the last clause of verse 11.

41. To that which is stated in verse 11.

42. Hebrew, *higdil.* Literally, that did magnify. The word *himself* is not in the text.

43. So *Ha-Keter* and Filwarg. According to this interpretation *higdil* means *magnify himself.*

44. Literally, he magnified to speak. In other words *higdil* is transitive, with the object missing. *Higdil* is short for *higdil le-dabber*. According to this interpretation our text reads: *Neither was it mine adversary that spoke arrogantly against me.*

45. A friend who turns into an enemy. See verse 16.

46. Hence David says: *Neither was it mine adversary that did magnify himself against me, then I would have hid myself from him.*

47. Our verse is in the singular. Hence I.E.'s comment.

A MAN MINE EQUAL. You are considered in my eyes as my equal.[48]

15. WE TOOK SWEET COUNSEL TOGETHER, IN THE HOUSE OF GOD WE WALKED WITH THE THRONG.

WE TOOK SWEET COUNSEL TOGETHER. We spoke of our secrets and found the experience pleasant.[49]

WITH THE THRONG. *Be-regesh* (with the throng) means, in one group.[50]

16. MAY HE INCITE DEATH AGAINST THEM, LET THEM GO DOWN ALIVE INTO THE NETHER-WORLD; FOR EVIL IS IN THEIR DWELLING, AND WITHIN THEM.

MAY HE INCITE. Rabbi Moses says that death is the subject in *yashi mavet* (may He incite death). The meaning of *yashi* [*mavet*] (may He incite death against them) is, may death demand them,[51] that is, may death take their lives.

Others say that *yashi* is related to the word *nashani* (hath made me forget)[52] in *hath made me forget* (Gen. 41:51).[53] The meaning [of our verse is] is, may they forget death and may the thought of death not enter their minds, so that they go down living into the grave. In this case[54] the word *yashi* is similar to *temchi* in (blot out) in *Neither blot out* (Jer. 18:23) and to the word *teshi* (thou wast unmindful) in *Of the Rock that begot thee thou wast unmindful* (Deut. 32:18).[55] The aforementioned is so even though[56]*yashi* [57] is ultimately accented.[58]

---

48. I consider you my equal. David's enemies were obviously not his equals. Hence I.E.'s comment.

49. Literally, and it was sweet for us.

50. *Regesh* means a group. See I.E. on Ps. 2:1. I.E. renders our clause, we walked in one group.

51. The root *nun, shin, heh* means to lend or to demand payment.

52. The root *nun, shin, heh* also has the meaning of, to forget.

53. In this case *mavet* (death) is the object in *yasahi mavet.*

54. If the root of *yashi* is *nun, shin, heh.*

55. Where the *yod* takes the place of the *heh.*

56. So *Ha-Keter.*

57. Literally, the word.

58. *Temchi* and *teshi* are penultimately accented. *Yashi* is ultimately accented. Nevertheless, *yashi* is similar to *temchi* and *teshi.* See Filwarg.

Others say that the word *yashi* is missing an *alef*.[59] It is related to *hishi'ani*[60] (beguiled me) (Gen. 2: 13). This interpretation is close to the correct meaning.
The meaning of our verse is; may death beguile them, so that they are not aware of it, and they go down living into the grave.[61]
Rabbi Moses says that the word *be-meguram* (in their dwelling) means, in their gathering. Compare the word *ba-megurah* (in the barn) in *is the seed yet in the barn* (Haggai 2:19).[62] However, in my opinion *be-meguram* means in the land of their sojourning.[63] The latter is parallel to *in the city* (Ps. 55:10).

17. AS FOR ME, I WILL CALL UPON GOD; AND THE LORD WILL SAVE ME.

AS FOR ME. I will call upon God, until He brings them down alive into the grave.

18. EVENING, AND MORNING, AND AT NOONDAY, WILL I COMPLAIN, AND MOAN; AND HE HATH HEARD MY VOICE.

EVENING. *Erev* (evening) refers to the beginning of the night. *Boker* (morning) refers to the beginning of the day. *Tzohorayim* (noonday) refers to the midpoint of the day. A person can determine these times by using his eyes.[64] However, one cannot see the sun's shadow at the midpoint of the day.[65] He can do so only after close to half an hour has past [from the day's midpoint].

19. HE HATH REDEEMED MY SOUL IN PEACE SO THAT NONE CAME NIGH ME; FOR THEY WERE MANY THAT STROVE WITH ME.

Mi-kerav li (so that none came neigh unto me] means, so that they did not touch me.[66]

---

59. It comes from the root *nun, shin, alef. Yashi* is spelled *yod, shin, yod*. It should be noted that the *kere* spells *yashi* with an *alef*.

60. From the root *nun, shin, alef*.

61. This interpretation, like the first one believes *mavet* (death) to be the subject in *yashi mavet*.

62. *Megurah* is a place where seed is gathered.

63. The root of *meguram* is *gimel, vav, resh*. The word *gur* means, dwell.

64. Morning, afternoon, and evening are times of prayer. Hence I.E. points out that each and every person can determine these times. Filwarg.

65. There is no shadow at noontime.

66. That is, they did not hurt me.

The *bet* of *ve-rabbim* (for they were many) in *ve-rabbim hayu immadi* (for were many that strove with me) is similar to the *bet* of *ve-lachmi* (my bread)[67] in *eat my bread* (Prov. 9:5). The word *many* refers to the angels. The meaning of *ki ve-rabbim hayu immadi* is, because of the many angels[68] that were[69] with us.[70]

20. GOD SHALL HEAR, AND HUMBLE THEM, EVEN HE THAT IS ENTHRONED OF OLD, SELAH, SUCH AS HAVE NO CHANGES, AND FEAR NOT GOD.

GOD SHALL HEAR. David goes back to speak about his enemies that have *evil in their dwelling* (16).

AND HUMBLE THEM. *Ve-ya'anem* (and humble them) is related to the word *oni* (poor). It means, and make them poor. However, it appears to me that the meaning of *ve-ya'anem* is; He shall bear witness against them. *Ve-ya'anem* is similar to *nega'anukha* (touched thee) in *we have not touched thee* (Gen. 26:29), for the meaning of *nega'anukha* is we touched you.[71]

EVEN HE THAT IS ENTHONED OF OLD. *Yoshev* (enthroned) means dwells. He that dwells of old[72] will truly bear witness against them.

SUCH AS HAVE NO CHANGES. Their star shall change from good to bad.[73]

GOD. Who has the power to change their luck.

---

67. Translated according to I.E. The *bet* usually means in. However, it has no translatable meaning in Prov. 9:5. Similarly *ve-rabbim* is to be rendered "many" not "in many."

68. According to I.E. *ki ve-rabbim* should be interpreted as if written *ki rabbim.*

69. Lit., are.

70. I.E.'s paraphrase. The Biblical text reads, *with me.* According to I.E. *ki ve-rabbim hayu immadi* should be interpreted as if written *ki rabbim hayu immadi.*

71. The *mem* suffix usually has the meaning of *otam.* Now in Hebrew one says, *ya'aneh bam,* not *ya'aneh otam.* We find the same with the word *nega'anukha* wherein the suffix *kha* has the meaning of *bekhah* rather than *otakh,* for the usual for touched you is naga *bekha* rather than *naga otekha.*

72. See Is. 57:19.

73. Their luck shall change from good to bad and remain that way.

21. HE HATH PUT FORTH HIS HANDS AGAINST THEM THAT WERE AT PEACE WITH HIM; HE HATH PROFANED HIS COVENANT.

HE HATH PUT FORTH. Each one of them sent forth his hands. *Shelomov* (at peace with him) should be interpreted as if written *be-anshe shelomov* (against the men that were at peace with him).[74] Compare *va-ani tefilah* (But I am all prayer)[75] (Ps. 109:4).

22. SMOOTHER THAN CREAM WERE THE SPEECHES OF HIS MOUTH, BUT HIS HEART WAS WAR; HIS WORDS WERE SOFTER THAN OIL, YET WERE THEY KEEN-EDGED SWORDS.

SMOOTHER After his words were smoother then cream [his heart was war].

THAN CREAM. The *mem*[76] of *machama'ot* is vocalized with a *pattach* because of the guttural[77] that follows it.

[HIS MOUTH] *Piv* (his mouth) should be interpreted as if written *divre piv* (the word of his mouth).[78]

BUT... WAR. *Karav* (war) is similar to the word *kerav* (war) in *Who traineth my hands for war* (Ps. 144:1).[79]

YET WERE THEY KEEN-EDGED SWORDS. *Petichot* means *keen-edged swords* or drawn swords. Compare, *patehcu* (have drawn out) in *the wicked have drawn out the sword* (Ps. 37:14).

74. Our verse literally reads: He hath put forth his hands against peace with him. I.E. says that this should be interpreted: He hath put forth his hands against the men who are at peace with him.

75. Lit. But I am prayer. According to Ibn Ezra "But I am prayer" is short for "But I am a man of prayer."

76. A prepositional *mem* prefix is usually vocalized with a *chirik*. Hence I.E.'s comment.

77. *The chet.*

78. Our clause literally reads, Smother than cream [was] his mouth. Hence I.E.'s comment.

79. In other words *kerav* means war.

23. CAST THY BURDEN[80] UPON THE LORD; AND HE WILL SUSTAIN THEE; HE WILL NEVER SUFFER THE RIGHTEOUSNESS TO BE MOVED.

CAST. David says the following to himself or to the righteous: *Cast thy burden (masakha)*[81] *upon the Lord.*

AND HE WILL SUSTAIN THEE. *Yekhalkelekha* (sustain thee) means, He will bear you. Compare, *yekhalkelukha* (contain Thee) in *the heavens cannot contain Thee* (1 Kings 8:27)[82] and *mekhalkel* (abide) in *But who may abide the day of his coming*[83] (Mal. 3:2).
Some say that *yehavekha* (thy burden) is similar to *netanekha* (hath given upon you) (Jer. 29:26).[84] It means, that which He placed upon you. Its meaning is, to the burden that God placed upon you.
Rabbi Moses says that *netanekha*[85] refers to the food which has been given to you up till now. God will similarly sustain you in the future.[86] *Yekhalkelekha* is similar to *va-yekhalkel* (sustained) in *And Joseph sustained* (Gen. 47:12). However, this interpretation is not in keeping with the meaning of this psalm.

24. BUT THOU, O GOD, WILT BRING THEM DOWN INTO THE NETHERMOST PIT; MEN OF BLOOD AND DECEIT SHALL NOT LIVE OUT HALF OF THEIR DAYS; BUT AS FOR ME, I WILL TRUST IN THEE.

BUT THOU. The *mem* of *toridem* (wilt thou bring down) refers to those whose words are softer than oil (v. 22).[87]

---

80. Hebrew, *yehavekha*.

81. I.E. paraphrases the clause. Scripture employs the word *yehavekha* for burden. I.E. employs the more common word, *masakha*. This is I.E.'s way of saying that *yehavekha* means, your burden.

82. I. E. renders this: The heavens cannot bear You.

83. I.E. renders this: "But who may bear the day of his coming."

84. Translated according to Ibn Ezra. I.E. renders Jer. 29:26: The Lord hath given (placed) upon you [the duties] of being a priest.

85. Rabbi Moses, like the previous interpretation, believes that *yehavekha* (thy burden) is similar to *netanekha* .

86. Rabbi Moses explains out clause as follows: Ascribe "what has been given to you up till now" to God. The Lord will likewise sustain you in the future.

87. The *mem* of *toridem* (wilt thou bring down) is a pronominal suffix meaning, them. According to I.E. the meaning of our verse is, You will bring down to the pit those whose words are softer than oil (v. 22).

SHALL NOT LIVE OUT HALF OF THEIR DAYS. You will not complete the number of their days.[88]

BUT AS FOR ME, I WILL TRUST IN THEE. That You will complete the number of my days as You promised me in Your Torah,[89] for I am Your servant. Or its meaning is, I will trust in You. I trust that You will bring them down [in the pit] at the midpoint of their days.

---

88. The days that they were destined to live. They will die prematurely.

89. See Ex. 23:26: *The number of Thy days will I fulfill.*

CHAPTER 56.

1. FOR THE LEADER; UPON JONATH-ELEM-REHOKIM. [A PSALM] OF DAVID MICHTAM; WHEN THE PHILISTINES TOOK HIM TO GATH.[1]

FOR THE LEADER; UPON JONATHAN-ELEM-REHOKIM. A psalm that is to be performed to the tune of a song opening with the words *Yonat-elem-rechokim.*[2] *Michtam* means something precious. [3] It is related to the word *ketem* (gold) in *the most fine gold* (Song of Songs 5:11).

2. BE GRACIOUS UNTO ME, O GOD, FOR MAN WOULD SWALLOW ME UP; ALL THE DAY HE FIGHTING OPPRESSETH ME.

WOULD SWALLOW ME UP. *Would swallow me up* is metaphoric. The reference[4] is to Avimelekh[5] or to his servants.[6]

3. THEY THAT LIE IN WAIT FOR ME WOULD SWALLOW ME UP ALL THE DAY; FOR THEY ARE MANY THAT FIGHT AGAINST ME,[7] O MOST HIGH.

1. For the incident referred to in this Psalm, see 1 Sam. 21:11ff.
2. See I.E. on Ps. 4:1.
3. *Mikhtam* thus means a *precious psalm*.
4. The one who would swallow up David.
5. King of Gath. See I.E. on Ps. 34:1.
6. See 1 Sam. 21:12.
7. Hebrew, *lochamim li*; literally, fight to me.

WOULD SWALLOW ME UP. David mocks his enemies and says: Why do my enemies spend all the day desiring to swallow me up, when I have many angels above who fight for me?[8] [Our text is to be so interpreted,] because when the word *milchamah* (war) is followed by a *lamed* it indicates [a war that is waged] to help [a friend in distress].[9] Compare, *ha-nilcham la-khem* (that fighteth for you) (Deut.3: 22). However when the word *milchamah* is followed by the word *im* (with) it has a negative connotation.[10]

4. IN THE DAY THAT I AM AFRAID, I WILL PUT MY TRUST IN THEE.

IN THEE. The word *elekha* is to be rendered *in Thee.*[11] Compare *el* (for)[12] in *For this child I prayed* (1 Sam. 2:27).

5. IN GOD-I WILL PRAISE HIS WORD- IN GOD DO I TRUST, I WILL NOT BE AFRAID; WHAT CAN FLESH DO UNTO ME?

IN GOD-I WILL PRAISE HIS WORD. The reference[13] is to God's word, which Samuel prophesied concerning David. Samuel prophesied that David would be king over Israel. Therefore *I trust in God* means, I trust that the Lord will fulfill His word.[14]

6. ALL THE DAY THEY TROUBLE MINE AFFAIRS; [15] ALL THEIR THOUGHTS ARE AGAINST ME FOR EVIL.

ALL THE DAY THEY TROUBLE MINE AFFAIRS. The word *ye'atzevu* (they trouble) is related to the word *itzavon* (toil) (Gen. 3:17). *Devarai ye'atzevu* (they trouble mine affairs) means, they trouble me because I trust in God.[16]

8. I.E. interprets of *lochamim li* (fight against me) as meaning, fight for me.

9. Hence the meaning of *lochamin li* (fight against me) is, fight for me.

10. It means fight with or fight against.

11. Hebrew, *alekha,* literally "on you." The word *elekha* literally means, to you. Hence I.E.'s comment.

12. *El* usually means, to. However, in 1 Sam. 2:27 it has the meaning of *al,* for (literally, on).

13. In God.

14. Since the first part of the verse speaks of God's word.

15. Hebrew, *devarai ye'atzevu.*

16. *Devarai ye'atzevu* literally means, my affairs they trouble. I.E. renders this, they trouble me because of my affairs, that is; they trouble me because of my trust in God.

7. THEY GATHER THEMSELVES TOGETHER, THEY HIDE THEMSELVES, THEY MARK MY STEPS; ACCORDING AS THEY HAVE WAITED FOR MY SOUL.

THEY GATHER THEMSELVES. The word *yagoddu* (they gather)[17] is related to the word *gedud* (a troop) (Gen. 49:19). My enemies gather themselves, so that they will be numerous and I will be unable to flee. *They mark my steps,* so that I do not escape.

8. BECAUSE OF INIQUITY CAST THEM OUT; IN ANGER BRING DOWN THE PEOPLES, O GOD.

BECAUSE. [*Al aven pallet lamo* (because of iniquity cast them out) means,] because of the iniquity which is in their hearts [help me escape them]. It might also mean, because of the iniquity which permeates them help me[18] escape them.[19] Though they[20] are many, bring them down in anger. David therefore says, *the peoples*.

9. THOU HAST COUNTED MY WANDERINGS; PUT THOU MY TEARS INTO THY BOTTLE; ARE THEY NOT IN THY BOOK.

MY WANDERINGS. *Nodi* (my wanderings) has the same meaning as *nedudai* (my wanderings).[21] Compare, *And dwelt in the land of Nod* (Gen. 4: 16).[22]

THOU HAST COUNTED. Its meaning is, You know how many times I have wandered from my place. It is poetic to combine *nodi* (my wanderings) with *ve-nodekha* (into Thy bottle).[23] The import of *Put Thou my tears in Thy bottle* is, God knows the number of the psalmist's drops, that is, the number of his tears.[24] This is the meaning of *ha-lo be-sifratekha* (are they not in Thy book).[25] The poet's tears are, as it were, gathered in a bottle. The latter is a figure of speech. Its meaning is, not a drop of my tears has been lost.

17. This is I.E.'s reading. Our texts of Psalms read *yaguru*. See *Minchat Shai*.

18. Literally, make me.

19. I.E. renders *pallet lamo* (cast them out) as, "their survivor." He interprets the latter as meaning, make me their survivor, that is, help me survive them.

20. David's enemies.

21. *Nedudai* is the usual term for *my wanderings*. Hence I.E.'s comment.

22. The land of wandering.

23. For they have a similar sound.

24. And placed them in a bottle.

25. I.E. renders *ha-lo be-sifratekha*, are they not among Thy numbered objects? See Rashi.

10. THEN SHALL MINE ENEMIES TURN BACK IN THE DAY THAT I CALL; THIS I KNOW, THAT GOD IS FOR ME.

THEN... Its meaning is as follows: When my enemies see that I call Your name they will be frightened.

[THIS I KNOW] *This I know* means, by this[26] I know.

11. IN GOD[27] - I WILL PRAISE HIS WORD - IN THE LORD[28] - I WILL PRAISE HIS WORD.

IN GOD. I will then proceed[29] with the help of God to praise the word spoken to me by the prophet Samuel. [30] [I will do so] time after time.[31]

12. IN GOD DO I TRUST, I WILL NOT BE AFRAID; WHAT CAN MAN DO UNTO ME.

IN GOD DO I TRUST. I will then trust in God forever.

13. THY VOWS ARE UPON ME, O GOD; I WILL RENDER THANK-OFFERINGS UNTO THEE.

UPON ME. Some say that the vow referred to is, *In God do I trust* (v. 12). However, David probably took a vow to bring burnt offerings. The latter interpretation is correct, for the following is the meaning of our verse: I am obligated to pay my vows for the good, which you did for me.

26. When his enemies turn back.

27. Hebrew *be-Elohim.* I.E. renders *be-Elohim* with God, that is, with God's help.

28. Hebrew *ba-Adonai.* I.E. renders *ba-Adonai* with the Lord, that is, with the Lords help.

29. Literally, say.

30. That I (David) would be king over Israel. See I Sam. 16:13.

31. The second half of the verse repeats the first half, to indicate permanence.

CHAPTER 57

1. FOR THE LEADER; AL-TASHHETH. [A PSALM] OF DAVID; WHEN HE FLED FROM SAUL IN THE CAVE. [1]

FOR THE LEADER; AL-TASHHETH... WHEN HE FLED FROM SAUL. This psalm was to be performed to the tune of a poem beginning with the words *al tashchet*.[2] David composed it in the cave.[3] He said: Even though I am in a cave I have no refuge but you.[4]

2. BE GRACIOUS UNTO ME, O GOD, BE GRACIOUS UNTO ME, FOR IN THEE HATH MY SOUL TAKEN REFUGE; YEA, IN THE SHADOW OF THY WINGS WILL I TAKE REFUGE; UNTIL CALAMITIES BE OVERPAST.

CALAMITIES. Some say that the word *havvot* (calamities) means an incident,[5] for David[6] was their king.[7]

3. I WILL CRY UNTO GOD MOST HIGH; UNTO GOD THAT ACCOMPLISHETH IT FOR ME.

I WILL CRY. David describes God as being *Most High* because he himself was in a very low state.

1. See 1 Sam. 24:3. Radak.
2. See I.E. on Ps. 4:1.
3. In the cave in which he sought refuge from Saul.
4. I.E.'s paraphrase of verse 2.
5. That is, incidents. The word *hoveh* means the present, that which now occurs. Filwarg.
6. Literally, he.
7. David had already been anointed as king of Israel. Hence he saw his persecution by Saul as a transitory incident. See Filwarg.

4. HE WILL SEND FROM HEAVEN, AND SAVE ME, WHEN HE WHO WOULD SWALLOW ME UP TAUNTETH. SELAH. GOD SHALL SEND FORTH HIS MERCY AND HIS TRUTH.

HE WILL SEND. David says *He will send from heaven,* because he earlier had described God as being *Most High*.

5. MY SOUL IS AMONG THE LIONS, I DO LIE DOWN AMONG THEM THAT ARE AFLAME; EVEN THE SONS OF MEN, WHOSE TEETH ARE SPARKS AND ARROWS, AND THEIR TONGUE A SHARP SWORD.

MY SOUL IS AMONG THE LIONS, I DO LIE DOWN AMONG THEM THAT ARE AFLAME. David says this because Saul's party surrounded him.

Lohatim (are aflame) is to be read as if written *be-tokh lohatim* (among them that are aflame).[8]

Shinnehem (whose teeth)... refers to those who speak evil of David[9] to Saul.

6. BE THOU EXALTED, O GOD, ABOVE THE HEAVENS; THY GLORY BE ABOVE THE EARTH.

BE THOU EXALTED. Show that You are exalted above the heavens by helping me. All the earth shall see Your glory, for those who hear[10] will speak of Your salvation.

7. THEY HAVE PREPARED A NET FOR MY STEPS, MY SOUL IS BOWED DOWN; THEY HAVE DIGGED A PIT BEFORE ME, THEY ARE FALLEN INTO THE MIDST THEREOF THEMSELVES. SELAH.

THEY HAVE PREPARED A NET FOR MY STEPS, MY SOUL IS BOWED DOWN. The word *kafaf* (bowed down) is an intransitive verb. *Nefesh* is employed as a masculine.[11] Compare, *nefesh* (souls) in *all the souls* (nefesh) *were seven* (shivah)[12] (Gen. 46:25). On

8. Our verse literally reads, "I do lie down them that are aflame." The *word* among is not in the text. Hence I.E.'s comment.

9. Literally, him.

10. What You did on my behalf.

11. The verb *kafaf* is a masculine. If *nefesh* were feminine then our text would read *kafefah nafshi*. The word *nefesh* is usually in the feminine. Hence I.E.'s comment.

12. *Shivah* is masculine. Hence here too the word *nefesh* is a masculine.

the other hand it is possible that *kafaf* is transitive. The meaning of *kafaf nafshi* (my soul is bowed down) is, each one of my enemies[13] bowed down my soul.[14]

A PIT. The word *shichah* (pit) has the same meaning as the word *shuchah* (pit) (Jer.19:20).[15] The word *keri'e* (the elect) (Numbers 16:2) [similarly] has the same meaning as *keru'e* (the elect) (Num 1:16).[16] The word *shichot* (pits) (Ps.119:85)[17] is similar.[18]
Nafelu be-tokhah selah (they are fallen into the midst thereof themselves. Selah.) means, they truly fell into it.[19]

8. MY HEART IS STEDFEST, O GOD, MY HEART IS STEDFEST; I WILL SING, YEA, I WILL SING PRAISES.

STEDFEST. The clause *My heart is stedfest* is repeated. [The repetition is another way of saying,] my heart is always steadfast.

STEDFEST. To sing and chant to God who has delivered me. I will say the following to my soul:[20]

9. AWAKE, MY GLORY; AWAKE, PSALTERY AND HARP; I WILL AWAKE THE DAWN.

AWAKE MY GLORY. When I awake to the dawn[21] I will likewise say to my psaltery awake.[22] The verb *urah* (awake) is intransitive. Compare, *ha'irah* (rouse Thee) in *rouse Thee, and awake to my judgment* (Ps. 35: 23).[23]

---

13. Hence the use of the singular *kafaf,* rather than the plural *kafefu.*

14. In this case *nefesh* is not necessarily a feminine, for *kafaf* does not govern *nefesh.* It refers to David's enemy. According to I.E. our verse reads: They have prepared a net for my steps; he (each one of my enemies) has bowed down my soul.

15. *Shuchah* is the more common term. Hence I.E.'s comment.

16. *Keru'e* is the more common form.

17. *Shichot* is a variant of *shuchot.* It is the plural of *shuchah.*

18. So Filwarg. The printed texts read *she-yashichu.* The latter cannot be explained and is clearly an error. Filwarg.

19. Reading *nafelu* rather than *she-nafelu.* Filwarg. .

20. *Awake my glory...* (v. 9).

21. Awake, my glory is a poetic way of saying to one's self, arise.

22. When I tell myself to get up, I will tell my psaltery get up.

23. See I.E. on Ps. 35:23.

10. I WILL GIVE THANKS UNTO THEE, O LORD, AMONG THE PEOPLES; I WILL SING PRAISES UNTO THEE AMONG THE NATIONS.

I WILL GIVE THANKS… AMONG THE PEOPLES. *Among the peoples* means, among the multitude of Israel. Compare, After *thee, Benjamin, among thy peoples* (Judges 5:14).

AMONG THE NATIONS. Who are not Israelites.

11. FOR THY MERCY IS GREAT UNTO THE HEAVENS, AND THY TRUTH UNTO THE SKIES.

FOR. It is possible that the meaning of *When he that would swallow me up taunteth*[24] (v. 4) is; *He will send forth His mercy* (ibid.), because he that would swallow me up taunts me.[25] This is what Scripture means by *For Thy mercy is great unto the heavens.*[26]
The psalmist says *Be thou exalted, O God, above the heavens* (v. 12) because the height of the heavens are searchable. However, God's mercy is unfathomable.

24. Literally, *He that would swallow me up taunteth.*

25. In other words, the meaning of *he that would swallow me up taunteth… He (God) will send forth His mercy* (v. 4) is, Because *he that would swallow me up taunteth… He (God) will send forth His mercy.*

26. *He (God) will send forth His mercy* means, God will send down Your help from the heavens.

CHAPTER 58

1. FOR THE LEADER; AL -TASHHETH. [A PSALM OF DAVID]; MICHTAM.

2. DO YE INDEED SPEAK AS A RIGHTEOUS COMPANY? DO YE JUDGE WITH EQUITY THE SONS OF MEN?

DO YE INDEED SPEAK AS A RIGHTEOUS COMPANY? Some say that the word *elem* (company) in [*ha-umnam elem tzedek tedabberun* (do ye indeed speak as a righteous company)] means a congregation.[1] Compare, *me'allemim allumim* (binding sheaves) (Gen. 37:7).[2] Rabbi Moses says that the meaning of *ha-umnam elem tzedek tedabberun* (do ye indeed speak as a righteous company) is, because you are dumbstruck[3] from speaking this righteous thing, that is, [from] speaking the truth.[4]

3. YEA, IN HEART YE WORK WICKEDNESS; YE WEIGH OUT IN THE EARTH THE VIOLENCE OF YOUR HANDS.

YEA, IN HEART YE WORK WICKEDNESS. [*Olot* means wickedness.] Compare, *And iniquity* (olatah) *stoppeth her mouth* (Job 5:16). *In heart ye work wickedness* means, the evil that you do is in your hearts.[5] This Psalm speaks of the judges.

1. Or a group or company.

2. This opinion renders *me'allemim allumim,* gathering a group of sheaves.

3. According to Rabbi Moses, *elem* (company) means, dumbstruck. He believes that our verse literally reads; because dumbstruck righteous you speak. Hence his interpretation.

4. According to Rabbi Moses, our verse should be understood as follows: because you are dumbstruck from speaking the truth and judging people with equity. [Yea, in your heart ye work wickedness...]

5. In other words, you do not do evil inadvertently. You plan it.

THE VIOLENCE OF YOUR HANDS. The reference is to the bloodshed, caused by graft. The meaning of *ye weigh out* [*the violence of you hand*] is, you weigh out the violence committed by your hands, so that no man is aware of it. The violence that you commit appears to be justly weighed out.[6]

4. THE WICKED ARE ESTRANGED FROM THE WOMB; THE SPEAKERS OF LIES GO ASTRAY AS SOON AS THEY ARE BORN.

ESTRANGED. *Zoru* (estranged) is a verb in the perfect. It follows the paradigm of *oru* (brightened) in *how mine eyes are brightened* (1 Sam. 14:29).[7] The meaning of *The wicked are estranged from the womb* is, the wicked are different in nature at birth from other new born children. [*The speaker of lies*] *go astray* [*as soon as they are born*] repeats the idea earlier mentioned.[8]

5. THEIR VENOM IS THE LIKE THE VENOM OF A SERPENT; THEY ARE LIKE THE DEAF ASP THAT STOPPETH HER EAR.

THEIR VENOM. The word *chamat* (venom) is in the construct. [9] However, Scripture omits the word to which it is connected. Compare, *u-shekhurat ve-lo mi-yayin* (And drunken, but not with wine) (Is. 51: 21).[10] *Chamat* means a fatal poison.[11] *Stoppeth her ear* refers to what follows,[12] namely, *Which hearkeneth not to the voice of charmers, Or the most cunning binder of spells* (v. 6).

7. BREAK THEIR TEETH, O GOD, IN THEIR MOUTH; BREAK OUT THE CHEEK-TEETH OF THE YOUNG LIONS, O LORD.

O GOD. The psalmist compares the wicked[13] to young lions because they tear with their teeth. The psalmist makes this comparison because the tongue is between the teeth.

6. You convince people that you acted justly and that your decisions were weighed in just scales. Radak.

7. The first letter of verbs in the *kal* perfect is usually vocalized with a kametz. Hence I.E.'s comment.

8. In the first part of the verse.

9. Our verse reads *chamot lamo* (their venom). *Chamat* means, venom of. Our verse thus literally reads: [The] venom of …is theirs; it is like the venom of a snake.

10. *Shekhurat* is in the construct. However, Scripture omits the word to which it is connected. *Shekhurat ve-lo mi-yayin* literally reads, drunken of... but not with wine.

11. Reading *sam* rather than *shem*. Filwarg.

12. Lit. The meaning of *Stoppeth her ear* refers to what the psalmist goes on to say.

13. Literally, them.

8. LET THEM MELT AWAY AS WATER THAT RUNNETH APACE; WHEN HE AIMETH HIS ARROWS, LET THEM BE AS THOUGH THEY WERE CUT OFF.

LET THEM MELT AWAY. The *alef* of *yimmasu* (let them melt away) is in place of the double letter.[14] Compare *baze'u* (divide) in *Whose land the rivers divide* (Is. 18:2).[15]

THAT RUNNETH APACE. Until they can not be found.
The word "archer" is missing [in the phrase: *when he aimeth* (yidrokh)].[16] It is similar to *he said to Joseph* (Gen. 48:1).[17] Our verse should be interpreted as if written, "As the archer aims his arrows at them." The psalmist mentions "his arrows" in place of his bow,[18] because the one who treads (bends) the bow, does so, to shoot the arrows.

THEY WERE CUT OFF. The word *yitmolalu* (they were cut off) is similar to *yemolel* (it is cut down) in *it is cut down, and withereth* (Ps. 90:6).[19]

9. LET THEM BE AS A SNAIL WHICH MELTETH AND PASSETH AWAY; LIKE THE UNTIMELY BIRTHS OF A WOMEN, THAT HAVE NOT SEEN THE SUN.

AS A SNAIL .The word *shabbelul* (snail) is found in the words of our ancients of blessed memory. Compare, *bara shabbelul* (he created the snail).[20] The *shabbelul* is a fishlike creature in the water that melts when it walks. There are those who say that the *lamed* of *shabbelul* is doubled and that the word is similar to *shibbolet* (*flood*) in *shibbolet mayim* (water flood) (Ps. 69:16).[21] This interpretation is also correct.

---

14. A *samekh*. The root of *yimmasu* is *mem samekeh, samekh. Yimmasu* might be connected to the root *mem, alef, samekh* (disgusted). Rashi makes this connection. Rashi renders our clause; Let them be despised in their own eyes from distress. Hence I.E.'s comment.

15. The *alef* in *baze'u* is in place of a *zayin*, for the root of *baze'u* is *bet, zayin, zayin*.

16. The noun which *aimeth* governs is omitted.

17. Translated literally. Here too Scripture omits the subject.

18. Our verse reads *yidrokh chitzav* (aimeth his arrows). *Yidrokh* means treads. *Yidrokh chitzav* literally means, treads his arrows. Hence I.E.'s comments.

19. Both words come from the root, *mem, lamed, lamed.*

20. *Midrash Shochar Tov*; 58:3.

21. *Shibbolet* is spelled with one *bet*. According to this interpretation our verse reads, *As a stream of water melts and passes away.*

I will now grammatically explain the word *eshet* (a woman).[22] Know that that the *heh* is the sign of the feminine. Compare, *atarah* (crown), *tifarah* (glory).[23] When the *heh* is switched with a *tav* the word is penultimately sounded both when the word is in the construct as in *tiferet yisra'el* (the beauty of Israel) (Lam. 2: 1), and also when the word is not in the construct. This is the case in *ateret tiferet* (a crown of beauty) (Is. 62:3).[24] The same applies to *eshet* (a woman).[25] Its primary form is *ishah* (a woman). It is pronounced *eshet* whether in the construct as in *eshet ish* (another man's wife) (Lev. 20:10) or in the absolute as in *eshet yefat to'ar*[26] (a women of goodly form) (Deut. 21:11).

10. BEFORE YOUR POTS CAN FEEL THE THORNS, HE WILL SWEEP IT AWAY WITH A WHIRLWIND, THE RAW AND THE BURNING ALIKE.

BEFORE YOUR POTS[27] CAN FEEL THE THORNS. Rabbi Hai of blessed memory says that the mature buds of the tree[28] are hard.[29] The wise men of Israel refer to them[30] as *evyonot* (caper berries) in their writings.[31] *Be-terem yavinu sitrotekhem atad…* [*ke-mo charon yisarenu*]) (before your pots can feel the thorns, [He will sweep it away with a whirlwind]) means, before the buds mature and turn into thorns, God will remove them with a whirlwind from their place.

Chai (the raw) means, when they have the power of life in them that is, when they are moist.

---

22. Our verse reads: *nefel eshet bal chazu shemesh* (the untimely births of a woman that have not seen the sun). *Eshet* appears to be a construct form. Thus *nefel eshet chazu shemesh* should be rendered, the untimely births of a women of, that have not seen the sun. This does not seem to make any sense. Hence I.E. goes on to explain that the word *eshet* which appears to be a construct is not really in the construct, for its *tav* is in place of a *heh*. In other words *eshet* is a variant of *isha* and *nefel eshet bal chazu shemesh* should be rendered, the untimely births of a woman (ishah), that have not seen the sun.

23. So *Ha-Keter.* Other printed versions have *ateret tiferet.* The *Ha-Keter* reading is to be preferred. The reading *ateret tiferet* probably arose because a scribe or printer wanted to "correct" the text which read *atarah tifarah* to *ateret tiferet* because I.E. later goes on to cite Is. 62:3 which reads *ateret tiferet.*

24. The word *ateret* looks like a construct but it is not. It is a variant of *atarah.*

25. It is not in the construct.

26. *Eshet yefat to'ar* is a variant of *ishah yefat to'ar.*

27. Hebrew, *sirotekhem.*

28. The thorn bush.

29. Our verse reads: *be-terem yavinu sirotekhem atad* (before your pots can feel the thorns). According to Rabbi Hai, *sirotekhem* means your flowers. It refers to the flowers of the thorn bush, which turn hard when they mature.

30. The product of the flowers.

31. Mature buds. See *Talmud Yerushalmi; Ma'asarot* 4:5.

AND THE BURNING ALIKE. *Kemo-charon yisarennu* (and the burning alike) means, like a man who uproots a tree from its place in his anger.[32]

11. THE RIGHTEOUS SHALL REJOICE WHEN HE SEETH THE VENGEANCE; HE SHALL WASH HIS FEET IN THE BLOOD OF THE WICKED.

The righteous shall rejoice is in contrast to "the righteous are dumbstruck (v. 2)."[33]

12. AND MEN SHALL SAY: VERILY THERE IS A REWARD FOR THE RIGHTEOUS; VERILY THERE IS A GOD[34] THAT JUDGETH IN THE EARTH.

A GOD THAT JUDGETH. *Elohim* (God) refers to the angels. For, from the place that is established for the angels[35] to dwell in,[36] come the decrees from the command of God the glorious, that befall the earth.

32. Literally, like a man storms a tree from its place in his anger. According to this interpretation our verse should be rendered as follows: Before your buds mature and turn into thorns, while they are yet full of sap, they will be uprooted [by God]. [God will act] like a man who in his anger uproots a tree.

33. See I.E. on verse 2.

34. Heb. *Elohim*.

35. Lit., them.

36. Heaven.

CHAPTER 59

1. FOR THE LEADER; AL TASHHETH. [A PSALM] OF DAVID; MICHTAM; WHEN SAUL SENT AND THEY WATCHED THE HOUSE TO KILL HIM.[1]

2. DELIVER ME FROM MINE ENEMIES, O MY GOD; SET ME ON HIGH FROM THEM THAT RISE UP AGAINST ME.

DELIVER ME… SET ME ON HIGH. You, who are the one who sets me on high, [2] for [You did so] when I in was a very low place.[3]

3. DELIVER ME FROM THE WORKERS OF INIQUITY, AND SAVE ME FROM THE MEN OF BLOOD.

DELIVER ME. From *the men of blood* is parallel *to kill him* (v. 1).

4. FOR LO, THEY LIE IN WAIT FOR MY SOUL; THE IMPUDENT GATHER THEMSELVES TOGETHER AGAINST ME; NOT FOR MY TRANSGRESSION, NOR FOR MY SIN, O LORD.

GATHER THEMSEVES. *Yaguru* means they gather. Compare *megurah* (barn)[4] in *is seed yet in the barn* (Haggai 2:19).

---

1. See 1 Sam 19:11.

2. In other words, *tesaggeveni* (set me on high) an imperfect, is to be interpreted as a participle (misgabbi). See Filwarg.

3. According to I.E. our verse is to be understood as follows: Deliver me from mine enemies, O my God; for you set me on high from them that rise up against me.

4. A place where produce is gathered.

Some say that the meaning of *the impudent gather themselves against me* is, the impudent gather round about the house.[5]

5. WITHOUT MY FAULT THEY RUN AND PREPARE THEMSELVES; AWAKE THOU TO HELP ME, AND BEHOLD.

WITHOUT MY FAULT THEY RUN AND PREPARE THEMSELVES. Its meaning is as follows: I did not trespass nor is there any sin or iniquity in me for which they desire to exact vengeance from me.

Awake Thou is parallel to *and they watched the house* (v. 1).[6]

6. THOU THEREFORE, O LORD GOD OF HOSTS, THE GOD OF ISRAEL, AROUSE THYSELF TO PUNISH ALL THE NATIONS; SHOW NO MERCY TO ANY INIQUITOUS TRAITORS. SELAH.

THOU. The meaning of *God of Hosts* [*the God of Israel*] is; You are the God of the Hosts who are in heaven above[7] and the God of the Hosts below, that is, of Israel.

SHOW NO MERCY TO ANY INIQUITOUS TRAITORS. From whatever nation they are.

7. THEY RETURN AT EVENING, THEY HOWL LIKE A DOG, AND GO ROUND ABOUT THE CITY.

THEY RETURN. The Psalmist compares them[8] to dogs that bark at night to protect the city. Those who "watch the house" (v. 1) act similarly.

8. BEHOLD, THEY BELCH OUT WITH THEIR MOUTH; SWORDS ARE IN THEIR LIPS: FOR WHO DOTH HEAR?

BEHOLD, THEY BELCH OUT. Like the barking dogs.

FOR WHO DOTH HEAR? They think that God does not hear their secret.[9]

5. See verse 1.

6. Those who watch the house stay awake. Filwarg.

7. The angels.

8. Those who came to watch the house and kill David.

9. Their intention to kill David.

9. BUT THOU O LORD, SHALT LAUGH AT THEM; THOU SHALT HAVE ALL THE NATIONS IN DERISION.[10]

BUT THOU O LORD SHALT LAUGH AT THEM. The latter is a metaphor.[11] The meaning of our verse is; You can destroy them at any time. Therefore do not kill them when they belch out (v. 8).[12]

10. BECAUSE OF HIS STRENGTH, I WILL WAIT FOR THEE; FOR GOD IS MY HIGH TOWER.

HIS STRENGTH. You are the God whose might is in His essence.[13]

I WILL WAIT FOR THEE. The word *eshmorah* (I will wait) is similar to the word *shimmurim* (waiting) in *It[14] was a night of waiting* (Ex. 12:42). [15] *I will wait for Thee* (eshmorah) is parallel to *and they watched* (va-yishmeru) *the house* (v. 1).[16] The psalmist therefore says, "Arouse Thyself "(v. 6).[17]

11. THE GOD OF MERCY WILL COME TO MEET ME; GOD WILL LET ME GAZE UPON MY ADVERSARIES.

GOD OF MERCY.[18] God is the cause of my mercy, for He knows that I did not sin against them. He will come to met me and punish them in accordance with their deeds.

GOD WILL LET ME GAZE UPON MY ADVERSARIES. *Yareni ve-shoraroi* [19] (will let me gaze upon my enemies) means, will let me see my desires fulfilled upon my adversaries.[20]

10. Lit. You shall mock all the nations.

11. Laugh and mock are not to be taken literally, for God does not laugh.

12. Let them live, so that You enjoy mocking them. You can kill them later. See verse 12.

13. God did not acquire His power. It is an essential "part" of Him. Hence it is true power.

14. Reading *hu*, rather then *hem. Hem* is a copyist's error. Filwarg. If we read *hem* then we should render, they are a night of waiting. In this case I.E. is paraphrasing Ex. 12:42.

15. Translated according to I.E.

16. Both words come from the same root.

17. Those who watched the house stayed awake all night. Hence the psalmist says; *arouse Thyself*, that is, awake. See I.E. on verse 6.

18. Literally, God of my mercy. Hence I.E.'s comment.

19. Lit., will let me see upon my enemies.

20. "Will let me see upon my enemies" is short for, will let me see my desires upon my enemies.

12. SLAY THEM NOT, LEST MY PEOPLE FORGET, MAKE THEM WANDER TO AND FRO BY THY POWER, AND BRING THEM DOWN, O LORD OUR SHIELD.

SLAY THEM NOT. The psalmist prayed to God that He not kill them in one moment, lest his people forget what God did to the wicked.

MAKE THEM WANDER TO AND FRO. To seek bread as dogs do, for the psalmist notes[21] that the dogs wander to and fro for food.
Ve-chelekha (by Thy power) refers to Israel.[22]

AND BRING THEM DOWN. From the status which their wealth bestowed upon them.

O LORD OUR SHIELD. God[23] is our true king. David alludes to Saul[24] who ordered him killed.[25]

13. FOR THE SIN OF THEIR MOUTH, AND THE WORDS OF THEIR LIPS, LET THEM EVEN BE TAKEN IN THEIR PRIDE, AND FOR CURSING AND LYING WHICH THEY SPEAK.

THE SIN. The word *sin* is connected to *and bring them down.*[26] Its meaning is; bring them down because of the sin of their mouth.[27]

LET THEM EVEN BE TAKEN IN THEIR PRIDE. In response to their saying, *For who doth hear*? (v. 8).

AND FOR CURSING AND LYING WHICH THEY SPEAK. Each one shall relate to the other, some of the curses and lies that they uttered.

21. In v. 15.

22. The word *chayil* means strength, army or multitude. I.E. renders *be-chelekha* (in Thy power) among Thy multitude. He renders *ha-ni'emo ve-chelekha* (Make them wander to and fro by Thy power), make them wander among Thy multitude (Israel).

23. Lit. He.

24. Shield alludes to king. See I.E. on Ps. 47:10.

25. The meaning of our verse is; God, not Saul who ordered me killed, is the true king.

26. In the previous verse.

27. And the words of their lips.

14. CONSUME THEM IN WRATH, CONSUME THEM, THAT THEY BE NO MORE; AND LET THEM KNOW THAT GOD RULETH IN JACOB, UNTO THE ENDS OF THE EARTH. SELAH.

CONSUME THEM. The word *consume* is repeated. Its meaning is, consume them little by little, so that they ultimately cease to exist.

Ruleth in Jacob is similar in meaning to the earlier mentioned phrase *God of Israel.*[28] Its meaning is as follows: The god's of the nations are idols. However, the God of Israel is a righteous judge.

15. AND THEY RETURN AT EVENING, THEY HOWL LIKE A DOG, AND GO ROUND ABOUT THE CITY.

AND THEY RETURN. Those that remain will return. They will then be like dogs in that they seek bread. Therefore: [*They wander up and down to devour…* (v. 16)] follows.

16. THEY WANDER UP AND DOWN TO DEVOUR, AND TARRY ALL NIGHT IF THEY HAVE NOT THEIR FILL.

NOT. The word *lo* (not) is to be read as if written twice. [The end of our verse is to be interpreted as follows:] If they do not have their fill, they do not sleep[29] all night. [30]

17. BUT AS FOR ME, I WILL SING OF THY STRENGTH; YEA, I WILL SING ALOUD OF THY MERCY IN THE MORNING; FOR THOU HAST BEEN MY TOWER AND A REFUGE IN THE DAY OF MY DISTRESS.

BUT AS FOR ME. *Thy strength* is parallel to *Because of His strength, I will wait for Thee* (v. 10).

Thy mercy is parallel to *The God of my mercy* (v. 11).[31]

In the morning is the reverse of *the dogs*, for they sleep during the day.[32]

---

28. V. 6. I.E.'s point is that Jacob and Israel mean the same thing.

29. I.E. renders *va-yalinu* (and tarry), and sleep. He renders the last part of our verse; *and do not sleep all night, if they have not their fill.*

30. They do not rest. If they do not have their fill they do not sleep at night but run to and fro searching for food.

31. See I.E. on verse 11.

32. I, in contrast to the dogs who sleep all day, will sing aloud of Thy mercy in the morning

FOR THOU HAST BEEN MY HIGH TOWER. For You heard my prayer: "Set me on high[33] from them that rise up against me (v. 2)."[34]

18. O MY STRENGTH, UNTO THEE WILL I SING PRAISES; FOR GOD IS MY HIGH TOWER, THE GOD OF MY MERCY.

O MY STRENGTH. The psalmist first mentions "His strength" (v. 10). The meaning of His strength is, God's strength is in His essence. [35] He also notes: God's mercy is the cause of my mercy.[36] It is for this reason that David says "for You are my strength" after saying *I will sing of Thy strength* (v. 17). [37] Our clause is similar to[38] *The Lord is my strength*[39] *and song* (Ex. 15:2).

The God of my mercy is parallel to *Thy mercy* (v. 17).

---

33. I.E. renders *misgav li* (My tower) as, the one who sets me on high. See I.E. on verse 2.

34. That is you heard my prayer; "Deliver me from mine enemies, O my God; for You set me on high from them that rise up against me." See I.E. on verse 2.

35. Lit., the strength is in His essence.

36. I.E.'s paraphrase of, *Thy mercy.*

37. David sings of God's might because David's strength, like his mercy, comes from the Lord.

38. *O my strength, unto Thee will I sing praises.*

39. The meaning of which is, my strength comes from the Lord.

CHAPTER 60.

1. FOR THE LEADER; UPON SHUSHAN EDUTH; MICHTAM OF DAVID, TO TEACH.

FOR THE LEADER; UPON SHUSHAN EDITH. This psalm was to be performed to the tune of a song beginning with the words *shushan edut.*[1]

Some say that *Shushan* is the name of a musical instrument. They say that the word *edut* means the same as the word *adi* (ornaments) (Ezk. 16:7). The word *edut* (insignia)[2] in the *crown and the insignia* (11 Kings 11:12) is similar to it.[3]

The meaning of *to teach* is, the singers should learn the poem in order to continually mention God's mercies, for after being weakened, David's hand was victorious.

2. WHEN HE STROVE WITH ARAM-NAHARAIM AND WITH ARAM-ZOBAH, AND JOAB RETURNED, AND SMOTE OF EDOM IN THE VALLEY OF SALT TWELVE THOUSAND.

WHEN HE STROVE. The word *be-hatzoto* (when he strove) is similar to *be-hatzotam* (when they strove) in *when they strove against the Lord* (Num. 26:10).

WITH ARAM-NAHARAIM. Some say that the meaning of *be-hatzoto* (when he strove) is *when he destroyed,* for *be-hatzoto* is related to the word *nitzim* (ruinous) as in *arim nitzim*

1. See I.E. on Ps. 4:1.

2. An insignia is a type of ornament.

3. According to this interpretation our verse should be rendered: For the Leader; A psalm to be played upon a musical instrument called *shushan,* a psalm as precious as an ornament (edut); a precious psalm (michtam)(See I.E. on 16:1) which is to serve as an instrument of teaching.

(ruinous heaps).[4] *And Joab returned* is a sign that David was weakened.[5] After this Joab defeated Aram.

3. O GOD, THOU HAST CAST US OFF, THOU HAST BROKEN US DOWN; THOU HAST BEEN ANGRY; O RESTORE US.

O GOD, THOU HAST CAST US OFF. David says *Thou hast cast us off* because he had not been defeated in war until now. The same applies to, *Thou hast broken us down.*[6]

[THOU HAST BEEN ANGRY; O RESTORE US.] I have previously noted that perfect and imperfect verbs imply a noun.[7] Compare, *when there befalls us war*[8] (Ex. 1:10) which is to be interpreted as if written, when events of war befalls us. [9] Similarly *anafta, teshovev lanu* (Thou hast been angry, O restore us) is to be read as if written, *anafta enef teshovev lanu* (Thou hast been angry with anger, restore us). [10]

4. THOU HAST MADE THE LAND TO SHAKE, THOU HAST CLEFT IT; HEAL THE BREACHES THEREOF; FOR IT TOTTERETH.

THOU HAST MADE THE LAND TO SHAKE. The reference is to Israel's reaction[11] to the report that David grew weak. It was like an earthquake.[12]

4. Scripture reads: *nitzim arim*. See 11 Kings 25:19; Is 37: 26. I.E. either quoted from memory and erred or he paraphrased. A scribal error is also possible.

5. For Scripture attributes the victory to Joab.

6. David says Thou *hast broken us* because he had not been defeated in war until now.

7. Perfect and imperfect verbs imply the noun that they govern. However, the noun is omitted in the text. See I.E. on 3:8.

8. Translated literally.

9. The word *mikrim* (events) is implied in the Hebrew verb *tikrenah* (befalls).

10 *Anafta* is a verb in the perfect. A noun should thus follow. Hence I.E. points out that the noun *enef* (anger) is implied in the verb *anafta.*

11. The land means the people of the land, the reference being to the people of the land of Israel.

12. Israel trembled upon hearing the bad news.

THOU HAST CLEFT IT. *Petzamtah* (Thou hast cleft it) has no "neighbor."[13] Its meaning to be ascertained from its context. The *heh* of *refah* (heal) is in place of an *alef*[14] for the letters *alef, heh, vav, and yod* interchange.
FOR IT TOTTERETH. When the mountains totter.

5. THOU HAST MADE THY PEOPLE TO SEE HARD THINGS; THOU HAST MADE US TO DRINK THE WINE OF STAGGERING.

THOU HAST MADE THY PEOPLE TO SEE. Here too a noun is implied in the verb. *Herita ammekha kashot* (Thou hast made Thy people to see hard things)[15] is to be read as if written, *herita ammekha marah kashah* (Thou hast made Thy people to see a hard sight).[16] Our verse is to be interpreted as follows: Thou hast made Thy people to see a hard sight; and it was as if we drank the wine of staggering[17].
Hishkitanu yayin tareleh (Thou hast made us to drink the wine of staggering) is similar to *sefer ha-miknah* (the deed of the purchase)[18] (Jer. 32:11). The same is the case here. *Yayin* (wine) is in the construct with *tarelah* (staggering).[19]

6. THOU HAST GIVEN A BANNER TO THEM THAT FEAR THEE, THAT IT MAY BE DISPLAYED BECAUSE OF THE TRUTH. SELAH.

THOU HAST GIVEN. You raised us up in past years,[20] because of our faith.[21]

13. The word is not found again in Scripture.

14. The root of the Hebrew word for heal is *resh, peh, alef.* Hence I.E.'s comment.

15. Literally, Thou hast made Thy people see hard. The word "things" is not in the Hebrew text.

16. The word *marah* (sight) is implied in the verb *herita.*

17. They didn't actually drink "the wine of staggering."

18. Sefer is in the construct with *ha-miknah. Yayin* is similarly in the construct with *tarelah.*

19. Even though it is not vocalized as a construct, for the construct form of the Hebrew word for wine is *yen.* Filwarg asserts that there is an error in the printed texts of I.E. He believes that the proof text quoted by I.E. is Jer. 32:12 rather than Jer. 32:11. Jer. 32:12 reads: *ha-sefer ha-miknah.* According to Filwarg, I.E. says the following: *ha- sefer ha-miknah* should be interpreted *ha-sefer, sefer ha-miknah,* for a word in the construct does not come with the direct object prefixed to it. He similarly believes that *yayin tarelah* is to be read *yayin, yen tarelah* for the word *yayin* is in the absolute and thus cannot be in the construct with *tarelah.* In other words *ha-sefer* and *yayin* are similar for they are both irregular and have to be explained as implying a word that is not in the text.

20. I.E. renders *Thou hast given a banner to them that fear Thee* as, You have turned those who fear You into a banner to be raised. The Hebrew reads *natata li-re'ekha.* This may be rendered, You have given to those who fear You, or You have made those who fear You. I.E. interprets *natata li-re'ekha* as, "You made those who fear You" because the word *li-re'ekha* (them that fear Thee) follows the word *natata.* Had the word *nes* (a banner) followed *natata* then he would have rendered the verse as *Thou hast given a banner to them that fear Thee.* See I.E. on Ps. 55:23.

21. I.E. interprets *because of the truth* to mean, because of their faith.

7. THAT THY BELOVED MAY BE DELIVERED, SAVE WITH THY RIGHT HAND,[22] AND ANSWER ME.

MAY BE. The word *yeminekha* (Thy right hand)] is lacking a *bet.*[23] Rabbi Moses says that *yeminekha* is the subject.[24] It is a metaphor.[25] It[26] is the reverse of *Therefore Mine own arm brought salvation unto Me* (Is. 63:5) .[27]

8. GOD SPOKE IN HIS HOLINESS, THAT I WOULD EXULT; THAT I WOULD DIVIDE SHECHEM, AND METE OUT THE VALLEY OF SUCCOTH.

GOD. I have noted many times, that a noun related to the verb, is implied in verbs in the perfect and the imperfect.[28] *Elohim dibber be-kodsho* (God spoke in His holiness) should be interpreted as if written *Elohim dibber be- devar kodsho* (God spoke with His holy word), that is, God spoke via prophecy to Samuel that my kingdom over Israel will, unlike that of Saul, endure.

Shechem refers to the city of Shekhem. [29] The same is the case with the word *Succoth.*[30] The meaning of *achallekah* (that I would divide)[31] is, it will always belong to me[32] and I will appoint my officials over it.[33]

22. Literally, "save Thy right hand." See next note.

23. Our verse reads: *Hoshi'ah yeminekha.* This literally means, save Thy right hand. It should have read *Hoshi'ah bi-yeminekha* (with Thy right hand). Hence I.E.'s comment.

24. Hence it does not have a *bet* prefixed to it. Rabbi Moses interprets *hoshi'ah yeminekha* as; Your right hand (shall) save.

25. For God has no hand.

26. *Save with Thy right hand.*

27. Is. 63:5 speaks of God's arm helping God. However, our verse speaks of God's arm bringing salvation to Israel.

28. See I.E. on verse 3. Also see I.E. on Ps. 3:8.

29 The word *Shekhem* might be taken to mean a portion. See Gen. 48:22.

30. It is the name of a city. See Gen. 33:17.

31. *Chelek* means a portion. I.E. renders *achallekah shekhem* as, I will take *shekhem* as my portion (chelek).

32. Literally, him.

33. For the city is mine.

9. GILEAD IS MINE, AND MANASSEH IS MINE; EPHRAIM ALSO IS THE DEFENSE OF MY HEAD; JUDAH IS MY SCEPTERE.

MINE. David speaks[34] of Shekhem and Succoth because the latter belong to Joseph.[35] Gilead,[36] Manasseh and Ephraim are therefore also mentioned. [37] [Scripture notes all of this,][38] because the house of Joseph was in the north of the Land of Israel. Judah was in the South. Scripture similarly reads: *Judah shall abide in his border on the south* (Josh. 18:5). The word *ma'oz* (the defense of) is in the construct.[39] Its vocalization does not change,[40] for it is a verb that comes from a double root.[41]

10. MOAB IS MY WASHPOT; UPON EDOM DO I CAST MY SHOE; PHILISTIA, CRY ALOUD BECAUSE OF ME.

MOAB IS MY WASHPOT. *Moab is my washpot* means; I will wash their country like a pot.[42]

We find that Scripture here states: *alai pleshet hitro'a'iy* (Philistia, cry aloud because of me).[43] Our verse says the opposite of what we expect it to say.[44] Rabbi Moses explains it as follows: Upon Edom who is mighty do I caste my shoe; Go ahead Philistia and imagine that you shout over me.[45] Our verse is similar to *Rejoice, O young man, in thy youth* (Ecc. 11:9)[46] and to *Come to Beth-el* [*and transgress*] (Amos 4:4).[47]

---

34. In the previous verse.

35. Shekhem belonged to the tribe of Ephraim and Succoth to the tribe of Manasseh. Ephraim and Manasseh were sons of Joseph. David is thus saying: I rule over Joseph.

36. Gilead belonged to the tribe of Manasseh

37. They too were in Joseph's territory. `

38. It speaks of Gilead, Manasseh, Ephraim and Judah.

39. With the word *roshi* (my head).

40. The *kametz* beneath the *mem* does not change to a *sheva*, as is the case in the construct, in words of similar vocalization.

41. Its root is *ayin, zayin, zayin.*

42. I will despoil Moab.

43. Literally, Philistia, shout over me i.e. Philistia, utter a victory cry over me. Now since our verse speaks of David defeating Israel's enemies our verse should have read *over Philistia do I cry aloud* (See Ps. 108:10) rather then, Philistia, shout over me.

44. Lit. It is reversed.

45. In other words, "Philistia, shout over me" was said sarcastically.

46. According to I.E. this is a sarcastic statement.

47. This too is a sarcastic statement.

11. WHO WILL BRING ME INTO THE FORTIFIED CITY?[48] WHO WILL LEAD ME UNTO EDOM?

[12. HAST NOT THOU, O GOD, CAST US OFF? AND THOU GOEST NOT FORTH, O GOD, WITH OUR HOSTS.]

WHO. I used to ask myself the following: Who will bring me to the city of Edom, which was besieged?[49] I used to tell myself that God would do this. God would lead me until Edom. Now the opposite of what I hoped for has come to pass for *Hast not Thou, O God cast us off?* The meaning of the latter is; what shall our armies do, if You do not go out with them?

13. GIVE US HELP AGAINST THE ADVERSARY; FOR VAIN IS THE HELP OF MAN.

GIVE US. The word *havah* means give. The *tav* of *ezrat* (help) is in place of a *heh*.[50] Compare *ve-shavat*[51] (then it shall return) in *then it shall return to the prince* (Ezk. 46: 17). David says: *For vain is the help of man*, because he earlier mentioned *our armies* (12).

13. THROUGH GOD WE SHALL DO VALIANTLY; FOR HE IT IS THAT WILL TREAD DOWN OUR ADVERSARIES.

THROUGH GOD. David prophesied via the Holy Spirit that he would ultimately triumph.

48. Hebrew *ir, matzor*. I.E. renders *ir matzor*, a besieged city.

49. I used to ask myself the following: Who will bring me victoriously into the city of Edom, which I besiege?

50. The word is usually written *ezrah*.

51. Here too the *tav* of *ve-shavat* is in place of a *heh*. The word is usually written *ve-shavah*.

CHAPTER 61

1. FOR THE LEADER; WITH STRING-MUSIC. [A PSALM] OF DAVID.

FOR THE LEADER... HEAR MY CRY, O GOD.[1] The word *neginat* (string-music) is short for *neginat piyyut* (tune of a poem).[2] The fact that the word *neginat* is vocalized with a *pattach* is proof of this.[3]

2. HEAR MY CRY, O GOD; ATTEND UNTO MY PRAYER.

HEAR MY CRY. Hear the cry that I offer in public, and *attend* unto *the prayer* that I offer in my heart. The latter[4] corresponds to the prayer of Hannah.[5]

3. FROM THE END OF THE EARTH WILL I CALL UNTO THEE, WHEN MY HEART FAINTETH; LEAD ME TO A ROCK THAT IS TOO HIGH FOR ME.

FROM THE END OF THE EARTH. Which is far from God's tent [*will I call unto thee... lead me to a rock that is* higher than me...] The meaning of our verse might also be, even though I am at the end of the earth, which is a very low place, lead me to a place a rock that is higher than I.[The end of our verse is to be so interpreted, for] the meaning of *tzur yarum mi-menni* (a rock that is too high for me) is, a rock that is higher than I. [6]

1. *Hear my cry, O God* is probably a transposition from the heading of verse 2.

2. This psalm was to be performed to the tune of a poem opening with the words *neginat piyyut.* See I.E. on Ps. 4:1.

3. A noun ending in a letter vocalized by a *pattach,* followed by a *tav,* is in the construct.

4. David's prayer which was offered in his heart.

5. See 1 Sam. 9-13: *So Hannah rose up....and prayed unto the Lord... she spoke in her heart; only her lips moved, but her voice could not be heard.*

6. The usual form for higher than me is *ram mi-meni.* Hence I.E.'s explanation.

4. FOR THOU HAST BEEN A REFUGE FOR ME, A TOWER OF STRENGTH IN THE FACE OF THE ENEMY.

FOR. You were always a tower of strength. I therefore desire to dwell in Your tent and to truly take refuge in the covert of Your wings.[7]

[5. I WILL DWELL IN THY TENT FOREVER; I WILL TAKE REFUGE IN THE COVERT OF THY WINGS. SELAH.]

6. FOR THOU, O GOD, HAST HEARD MY VOWS; THOU HAST GRANTED THE HERITAGE OF THOSE THAT FEAR THY NAME.

FOR. The *lamed* placed in front of the word *nedarai* (my vows)[8] is superfluous. It is like the *lamed* placed in front of the word *avshalom*[9] (Absalom) in, *the third, Absalom* (1 Chron. 3:2).

The meaning of *For Thou, O God, hast heard my vows* is,[10] I uttered a vow that I will dwell in Your tent if You fulfill my request.[11]

Thou hast granted the heritage [*of those that fear Thy name*] means, I will dwell in the Land of Israel, which You have given as a heritage to those who fear Your name.[12]

7. MAYEST THOU ADD DAYS UNTO THE KINGS DAYS! MAY HIS YEARS BE AS MANY GENERATIONS!

MAYEST THOU ADD DAYS UNTO THE KINGS DAYS. Its meaning is as follows: David requests[13] to live[14] many years so that he will dwell in the house of God in order to serve Him. Our verse is parallel to [*I will dwell in Thy tent*] *for ever* (v. 5). *Tosif* (*May-*

7. See verse 5.

8. *Li-nedarai* (my vows) literally means, to my vows. Hence I.E.'s comment.

9. Which is superfluous.

10. Lit. The meaning is.

11. To return me to the Land of Israel. Radak.

12. In other words, *Thou hast granted the heritage* [*of those that fear Thy name*] is connected to *I will dwell in Thy tent forever; I will take refuge in the covert of Thy wings*. I.E. should be understood as follows: The meaning of *I will dwell in Thy tent forever; I will take refuge in the covert of Thy wings… Thou hast granted the heritage of those that fear Thy name* is: I will dwell in the Land of Israel, which You have given as a heritage to those who fear Your name

13. Reading *she-yevakkkesh*.

14. Reading *she-yichyeh*. See Filwarg.

est Thou add) is similar to *tosif* (prolongeth) in *The fear of the Lord prolongeth days* (Prov. 10:27). However, the *tav* of *tosif* [in our verse] refers to God.[15]

8. MAY HE BE ENTHRONED BEFORE GOD FOREVER! APPOINT MERCY AND TRUTH, THAT THEY MAY PRESERVE HIM.

MAY HE BE ENTHRONED… THAT THEY MAY PRESERVE HIM. The word *man* (appoint)[16] follows the paradigm of the word *tzav*[17] (command) in *Command the children of Israel* (Num. 28:2).[18] The word *asher* has been omitted.[19] Compare, *im levavam shalem* (in behalf of them whose heart is whole) (2 Chron. 16:9).[20] There are many such instances. Our text should be read as follows: *appoint mercy and truth that they may preserve him. The* word *man* (appoint) is similar to *va-yeman* (prepared) in *And the Lord prepared.* [21]

9. SO WILL I SING PRAISE UNTO THY NAME FOREVER, THAT I MAY DAILY PERFORM MY VOWS.

SO. As I do with this psalm, *so will I sing praise unto Thy name forever* and I will daily perform my vows. [22]

15. The *tav* of *tosif* in our verse is a second person prefix while that in Proverbs is a third person prefix. Hence *tosif* in our verse means, You (God) *will add.* However, *tosif* in Proverbs means, *it will add* (or prolong).

16. From the root *mem, nun, heh.*

17. From the root *tzadi, vav, heh.*

18. Both words come from a root that ends in a *heh.* Both words drop the *heh* and are vocalized with a *pattach* beneath the first letter.

19. Our text reads *chesed ve-emet man yintzeruhu* (appoint mercy and truth, that they may preserve him). The latter literally reads: appoint mercy and truth, they may preserve him. The word "that" is not in the Hebrew text. I.E. believes that our verse should be interpreted as if the word "that" (asher) was in the text. Our verse should be interpreted as if written, *chesed ve-emet man* ***asher yintzeruhu***, appoint mercy and truth, **that** they may preserve him.

20. *Im levavam shalem* should be read as if written *asher im levavam shalem.*

21. Both words come from the same root.

22. The Hebrew literally reads: to perform my vows daily. I.E. renders the latter as, and I will perform my vows daily.

CHAPTER 62

1. FOR THE LEADER; FOR JEDUTHUN. A PSALM OF DAVID.

FOR THE LEADER; FOR JEDUTHUN. A psalm which is to be performed to the tune of poem beginning with the word *li-yeduthun.*[1] It was composed by the poet Jeduthan. On the other hand it may refer to a poem that someone composed regarding Jeduthan. It is far fetched to explain *Jeduthun* as being the name of a musical instrument.

2. ONLY FOR GOD DOTH MY SOUL WAIT IN STILLNESS; FROM HIM COMETH MY SALVATION.

ONLY FOR GOD. *Only* means the following:[2] For whom[3] does my soul wait for salvation to come to it? [It waits] only for God. [4]
The word *dumiyyah* (wait) is similar to the word *dom* (resign) in *Resign*[5] *thyself unto the Lord* (Ps. 37:7) and *dommu* (tarry) in *Tarry until we come to you* (1 Sam.14: 9). *Dumiyyah* follows the vocalization of *bokhiyyah (*weep) in *For these things do I weep* (Lam. 1:16).

1. See I.E. on Ps. 4:1. It appears that I.E.'s version of psalms read: *li-yedutun.* Our texts of Psalms read: *al yedutun.* See *Minchat Shai.* However, it is possible that the reading *li-yedutun* is due to a slip of the pen or a scribal error.

2. *Only...* is an answer to the question: *For whom does my soul wait for salvation to come to it?* The question is not stated but is implied in the statement: *Only for God doth my soul wait in stillness.*

3. Reading *le-mi* rather than *le-mah.*

4. The order of the words in I.E. is as follows: "The meaning of only is: For whom does my soul wait? -The word *dumiyyah* (wait) is similar to the word *dom* (resign) in *Resign thyself unto the Lord* (Ps. 32:7) and to *dommu* (tarry) in *Tarry until we come to you* (1 Sam.14: 9). *Domiyah* follows the paradigm of *bokhiyyah* (weep) in *For these things do I weep* (Lam. 1:16), for salvation to come to it. - Only to God alone. "

5. I.E. renders this as, wait.

3. HE ONLY IS MY ROCK AND MY SALVATION, MY HIGH TOWER, I SHALL NOT BE GREATLY MOVED.

HE ONLY IS MY ROCK. I have no savior outside of the Lord. David says[6] that God is his salvation because he earlier stated: *From Him cometh my salvation* (v. 2).

Lo emmot rabbah (I will not be greatly moved) is short for *lo emmot el tehom rabbah* (I will not slip into the great deep). The great deep is the reverse of *my high tower*.[7] [We may interpret *rabbah* as being short for *tehom rabbah*] because we find the word *tehom* (deep) in the feminine.[8] Compare *tehom romematehu*[9] (the deep made it grow) (Ezek. 31:4).

4. HOW LONG WILL YE SET UPON A MAN, THAT YE MAY SLAY HIM, ALL OF YOU, AS A LEANING WALL, A TOTTERING FENCE?

HOW LONG? *I shall not be moved* refers to the thoughts of people who imagine that David will slip. David therefore chastises them by saying *How long will ye set upon a man*? *Tehotatu* (will ye set on a man) is related to the word *havvot* (events), in "Your tongue imagines events" (Ps. 52:4).[10] [*Tehotatu al ish* (will ye set on a man) means,] you think about a man.[11]

The *resh* of *terotzechu* (that you may slay him) is vocalized with a *kametz*.[12] *Terotzechu* is therefore a *pual*. [13] It is like the word *ruchatzt* [14] (washed) in *neither wast thou washed in water* (Ezek. 16:4), for the *pu'al* is vocalized with *kametz, shuruk* or *cholam*.[15]

Terotzechu (that ye may slay him) [16] was uttered in prayer.[17]

---

6. Literally, here states.

7. According to I.E our verse reads: [God] is my rock, my high tower I will not slip into the deep pit.

8. The word *rabbah* (greatly) is in the feminine. Hence the noun *tehom* which it describes has to be a feminine. The problem is that *tehom* has the form of a masculine and appears as such in Scripture. See Job 28:14. Hence I.E.'s comment.

9. *Romematehu* is a feminine. Hence the word *tehom* which it governs is a feminine.

10. Translated according to I.E. See I.E. on 52:4.

11. You think evil thoughts regarding a man.

12. A *kametz katan* beneath the *resh*.

13. And not a *piel*. If *terotzechu* was a *piel* then it would have been vocalized with a *pattach* beneath the *resh*.

14. Which is a *pu'al*.

15. It is usually vocalized with a *shuruk*. Hence I.E.'s comment.

16. I.E. renders *terotzechu*, may you will be murdered.

17. I.E. interprets our verse as follows: How long will ye set upon a man? May you all be slain, may you be as a leaning wall, as a tottering fence.

Ke-kir natuy (as a leaning wall) means, may you be as a leaning wall. *Natuy* (leaning) follows the paradigm of *atzum* (mighty). [18] On the other hand *natuy* might be a transitive verb.[19] The word *ha-dechuyah* (tottering)[20] is proof, for Scripture repeats itself.[21]

5. THEY ONLY DEVISE TO THRUST HIM DOWN FROM HIS HEIGHT, DELIGHTING IN LIES; THEY BLESS WITH THEIR MOUTH, BUT THEY CURSE INWARDLY. SELAH.

FROM HIS HEIGHT. The word *se'eto* (his height) is similar to *se'eto* (his majesty) in *Shall not His majesty terrify you* (Job 13:11) and *naso essa* (I should pardon) in *that I should in any wise pardon them.*[22]

David complains[23] that his enemy wants to thrust him down behind a tottering fence with their lies.

6. ONLY FOR GOD WAIT THOU IN STILLNESS, MY SOUL; FOR FROM HIM COMETH MY HOPE.

ONLY FOR GOD. Howbeit, I say to my soul: *My soul,* wait only for God.

7. HE ONLY IS MY ROCK AND MY SALVATION, MY HIGH TOWER, I SHALL NOT BE MOVED.

He has been my rock and my salvation many times.

8. UPON GOD RESTETH MY SALVATION AND MY GLORY; THE ROCK OF MY STRENGTH, AND MY REFUGE, IS IN GOD.

UPON GOD. Since God is my salvation and rock,[24] I do not have to try to seek ways to save myself and be glorified for doing so. On the contrary, it is for God to save me and glorify me.

18. It is an adjective.
19. In the *pa'ul.*
20. *Dechuyah* is a transitive verb in the *pa'ul.*
21. *Natuy* is parallel to *dechuyah.* Both are verbs in the *pa'ul.*
22. All these words come from the root *nun, sin, alef* (raise, lift up, exalt).
23. Literally, mentions.
24. Literally, this being so.

9. TRUST IN HIM AT ALL TIMES, YE PEOPLE; POUR OUT YOUR HEART BEFORE HIM; GOD IS A REFUGE FOR US. SELAH.

TRUST IN HIM. After the psalmist chastises those who plan evil, he goes back to speak to God's people. He tells them: Trust in God. The psalmist therefore employs the plural.

GOD IS A REFUGE FOR US. SELAH. The poet says *for us,* for he is included in God's people.[25] The psalmist employs the phrase *God is a refuge* because he earlier said:[26] *And my refuge, is in God* (v. 8).

10. MEN OF LOW DEGREE ARE VANITY, AND MEN OF HIGH DEGREE ARE A LIE; IF THEY BE LAID IN THE BALANCES, THEY ARE TOGETHER LIGHTER THAN VANITY.

ARE VANITY. Do not put your trust in men, for they are a vanity and a lie. If men were placed in a scale, then the men would weigh less then the vanities and lies.[27] The afore-mentioned is a parable. Its meaning is, as David's son Solomon said; men are *a vanity of vanities* (Kohelteh 1:2).

11. TRUST NOT IN OPPRESSION, AND PUT NOT VAIN HOPE IN ROBBERY; IF RICHES INCREASE, SET NOT YOUR HEART THEREON.

TRUST NOT IN OPPRESSION. Our Psalm is to be understood as follows: Scripture first stated, do not put your trust in man to save you (v. 10). It then states[28] do not put your trust in your money and believe that it will stand by you in your time of trouble. This is the meaning of *chayil ki yanuv [al tashitu lev]...* (If riches increase [set not your heart thereon.]) *Chayil* (riches) is similar to the word *chayil* (wealth) in *hath gotten me this wealth* (Deut. 8:17). *Yanuv* means increase. It is similar to the word *tenuvah* (fruit-age) (Is. 27: 6).[29]

25. Mentioned in the previous verse.

26. Literally, because it is parallel.

27. If men were placed on one side of a scale and vanities and lies on the other side then the men would weigh less then the vanities and lies.

28. In our verse.

29. Thus *chayil ki yanuv* (if riches increase) means, if riches bear fruit (increase).

The psalmist mentions *oppression* and *robbery* because most of the money acquired by people is by one of these ways. *Oshek* (oppression) refers to money acquired by seduction and cheating. Robbery refers to money acquired by force.

The meaning of *tehbalu* (put… vain hope) is, you add vanity[30] upon vanity.[31]

12. GOD HATH SPOKEN ONCE, TWICE HAVE I HEARD THIS: THAT STRENGTH BELONGETH UNTO GOD.

ONCE. God has previously charged us, once and twice, that strength belongs to God alone and that He alone will forever give strength or wealth.

Strength belongeth unto God is parallel to *The rock of my strength* (v. 8).

13. ALSO UNTO THEE, O LORD, BELONGETH MERCY; FOR THOU RENDEREST TO EVERY MAN ACCORDING TO HIS WORK.

ALSO UNTO THEE. The psalmist then goes on to praise God who does acts of mercy for human beings. He cautions and informs people that God will recompense each and every person in accordance with his deeds. Some say that the meaning of *ki* (for) in *ki attah* (for Thou) is "even though" as in *ki am kesheh oref hu* (even though they are a stiff-necked people) (Ex. 34:9).[32] [According to the latter the meaning of our verse is:] *Also unto Thee, O Lord belongeth mercy* even though Thou ultimately *renderest to every man according to his work.*[33]

30. Vain hope.

31. I. E. explains *u-vegazel al tehbalu* (and put not vain hope in robbery) as, do not add vanity to vanity by committing robbery

32. Translated according to I.E. See I.E. on Ex. 34:9.

33. God is merciful even though he ultimately punishes the wicked.

CHAPTER 63

1. A PSALM OF DAVID, WHEN HE WAS IN THE WILDERNESS OF JUDAH.

IN THE WILDERNESS OF JUDAH. The following is the theme of this psalm: David greatly desired to go to *kiryat-ye'arim* the place of the Ark.[1] [However; he could not do so,] because he was hiding from Saul.

2. O GOD, THOU ART MY GOD, EARNESTLY WILL I SEEK THEE; MY SOUL THIRSETH FOR THEE, MY FLESH LONGETH FOR THEE, IN A DRY AND WEARY LAND, WHERE NO WATER IS.

O GOD, THOU ART MY GOD, EARNESTLY WILL I SEEK THEE. *Ashachareka* (earnestly will I seek thee) is similar to the word *shochar* (dilligently seeketh) in *diligently seeketh good* (Prov. 11:27). On the other hand it might be similar to *shachar* (morning) (Ps. 57:9). It is like the word *le-vakker* (to visit early) in *and to visit early in His temple* (Ps. 27:4) which is related to the word *boker* (morning).[2]

MY FLESH LONGETH FOR THEE. My soul thirsts for You, as one thirsts for water. My flesh is dry (kamah).[3] *Kamah* (longeth) is to be rendered *dry,* for the word has no "neighbor" in Scripture.[4]

1. The Ark had as of yet not been brought to Jerusalem. It was in *kiryat-ye'arim.* See 1 Sam 7:1 and 1 Chron. 1:54.

2. Similarly *ashachareka* means, I will seek you in the morning.

3. I.E. renders, *kammah lekha besari* (my flesh longeth for Thee) as, my flesh is dry for You, that is, my flesh thirsts for You.

4. *Kamah* is not found elsewhere in Scripture. It is to be translated in accordance with its context.

IN A DRY AND WEARY LAND. I am, as it were, in a dry and weary land that has no water. Scripture reads *eretz ayef* (weary land), for the word *eretz* (land)[5] is found in the masculine.[6] Compare, *netam*[7] *aretz* (the land burnt up) (Is. 9:18). There are many such instances.[8]

3. SO HAVE I LOOKED FOR THEE IN THE SANCTUARY, TO SEE THY POWER AND THY GLORY.

SO. I contemplate in my heart[9] and I see You.[10] I picture myself in the sanctuary and I see Your power, that is, the ark. Compare, *And delivered His strength*[11] *into captivity* (Ps. 78:61).

AND THY GLORY. The manifestation of God's presence.[12]

4. FOR THY LOVINGKINDNESS IS BETTER THAN LIFE; MY LIPS SHALL PRAISE THEE.

FOR THY LOVINGKINDNESS IS BETTER THAN LIFE. It is more precious than life for me to behold Your loving kindness, that is, Your resting among Israel. My lips shall therefore praise You.

5. SO WILL I BLESS THEE AS LONG AS I LIVE; IN THY NAME WILL I LIFT UP MY HANDS.

SO WILL I BLESS THEE. I will bless You in this manner, as long as I exist. I will lift up my hands while blessing Your name. There are many such instances in Scripture.[13]

5. *Ayef* is masculine. Hence I.E.'s comment.

6. Hence it can be modified by an adjective (ayef) that is in the masculine.

7. *Netam* is in the masculine.

8. Where *eretz* is treated as a masculine.

9. I think about You.

10. I picture You in my mind.

11. The reference is to the ark.

12. Hebrew, *shekhinah.* God's presence over the ark. So Radak.

13. Where the raising of the hands is tied to a blessing. See Num. 9: 22.

6. MY SOUL IS SATISFIED AS WITH MARROW AND FATNESS; AND MY MOUTH DOTH PRAISE THEE WITH JOYFUL LIPS.

AS WITH …FATNESS. The world *chelev* (marrow) is similar to the word *chelev* (fat of) in *the fat of the land* (Gen. 44:18). A *bet*[14] is missing from the word *chelev.*[15] Compare *savati... elim* (I am full of...rams) (Is.1: 11).[16]
The meaning of *with joyful lips*[17] is, I will sing to You in all languages that I know.[18] The meaning of *And my mouth doth praise thee with joyful lips* might also be: My mouth which shall praise You, will be the cause of all lips praising You.[19] Our verse is connected with that which follows.

7. WHEN I REMEMBER THEE UPON MY COUCH, AND MEDITATE ON THEE IN THE NIGHTWATCHES.

WHEN. When I remember You, my soul is satisfied with pleasure.

NIGHTWATCHES. There are three night watches.[20] I am obligated to render thanks to You, for You have been my help (v. 8). I chant like a singing bird when I am in the shadow of Your wings (ibid.)

9. MY SOUL CLEAVETH UNTO THEE; THY RIGHT HAND HOLDETH ME FAST.

CLEAVETH. My soul has no love but You. You too have helped me to cleave unto You. The latter is the meaning of *Thy right hand holdeth me fast.*

---

14. An inseparable prepositional prefix.

15. Our verse literally reads, as marrow and fatness. With a *bet* before *chelev* our verse reads, as with marrow and fatness.

16. *Savati... elim* literally means, I am full rams. I.E. believes that the phrase should be interpreted as if written *savati...ve- elim,* I am full of rams.

17. Hebrew, *sifte renanot.*

18. I.E. renders *sifte* (lips) as languages. See Gen 11:1; *safah echat* (one language). He renders *renanot* as, singing. Our verse literary reads: *And joyful lips* (languages) *my mouth doth* (or will) *praise Thee*. I.E. renders this as: My mouth shall sing praises to You joyfully, in all languages that I know.

19. This interpretation renders *sifte* as lips. It explains: *And joyful lips my mouth doth* (or will) *praise Thee* as follows: And singing lips will result because my mouth will praise You.

20. *Berakhot* 3a.

10. BUT THOSE THAT SEEK MY SOUL, TO DESTROY IT, SHALL GO INTO THE NETHERMOST PARTS OF THE EARTH.

BUT THOSE. David does not mention the name of the slanderers and those who reveal his secrets to Saul. He merely alludes to them with the words *But those that seek my soul.* The word *sho'ah* (destruction) is similar to *sho'ah* (destruction) in *Let destruction come upon him* (Ps. 35:8).

SHALL GO. They shall go unto the nethermost parts of the earth, to destruction and below it.

11. THEY SHALL BE HURLED TO THE POWER OF THE SWORD; THEY SHALL BE A PORTION FOR FOXES.

THEY SHALL BE HURLED.[21] The hurlers shall hurl[22] each one of them them. [23] Compare, *And he said to Joseph*[24] (Gen. 48:1).

12. BUT THE KING SHALL REJOICE IN GOD; EVERY ONE THAT SWEARETH BY HIM SHALL GLORY; FOR THE MOUTH OF THEM THAT SPEAK LIES SHALL BE STOPPED.

BUT THE KING. Some say that *the king* refers to Saul.[25] However, I believe that the reference is to David. The meaning of *every one that sweareth by Him* is, everyone that swears by Him[26] in truth. Compare, *Every tongue shall swear* (Is. 45:23). *Them that speak lies* (v. 12) is proof of this. Some say that David says *that sweareth by Him* because of the oath taken by Saul.[27]

21. Hebrew, *yaggiruhu*. Literally, they shall hurl him.

22. Our verse literally reads: They shall hurl him (yaggiruhu) by the power of the sword. The subject of the verb *yaggiruhu* is missing. Hence I.E.'s comment.

23. *Yaggiruhu* (they shall be hurled) has a singular suffix. It literally means, they shall hurl him. However, the verse speaks of David's enemies. Hence I.E.'s comment.

24. Translated literally. Here too the subject of *va-yomer* is missing. The verse should be interpreted as follows: and the one who said, said to Joseph. See I.E. on Gen. 48:1.

25. David hoped that after those who spoke evil of him to Saul would perish, Saul would become righteous and cease persecuting. Filwarg.

26. God.

27. Not to harm David. See 1 Sam. 19:6. However, Saul broke his word.

CHAPTER 64

1. FOR THE LEADER. A PSALM. A SONG OF DAVID.

2. HEAR MY VOICE, O GOD, IN MY COMPLAINT; PRESERVE MY LIFE FROM THE TERROR OF THE ENEMY.

HEAR MY VOICE, O GOD, IN MY COMPLAINT. The meaning of *hear my voice* is, [hear my voice which implores You to] *preserve my life.*[1]

3. HIDE ME FROM THE COUNCIL OF EVIL DOERS; FROM THE TUMULT OF THE WORKERS OF INIQUITY.

HIDE ME FROM THE COUNCIL.[2] The Council [of evil doers] takes place in secret. Hence Scripture reads, *Hide me.*[3]

TUMULT. *Rigshat* (tumult) is similar to *rageshu* (uproar) in *Why are the nations in an uproar* (Ps. 2:1). [4]

4. WHO HAVE WHET THEIR TONGUE LIKE A SWORD, AND HAVE AIMED THEIR ARROW, A POISONED WORD.

WHO HAVE WHET. The word *shananu* (who have whet) is similar to the word *shannun* (sharp) in *and a sharp sword* (Prov. 25:18).

1. The meaning of our verse is; *hear my voice* that implores you to *preserve my life.*

2. Hebrew, *sod.* Literally, the secret, that is, the secret council. See Radak.

3. Rather than save me. Hide me in a secret place from the council taken in secret is more poetic than, save me in a secret place from the council taken in secret.

4. I.E. translates *rigshat* (tumult) as a gathering. See I.E. on Ps. 2:1. He renders *me-rigshat po'ale aven* (from the tumult of the workers of iniquity) "from the gathering of the workers of iniquity."

AND HAVE AIMED THEIR ARROW.[5] The meaning of *darekhu chitzam*[6] (and have aimed their arrow) is, they bend their bow with arrows.[7] I have previously explained the aforementioned in my comments on the verse reading *When he bends* (yidrokh) *his arrows* (Ps. 58:8).

Some say that *a poisoned word*[8] refers back to *their tongue*. However, it is possible that the meaning of *davar mar* (a poisoned word) is; this act[9] is a poisoned thing.[10]

5. THAT THEY MAY SHOOT IN SECRET PLACES AT THE BLAMELESS; SUDDENLY DO THEY SHOOT AT HIM, AND FEAR NOT.

THAT THEY MAY SHOOT IN SECRET PLACES. I therefore ask: *hide me* (v. 3).

AND FEAR NOT. God who sees them.

6. THEY ENCOURAGE ONE ANOTHER IN AN EVIL MANNER; THEY CONVERSE OF LAYING SNARES SECRETLY; THEY ASK, WHO WOULD SEE THEM.

THEY ENCOURAGE. One another[11] to do evil.

7. THEY SEARCH OUT INIQUITIES, THEY HAVE ACCOMPLISHED A DILIGENT SEARCH; EVEN IN THE INWARD THOUGHT OF EVERY ONE, AND THE DEEP HEART.

THEY SEARCH OUT. *Yachpesu* (they search out) is a *kal*. The *yod* prefix that indicates that *yachpesu* is an imperfect is vocalized with a *pattach* because it precedes a guttural.[12]

5. Hebrew, *darekhu chitzam*. The latter literally means; they bend their arrow. Hence I.E.'s comment.

6. The latter literally means; they bend their arrow.

7. They bend their bow in order to shoot their arrows (I.E. on Ps. 58:8). Thus to bend the arrow is another way of saying, to aim the arrow.

8. Heb. *Davar mar*.

9. The term *davar* can mean a word or a thing.

10. According to this interpretation our verse reads: Who have whet their tongue like a sword, and have aimed their arrow. [They committed] a poisoned deed.

11. Our verse reads *yechazzeku lahem*. This literally means: They encourage (or they strengthen) to them. I. E. explains that this is to be interpreted as, they encourage each other.

12. The *chet*.

Compare *ya'alzu* (exult) in *Let the saints exult in glory* (Ps. 149:5).[13]

INIQUITIES. The word *olot* (iniquities) is related to the word *avel* (iniquity) (Lev. 19:15).[14] Compare, *ve-oloto* (and iniquity) in *And iniquity stoppeth her mouth* (Job 5:16).

[ACCOMPLISHED (Tammenu).] According to the Spanish grammarians[15] the word *tammenu* (consumed) in *Surely the Lord's mercies are not consumed* (Lam. 3:22) is a variant of *tammemu* (consumed).[16] The *nun* of *tammenu* is in place of the doubled letter.[17] The fact that Scripture goes on to say *Surely His compassion fail not* (khalu) (ibid.) is proof of this.[18] The fact that we do not find this root[19] among the verbs whose middle letter is silent[20] is a second proof.[21] The wise men of France call such stems[22] two letter roots. A third proof of the aforementioned[23] is the fact that *tammenu* (accomplished) in *they have accomplished a diligent search* which does not have an *etnach*[24] is vocalized with a *kametz.*[25] If *tammenu* was similar to the word *shavnu*[26] (returned) in *we had now returned* (Gen. 43:10), then *tammenu* would have been vocalized with a *pattach.*[27]

---

13. *A yod* prefix in the *kal* is usually vocalized with a *chirik*. Hence I.E.'s comment.

14. Both words come from the root *ayin, vav, lamed.*

15. Rabbi Jonah ibn Janach; *Sefer Ha-Rikamh*. Also see Radak.

16. From the root *tav, mem, mem*. If *tammenu* comes from the root *tav, vav, mem* then the word is a first person plural in the perfect, with the meaning of, we have finished. If it comes from the root *tav, mem, mem,* then it means they have finished, or they have accomplished.

17. A *mem.*

18. *Tammenu* (consume) is parallel) to *khalu* (fail not). *Khalu* is a third person plural perfect. Hence *tammenu* in is a variant of *tamemu* (consumed).

19. If the suffix *nu* in the word *tammenu* is a first person plural, then the word *tammenu* comes from the root *tav vav, mem.* However, the root *tav vav mem* does not seem to exist.

20. A root whose middle letter is a *vav.*

21. That *tammenu* (consumed) is a variant *tammemu.*

22. Roots whose middle letter is a *vav.*

23. That *tammenu* (consumed) is a variant *tammemu.*

24. A note that indicates a break in the sentence. If *tammenu* had an *etnach* beneath it, then it would be possible to explain the word as coming from the root *tav, vav, mem*, for in such cases the *pattach* changes into a *kametz.*

25. So Filwarg. The first stem letters of verbs in the third person plural perfect are vocalized with a *kametz. Tammenu* is spelled with a *pattach* in our version of Scripture. However, it was spelled with a *kametz* in I.E.'s version of Scripture. See *Minchatt Shai.* Also see Radak.

26. A first person plural perfect, from the root *shin, vav, bet.*

27. Like *shavnu*. So Filwarg. The printed texts have *kametz.* This is an obvious error, for the word *shavnu* is vocalized with a *pattach.*

The meaning of *tammenu chefes mechupas* (they have accomplished a diligent search) is they have concluded seeking that which they sought. All of this in secret.[28] This is the meaning of *even in the inward thought of every one, and the deep heart.*

8. BUT GOD DOTH SHOOT AT THEM WITH AN ARROW SUDDENLY; THENCE ARE THEIR WOUNDS.

BUT GOD DOTH SHOOT AT THEM. *But God doth shoot at them* is in contrast to *That they may shoot* (v. 5).

SUDDENLY. The latter is in contrast to *suddenly do they shoot at him* (5).

9. SO THEY MAKE THEIR OWN TONGUE A STUMBLING UNTO THEMSELVES; ALL THAT SEE THEM SHAKE THE HEAD.

SO THEY MAKE… A STUMBLING. *So they make their own tongue a stumbling* refers to those[29] *who have whet* [their tongue] *like a sword* (v.4).

10. AND ALL MEN FEAR; AND THEY DECLARE THE WORK OF GOD, AND UNDERSTAND HIS DOING.

AND ALL MEN FEAR. The reference is to every person, who saw the acts of God, in punishing the wicked, for intending to do evil to the righteous and blameless.

11. THE RIGHTEOUS SHALL BE GLAD IN THE LORD, AND SHALL TAKE REFUGE IN HIM; AND ALL THE UPRIGHT IN HEART SHALL GLORY.

THE RIGHTEOUS SHALL BE GLAD. *The righteous,* that is, the blameless shall be glad and grow in courage. Our clause is in contrast to *that they may shoot in secret places at the blameless* (v. 5).

28. They have secretly accomplished seeking that which they sought.

29. Lit. Is parallel to, or stands in contrast to.

CHAPTER 65

1. FOR THE LEADER. A PSALM. A SONG OF DAVID.

2. PRAISE WAITETH FOR THEE, O GOD, IN ZION; AND UNTO THEE THE VOW IS PERFORMED.

PRAISE WAITETH FOR THEE. David composed this psalm when the ark was [in Zion].[1] On the other hand it is possible that one of the poets composed it when the temple was built.[2] The latter appears correct to me. The word *dumiyyah* (waiteth) is related to the word *demut* (image).[3] It is also possible that *dumiyyah* is related to the word *dumiyyah* (wait) in *Only for God doth my soul wait in stillness* (Ps. 62:2).[4] It has the meaning of *dom* (wait) in *Wait for the Lord and fear him*[5] (Ps. 37:7) and *dommu* (tarry) in *Tarry until we come to you* (1 Sam.14:9). The meaning of our verse is: Praise waits for You in Zion, from the people who come there to praise You, in the place of the ark. There will a vow be paid untoYou.

3. O THOU THAT HEAREST PRAYER UNTO THEE DOTH ALL FLESH COME.

O THOU THAT HEAREST PRAYER. For the Holy Temple, as Solomon mentioned in his prayer was called a house of prayer for all people.[6] The psalmist therefore says *unto Thee,* that is, unto Your place[7] *doth all flesh come.*

1.Hence the psalm speaks of God being praised in Zion.

2. During the reign of King Solomon.

3. According to I.E., *lekha dumiyyah tehillah Elohim, be-tziyon* (Praise waiteth for Thee, O God in Zion) should be rendered: Praise which describes You is in Zion.

4. In this case *lekha dumiyyah tehillah* means, *Praise waiteth for Thee.*

5. Translated according to I.E. See I.E. on Ps. 37:7.

6. 1 Kings 8:41-43.

7. Your temple.

4. THE TALE OF INIQUITIES IS TOO HEAVY FOR ME; AS FOR OUR TRANSGRESSIONS, THOU WILT PARDON THEM.

THE TALE OF INIQUITIES. This is tied [to the preceding verse].[8] It is written above: *Unto thee doth all flesh come* because *Thou hearest prayer* (v. 3), for You heard my prayer when I confessed my sins[9] and You pardoned all of our transgressions.[10]
This psalm was composed by the poet in a year of drought. They prayed to God and God heard their prayer.
The tale of iniquities is too heavy for me are the words of the poet who prays. The poet says: I confess that I committed many sins.[11] I and my people transgressed.[12] Therefore the straits of the drought came upon us.

5. HAPPY IS THE MAN WHOM THOU CHOOSEST, AND BRINGEST NEAR, THAT HE MAY DWELL IN THY COURTS; MAY WE BE SATISFIED WITH THE GOODNESS OF THY HOUSE, THE HOLY PLACE OF THY TEMPLE.

HAPPY IS THE MAN WHOM THOU CHOOSEST.[13] The word *asher* (whom) is missing.[14] Compare, *le-khol yavo gevuratekha* (to all will come Your might) (Ps.71:18).[15] The aforementioned is to be read as if written *le-khol asher yavo gevuratekha*] (to all *who* will come, Your might]. Our verse is to be interpreted as if written *ashre asher tivchar bo* (happy is the man *whom* Thou choosest). The clause is to be understood as follows: Happy is he, whom You choose and bring near, that he may dwell in Your courts.
May we be satisfied refers to the pleasure that the soul experiences in the service of God in the Holy Temple.

8. Verses 3 and 4 are to be interpreted as one verse.

9. I.E.'s interpretation of: *The tale of iniquities is too heavy for me.*

10. I.E.'s interpretation of: *as for our transgressions, Thou wilt pardon them.*

11. I.E.'s explanation of *The tale of iniquities is too heavy for me.*

12. I.E.'s interpretation of *As for our transgressions, Thou wilt pardon them.*

13. Literally, Happy Thou choosest. See next note.

14. Our verse opens *ashre tivchar* (happy is the man whom Thou choosest). *Ashre tivchar* literally means happy Thou choosest. This makes no sense. Hence I.E. points out that it should be read as if written *ashre asher tivchar* happy is the one whom Thou choosest.

15. Translated literally.

The word *be-tuv* (with the goodness) is to be read as if written twice. [16] The end of our verse is to be read as if written, with the goodness of the holy of Thy temple.[17] The meaning of the latter is, with the goodness of the glory,[18] for that is what holy refers to.[19] Others interpret our verse as follows: May we be satisfied in the goodness of Your house, You who are the holy one in Your Temple.[20]

6. WITH WONDROUS WORKS[21] DOST THOU ANSWER US IN RIGHTEOUSNESS, O GOD OF OUR SALVATION; THOU THE CONFIDENCE[22] OF ALL THE ENDS OF THE EARTH, AND OF THE FAR DISTANT SEAS.

WITH WONDROUS WORKS. The meaning of [the last part of our verse] is,[23] when a nation serves God then it will live in security, without hunger or fear of any enemy. The meaning of [the first part of our verse] is, when we fear You then You will answer us to save us.[24]
The meaning of *be-tzedek* (*in righteousness*) is to be interpreted as if written *be-tzidkadekha* (in Your righteousness). On the other hand *be-tzedek* (in righteousness) might mean because of the righteousness[25] which we practiced, that is, we repented and you forgave our transgressions.[26]
Rabbi Moses says that *The confidence of all the ends of the earth* means, the confidence of all people.[27] It is similar to, *And all countries came into Egypt to Joseph to buy corn* (Gen. 42:57.[28]

---

16. Literally, *be-tuv* also serves another word.

17. The end of our verse literally reads: the holy of Thy temple.

18. God's glory (the shekihnah) which was manifest in the temple.

19. Literally, for that is what is holy. According to this interpretation our verse concludes: May we be satisfied with the goodness of Thy house, with the goodness of the holy of Thy Temple, that is, with the goodness of the glory which rests in Thy Temple.

20. According to this interpretation, the holy of Thy temple means, You who are the holy one in Your Temple.

21. Hebrew, *nora'ot*. I.E. renders this as, "greatly fearful' or very fearful. Hence his comment.

22. Hebrew, *mivtach*. Literally, the security. Hence I.E.'s explanation.

23. *Thou the confidence of all the ends of the earth, and of the far distant seas.*

24. I.E. renders our verse: [When we are] *greatly fearful, You answer us in righteousness O God of our salvation.*

25. In other words *be-tzedek* (in righteousness) means, because of the righteousness.

26. The order of the words in our text is, *in righteousness dost Thou answer us*. This interpretation interprets the aforementioned as follows: Because of the righteousness [which we practiced] You forgave our sins *(dost thou answer us).*

27. In other words *of the earth* means, the inhabitants of the earth.

28. *And all countries came into Egypt* means, and all the inhabitants of the countries came to Egypt.

[*All ends of the earth* refers] to people in the far distance. The meaning of our clause is: You will save those who live at the ends of the earth and those who are on the seas[29] whom no human being has the power to save.

According to my opinion,[30] *katzve* (ends of) does not speak of physical entities for *katzve* refers to [what lies] beyond that which is physical. Hence it does not refer to anything physical.[31] Compare, *The creator of the ends of the earth* (Is. 40:28).

Scripture reads *and of the far distant seas* because half of the earth's globe is covered by seas. Scripture reads *rechokim* (far distant),[32] because there are many seas.

7. WHO BY THY STRENGTH SETTEST FAST THE MOUNTAINS, WHO ART GIRDED ABOUT WITH MIGHT.

WHO... SETTEST FAST . Scripture mentions *the mountains,* because it earlier mentioned the earth. It mentions the mountains,[33] because they are like pillars.

Scripture reads *Who art girded about with might,* because God's strength is seen in the high mountains which He created. They are therefore called *the mountains of God* (Ps. 36:7).

In my opinion Scripture first says *Thou the confidence of all the ends of the earth* (v. 6).[34] The meaning of the aforementioned is; You are the confidence of that which is not seen.[35] It [then goes on to say] Your might is seen in the great bodies.[36]

8. WHO STILLEST THE ROARING OF THE SEAS, THE ROARING OF THEIR WAVES, AND THE TUMULT OF THE PEOPLES.

WHO STILLEST. The word *mashbi'ach* (stillest) is similar to the word *teshabbechem* (Thou stillest them) (Ps. 89:10). *Mashbi'ach* means, "stills."[37] Our clause is similar to *Thou rulest the proud swelling of the* sea (ibid).

---

29. So Radak.

30. According to this interpretation, the end of verse 6 does not deal with people living at the ends of the earth but speaks of God's power over nature. It speaks of God being the support of the horizon and the far seas. It then goes on to speak of God as supporting the mountains.

31. Literally: Because they *(katzve)* are the ends of all bodies; they are not bodies. In other words, *katzve* refers to that which lies beyond the earth. According to I.E. "the ends" refers to the lines (the spheres) that surround the earth. See I.E. and Radak on Isaiah 40:28.

32. *Rechokim* is a plural. Hence I.E.'s comment.

33. Rather than any other aspect of the earth.

34. Hebrew *mivtach*. The word may be taken to mean the security, or the support.

35. See note 31. The reference might also be to the distant seas.

36. The mountains.

37. Or, *who stillest.*

[Scripture says *Who stillest the roaring of the seas,* because] it earlier spoke of the far distant seas.[38]

The tumult of the peoples means the tumult of the people who are compared to the seas.[39] Compare, *The waters of the River, mighty and many* [40] (Is. 8:7). God will deliver them from the drought and from the enemy.

9. SO THAT THEY THAT DWELL IN THE UTTERMOST PARTS STAND IN AWE OF THY SIGNS; THOU MAKEST THE OUTGOINGS OF THE MORNING AND EVENING TO REJOICE.

SO THAT THEY THAT DWELL IN THE UTTERMOST PARTS. [*They that dwell in the uttermost parts*] is in contrast to the Holy Temple.[41]

OF THY SIGNS. The reference is to the power of the rain. Compare, *Who doeth great things past finding out* (Job 9:10).[42]

The meaning of *Thou makest the outgoings of the morning* [*and evening to rejoice*] is people rejoice because the signs[43] which go out and are seen in the morning[44] and evening.[45] The word *tarnin* (Thou makest to rejoice) is thus a verb governing two actions.[46] Rabbi Moses says that *Thou makest the outgoings of the morning* [*and evening to rejoice*] speaks of the beginning of the day and night.[47] The end of one is the beginning of the other. This is the cause of the joy.

38. V. 6.

39. In other words, *The tumult of the peoples* refers to the enemies of Israel.

40. The reference is to the Assyrian army.

41. Not only those who are in the Holy Temple will stand in awe of Your signs, but also those who dwell in the outermost parts of the earth shall do so.

42. This is the way the Talmud interprets the verse. See *Ta'anit* 2a.

43. The heavenly bodies.

44. The sun.

45. The moon and stars.

46. That is, *tarnin* is a *hifil.* It applies to God and to the signs, that is, God causes the signs to rejoice.

47. In other words, *The outgoings of the morning and evening* does not speak of the signs which appear during the day and night, but to the beginning of the day and night.

10. THOU HAST REMEMBERED THE EARTH AND WATERED HER, GREATLY ENRICHING HER, THOU PREPAREST THEM CORN, FOR SO PREPAREST THOU HER.

THOU HAST REMEMBERED. This verse is proof that Zion suffered a year of drought and the enemy contemplated coming to Zion, to besiege her. However, God remembered the Land of Israel which is His land.[48]

Some say that the meaning of *va-teshokakeha* means, *and watered her*. However, this is incorrect.[49] The phrase *ve-nafesho shokekah*[50] (and his soul hath appetite) (Is. 29:8) is proof.[51] On the contrary, our verse is like *va-yarum tola'im va-yivash* (Ex.16:20). The meaning of the latter is, and it had bred worms and rotted.[52] There are many such instances.[53] Our verse is to be understood as follows: You remembered the earth which had desired [water].[54] This is the reason why our psalm reads: You remembered.

GREATLY. The *tav* of *rabbat* (greatly) is like the *tav* of *ve-shavat*[55] (then it shall return) in *then it shall return to the prince* (Ezek. 46:17). The term being described is missing.[56] "Great (rabbah)" is similar in meaning, to a great thing.[57]

ENRICHING HER. If *tashrennah* (enriching her) belongs to the heavy conjugation[58] then a *chirik* should have been placed beneath the *shin*.[59] However, if *tashrennah* is a *kal*

---

48. And watered it.

49. For the root of the Hebrew word for watered is *shin, kof, heh*. However, the root of *va-teshokakeha* is *shin, kof, kof.*

50. From the root, *shin, kof, kof.*

51. The phrase *ve-nafesho shokekah* shows that the word *va-teshokakeha* does not mean, watered. On the contrary it shows that it means, to desire.

52. According to I.E. *va-yarem (bred)* is a pluperfect. See I.E. on Ex. 16:20.

53. Of the use of the pluperfect in Scripture.

54. I.E. renders *va-teshokakeha,* and desired it (water). Our verse literally reads Thou hast remembered the earth, and she desired it (water). Now if God remembered the earth: Why would it desire water? Hence, I.E. takes *va-teshokakeha* as pluperfect meaning, she had desired it. Our verse is to be understood as follows: Thou hast remembered the earth; [before You remembered her] she had desired it (water).

55. *Ve-shavat* is a variant of *ve-shavah*. Similarly, *rabbat* is a variant of *rabbah.*

56. *Rabbat* is an adjective. According to I.E. *rabbat* (greatly) is not in the construct with *tashrennah* (enriching her). Hence he believes the word which it is describing is not in the text.

57. In other words great is short for "a great thing." I.E. reads our verse as follows: Thou hast remembered the earth... enriching her with a great thing, with the river of God, that is full of water.

58. The *hifil.*

59. The word should have read *ta'ashirennah.*

then it is a transitive verb.[60] It is like *yasor* (he will take the tenth) (1 Sam. 8:17) which is spelled with a *sin*.[61] We find this to be the case in the three forms.[62]

THE RIVER. Which is made up of rain.
The *mem* of *deganam* (them corn)[63] refers to *Thou hast remembered the earth* (v. 10).[64]

FOR SO PREPARES THOU HER. The reference is to the earth.

11. WATERING HER RIDGES ABUNDANTLY, SETTLING DOWN THE FURROWS THERE-OF, THOU MAKEST HER SOFT WITH SHOWERS; THOU BLESSEST THE GROWTH THEREOF.

HER RIDGES. *Telameha* (her ridges) is similar to *telem* (furrow) in *with his band in the furrow* (Job 39:10).[65]
Some say that the meaning of *nachet gedudeha* (settling down the furrows there-of) is, bring down the furrows there-of.[66] Compare *gedudot* (cuttings) in *Upon all the hands are cuttings* (Jer. 48:37). *Gedudot* refers to the lines made by the plow. Scripture compares them to cuttings. The meaning of bring *down the furrows there-of* is, saturate the furrows with water.[67]
Some say that the word *gedudeha* is related to *gedud yegudenu* (a troop shall troop upon him) (Gen. 49:19). The reference is to the rain,[68] that is, to the streams.[69]

60. The root *ayin, shin, resh* (rich) in the *kal* is usually intransitive. Hence I.E.'s comment.

61. Not with a *shin*. There are no vowels in the text of I.E. Hence I.E. is telling us how the word is to be read. See Filwarg.

62. The root *ayin, sin, resh* (ten) comes in the *kal, piel and hifil*. In all of these forms it is transitive. Hence it is possible that the root *ayin, shin, resh* (rich) is transitive in both the *kal* and *hifil*.

63. *Deganam* (them corn) literally means, their corn. According to I.E. the reference is to the corn of the people of the earth.

64. The meaning of which according to I.E. is, *Thou hast remembered the people of the earth*.

65. *Telem* refers to the ridges of the furrows.

66. That is, bring down the rain into the furrows.

67. God will bring down the rain into the furrows. Radak.

68. According to this interpretation *nachet gedudeha* (settling down the furrows there-of) is, bring down her troops (of water).

69. The streams produced by the rains.

12. THOU CROWNEST THE YEAR WITH THY GOODNESS; AND THY PATHS DROP FATNESS.

[*Thou crownest the year with Thy goodness*] so that this year stands out from other years,[70] like a queen wearing a crown is distinguished from the rest of the women.[71]
And Thy paths is metaphoric.[72] The word *me'agel* (path) refers to the places where the rain water of the pools gathers. [73]

13. THE PASTURES OF THE WILDERNESS DO DROP; AND THE HILLS ARE GIRDED WITH JOY.

The[74] pools[75] are in inhabited places. *Ne'ot midbar* (the pastures of the wilderness) is similar to *ne'ot ha-ro'im* (the pastures of the shepherds) (Amos.1:2).

[AND THE HILLS ARE GIRDED WITH JOY.] The hills will be girded with joy when the herbage and the grass are seen.

14. THE MEADOWS ARE CLOTHED WITH FLOCKS; THE VALLEYS ALSO ARE COVERED OVER WITH CORN; THEY SHOUT FOR JOY, YEA, THEY SING.

CLOTHED. [*Laveshu karim ha-tzon* (the meadows are clothed with flocks)] is similar to *im chelev karim* (with fat of lambs) (Deut. 32:14).[76] The flocks will be numerous. The Rabbis said that our clause is a euphemism.[77] However, it appears to me that the word

70. Literally, is among the other years.

71. Literally, like a queen wearing a crown among the women.

72. *Paths* are a metaphor for the pools of rain water. They are described as God's paths for the rain comes from the clouds which are, metaphorically speaking, God's paths. Radak.

73. See Josh. 15:19.

74. Lit. Your.

75. The pools (paths) mentioned in the previous verse.

76. *Karim* in Deut. 32:14 means, lambs. So too the word *karim* in our verse. Furthermore, Deut. speaks of fat lambs. So does our verse, for according to this interpretation *laveshu karim ha-tzon* means, the sheep are clothed in fat.

77. The Rabbis interpret our verse as referring to the coupling of sheep. They render our verse; the sheep are clothed with rams.

karim (flocks) is similar to the word *kar* (pastures) in, *in large pastures* (Is. 30:23).[78] The fact that Scripture reads *the valleys* is proof of this.[79]

COVERED. The word *ya'atfu* (covered) is related to the word *mitattef* (cover). It means will be clothed. The word *yitro'a'u* (they shout for joy) is related to the word *teru'ah* (shouting) (Job 8:21). Our verse is similar to *The mountains and the hills shall break forth before you into singing* (Is. 55:12).

78. In other words *karim* means, meadows and not sheep.

79. The fact that the *valleys also are covered over with corn* follows the clause dealing with *karim,* indicates that *karim* is to be rendered, meadows.

CHAPTER 66

1. FOR THE LEADER. A SONG, A PSALM. SHOUT UNTO GOD, ALL THE EARTH.

FOR THE LEADER... SHOUT UNTO GOD. The psalm does not mention the name of the author. This psalm was also[1] most probably composed by one of the poets,[2] for it is in the plural and we do not find this to be the case in most of the psalms that were written by David.

2. SING PRAISES UNTO THE GLORY OF HIS NAME; MAKE HIS PRAISE GLORIOUS.

SING PRAISES. The meaning of *simu* [*khavod tehillato*[3]] (make his praises glorious) is, extol [4] [Him], because God's praise is your Glory, that is, you will become glorious in His praise. [5]

3. SAY UNTO GOD: HOW TREMENDOUS IS THY WORK! THROUGH THE GREATNESS OF THY POWER SHALL THINE ENEMIES DWINDLE AWAY BEFORE THEE.

SAY UNTO GOD. [*Mah nora ma' asekha* (how tremendous is Thy work) means,] *How tremendous* is each one of Your works.[6]

1. Like other such psalms.

2. An unidentified poet. See I.E.'s introduction to the Book of Psalms.

3. Literally, put glory His praise.

4. The word *simu* (make) literally means put. Here it has the meaning of declare, or extol.

5. I.E. renders our verse as follows: Extol Him, glory is His praise. He explains this as: Extol him because His praise is your glory.

6. *Nora* (tremendous) is a singular. *Ma'asekha* is a plural. The noun and the adjective governing it are thus inconsistent. I.E. explains the combination of the plural and singular as referring to each one of the plural.

Compare, *Its branches* (banot)[7] *run* (tza'adah)[8] over *the wall* (Gen. 49:22). [9]
The meaning of *yekhachashu* (shall dwindle),[10] is they shall bear witness that lies and deceit are in their hands.[11]

4. ALL THE EARTH SHALL WORSHIP THEE, AND SHALL SING PRAISES UNTO THEE; THEY SHALL SING PRAISES TO THY NAME. SELAH.

ALL. Scripture earlier said *Thine enemies*. The reference was to enemies who are close by. The psalmist now speaks of *All the earth*.[12]
There is no difference between *They shall sing praises* to Thee[13] and *And shall sing praises unto Thee*.[14] Scripture repeats itself.

5. COME, AND SEE THE WORKS OF GOD; HE IS TERRIBLE IN HIS DOING TOWARD THE CHILDREN OF MEN.

COME. One person shall say to the other person *lekhu*. The meaning of *lekhu* is come.[15] Compare *lekhu* (come) in *Come, now, and let us reason together* (Is. 1:18). The [literal] meaning of *lekhu* is, go to us.

TERRIBLE. The word *nora* (terrible) is connected to *alilah* (doing).[16] The meaning of *nora alilah* (He is terrible in his doing) is, the deed is terrible.[17]
The one who says that the *heh* of *alilah* (doing) is superfluous and that the word has the meaning of *elyon* (high)[18] is in error, for the *heh* indicates that the word is in the feminine. We do not find a superfluous *heh* at the end of a noun unless the word is penultimately

7. *Banot* is a plural.

8. *Tza'adah* is a singular.

9. According to I.E. this verse should be rendered, each one of its branches run over the wall.

10. From the root *kaf, chet, shin* meaning to deceive.

11. According to I.E., *yekhachashu* means, will admit to their deceit.

12. Those who are distant.

13. "To Thee" is I.E.'s paraphrase of *to Thy name*.

14. There is no difference between *They shall sing praises to Thy name* and *And shall sing praises unto Thee*.

15. The literal meaning of *lekhu* is, go. Hence I.E.'s comment.

16. *Nora* is an adjective modifying *alilah*. The word *alilah* means, deed.

17. That is, His deeds are terrible. God terrifies the sinner so that he comes to fear Him. See Radak. I.E. renders our verse: Come, and see the works of God; the terrible deeds upon the children of men.

18. This interpretation renders *nora alilah*, terrible is the Most High.

accented. *Sorek* (a noble vine) (Jer. 2:21) and *sorekah* (choice vine)[19] (Gen. 49: 11) is like *tzedek* (righteous) (Deut. 16:18) and *tzedakah* (righteousness) (Gen. 15:6).[20]

6. HE TURNED THE SEA INTO DRY LAND; THEY WENT THROUGH THE RIVER ON FOOT; THERE LET US REJOICE IN HIM.

HE TURNED. The psalmist relates the ancient deeds of God.
Through the river refers to the Jordan. Israel joyfully passed the Jordan and the ark stood in it.[21]

7. WHO RULETH BY HIS MIGHT FOREVER; HIS EYES KEEP WATCH UPON THE NATIONS; LET NOT THE REBELLIOUS EXALT THEMSELVES. SELAH.

WHO RULETH. The word *olam* (forever) in Scripture always means time and eternity. The meaning of *moshel olam* (Who ruleth ...forever) is, God rules forever. The meaning of our verse is: God by his great might rules eternally and His rule is over the nations, that is, he sees them.[22] It is wrong to interpret the *bet* of *bi-gevurato* (by His might) as the *bet* in *meshol banu* (rule thou over us) (Judges 8:22),[23] for such an interpretation makes no sense.[24]
Scripture notes that God's rules over the sea and the dry land.[25] Hence, Let not the rebellious that revolt against God exalt themselves.

8. BLESS OUR GOD, YE PEOPLES, AND MAKE THE VOICE OF HIS PRAISE BE HEARD.

BLESS OUR GOD, YE PEOPLES. *Ye peoples* refers to the nations, such as the Jebusites, that were under Israel's control. On the other hand it may be directed to everyone.[26] All

19. *Sorekah* is the feminine form of *sorek*. Thus the *heh* of *sorekah* is not superfluous.

20. *Ttzedakah is* the feminine form of *tzedek*. Thus the *heh* of *tzedakah* is not superfluous.

21. See Joshua 3:10-17.

22. I.E.'s interpretation of Who *ruleth by His might forever; His eyes keep watch upon the nations.*

23. The *bet* in *banu* has the meaning of *over*. Thus it is theoretically possible to interpret *bi-gevurato* as meaning, over His might

24. If we interpret *bi-gevurato* as, over His might, then our verse reads, "Who ruleth over His might forever." The latter, according to I.E. makes no sense.

25. Verse 6.

26. All nations. It does not only refer to the Jebusites.

of us[27] are obligated to bless God. Some say that *ye peoples* refer to Israel. Compare, *After thee, Benjamin, among thy peoples* (Judges 5:14). The latter interpretation is correct.

10. FOR THOU, O GOD, HAST TRIED US; THOU HAST REFINED US, AS SILVER IS REFINED.

FOR. Our verse is metaphoric. It speaks of a trouble that befell Israel. God tested Israel, to know what is in their heart. The latter[28] too is metaphoric, because everything is revealed to God before it occurs, for He sees the heart of the one who thinks.[29]

11. THOU DIDST BRING US INTO THE HOLD; THOU DIDST LAY CONSTRAINT UPON OUR LOINS.

THOU DIDST BRING US INTO THE HOLD. Such as a fortress or evil.

CONSTRAINT. The word *mu'akah* (constraint) is similar in meaning to *akat* (oppression) in *akat rashah* (the oppression of the wicked) (Ps. 55:4). It means, trouble. This is the way the Targum[30] renders it. The word *mu'akah* is a noun. On the other hand it might be a *pa'ul* lacking an adjective. It refers to something that acts as a constraint[31] on the[32] loins.

12. THOU HAST CAUSED MEN TO RIDE OVER OUR HEADS; WE WENT THROUGH FIRE AND THROUGH WATER; BUT THOU DIDST BRING US OUT UNTO ABDUNDANCE.

THOU HAST CAUSED MEN TO RIDE OVER OUR HEADS. Its meaning is; You caused men to ride over our high places.[33]

27. All peoples.

28. The clause for *Thou, O God, hast tried us.*

29. God knows how a person will react to a test. In Genesis, I.E. argues that the purpose of a test is to reward the one who is tested. See I.E. on Gen. 22:1.

30. The *Targum* renders the word *tzarah* (trouble) by the Aramaic word *aka.* Targum on Ps. 55:4.

31. Such as chains. *Targum.*

32. Literally, their.

33. Lit. Its meaning is; for he rides over his high places.

[WE WENT THROUGH FIRE AND THROUGH WATER.] We were like those who went through fire or water.[34] Compare, *whosesoever strikes his father and mother.*[35] The meaning of *unto abundance* is, into the air, for a person is dried by fire[36] and is swept away by water. [37]

13. I WILL COME INTO THY HOUSE WITH BURNT-OFFERINGS, I WILL PERFORM UNTO THEE MY VOWS.

I WILL COME. These are the words of the poet [speaking on behalf of himself.] Or, the poet speaks on behalf of the one who conducts the war.

14. WHICH MY LIPS HAVE UTTERED, AND MY MOUTH HATH SPOKEN, WHEN I WAS IN DISTRESS.

WHICH MY LIPS HAVE UTTERED. *Asher patzu sefatai* (which my lips have uttered) refers to a vow. Compare, *for I have opened* (patziti) *my mouth unto the Lord* (Judges 11:35).

15. I WILL OFFER UNTO THEE BURNT-OFFERINGS OF FATLINGS, WITH THE SWEET SMOKE OF RAMS; I WILL OFFER BULLOCKS WITH GOATS. SELAH.

FATLINGS. The word *mechim* (fatlings) is vocalized like the word *metim* (the dead). The noun is missing.[38] Our verse should be understood as follows: [*I will offer unto Thee*] *burnt offerings* of fat sheep,[39] sheep full of marrow.[40]

RAMS. Large sheep.

---

34. In other words the *vav* prefixed to *va-mayim* (through water) is to be rendered as "or" rather than "and."

35. Translated literally. According to I.E. *whosesoever strikes his father and mother* should be rendered: *whosesoever strikes his father or his mother,* for the *vav* prefixed to *immo* (his mother) is to be translated as "or" rather than "and."

36. He thus lacks air.

37. He thus lacks air.

38. *Metim* is an adjective. It means, full of marrow. According to I.E. our verse literally reads: I will offer unto Thee burnt-offerings full of marrow (mechim). However, it does not does not tell us what specific type of animal *mechim* is describing.

39. The missing noun is *kevasim* (sheep). Thus our text should be read as if reading *kevasim mechim.*

40. Sheep full of marrow refers to fat sheep. So too Rashi.

The word *selah* means in truth.[41]

16. COME, AND HEARKEN, ALL YE THAT FEAR GOD, AND I WILL DECLARE WHAT HE HATH DONE FOR MY SOUL.

COME, AND I WILL DECLARE WHAT HE HATH DONE FOR MY SOUL. I will declare what God has done for my soul.[42]

17. I CRIED UNTO HIM WITH MY MOUTH, AND HE WAS EXTOLLED WITH MY TONGUE.

I CRIED UNTO HIM WITH MY MOUTH. The word *pi* (my mouth) is missing a *bet.*[43] It is similar to the word *sheshet* (six)[44] in for *in six days the Lord made heaven and earth* (Ex.20:11). *Elav pi karati* should be interpreted as if written *elav be-fi karati* (I cried unto Him with my mouth).

AND HE WAS EXTOLLED WITH MY TONGUE.[45] Additional praise was beneath my tongue. The allusion is to the heart. Some say that Scripture repeats itself.[46]
Ve-romam (and he was extolled)[47] is vocalized like *u-morak* (shall be scoured) in it *shall be scoured, and rinsed in water* (Lev .6:21).

18. IF I HAD REGARDED INIQUITY IN MY HEART, THE LORD WOULD NOT HEAR.

INIQUITY. God would not have listened to me, if I had iniquity in my heart, when I called to Him with my mouth. The fact that there was no iniquity in my heart is a sign of this.

---

41. See I.E. on Ps. 3:5.

42. In other words, the pronoun *He* in *What He hath done for my soul* refers to God.

43. Our verse reads: *elav pi karati.* The latter literally means, "Unto him my mouth I called" This makes no sense. Hence I.E.'s comment.

44. The word *sheshet* (six*) is* to be interpreted as if written *be-sheshet* (in six). Ex. 20:11 literally, reads: *for six days the Lord made heaven and earth.* It is to be read as if written, *for in six days the Lord made heaven and earth.*

45. Literally, and praise was beneath my tongue. Hence I.E.'s comment.

46. *I cried unto him with my mouth* means the same as and *praise was beneath my tongue.*

47. Literally, and praise.

19. BUT VERILY GOD HATH HEARD; HE HATH ATTENDED TO THE VOICE OF MY PRAYER.

The word *akhen* (but verily) is similar to the word *akhen* (surely) in *Surely the thing is known* (Ex. 2:14).

20. BLESSED BE GOD, WHO HATH NOT TURNED AWAY MY PRAYER, NOR HIS MERCY FROM ME.

BLESSED BE GOD. Who helped me to pray and did not turn away my prayer.

HIS MERCY. That I should pray to him.[48]

48. God's mercy consists in allowing the psalmist to pray to Him.

CHAPTER 67.

1. FOR THE LEADER; WITH STRING-MUSIC. A PSALM, A SONG.

FOR THE LEADER. This is another psalm whose author is unknown to us.

2. GOD BE GRACIOUS UNTO US, AND BLESS US; MAY HE CAUSE HIS FACE TO SHINE TOWARD US; SELAH.

GOD BE GRACIOUS UNTO US. *Yechannenu* (be gracious unto us) is similar to *channunu* (grant them graciously) in *grant them graciously unto us* (Judges 21:22) and to *chanan* (graciously given) in *Whom God hath graciously given* (Gen. 33:5).[1]
The meaning of *and bless us* is, add[2] to that which You have graciously given us.[3]
The meaning of *may He cause his face to shine toward us* is, May we find favor in God's eyes whenever we request something from Him.

3. THAT THY WAY MAY BE KNOWN UPON EARTH, THY SALVATION AMONG ALL NATIONS.

THAT THY WAY MAY BE KNOWN. It will then be known, that it is the way of God to bless the few and to save them.

4. LET THE PEOPLE GIVE THANKS UNTO THEE, O GOD; LET THE PEOPLES GIVE THANKS UNTO THEE, ALL OF THEM.

GIVE THANKS. Nations will then also give thanks unto You.

1. In other words *Yechannenu* means, be gracious unto us.

2. Literally, He should add.

3. According to I.E. a blessing is an addition of the good. See I.E. on Gen. 2:3.

5. O LET THE NATIONS BE GLAD AND SING FOR JOY; FOR THOU WILT JUDGE THE PEOPLES WITH EQUITY, AND LEAD THE NATIONS UPON THE EARTH. SELAH.

BE GLAD. Its meaning is: [*O let the nations be glad and sing for joy,*] because of the good that You will do for us.

6. LET THE PEOPLES GIVE THANKS UNTO THEE, O GOD; LET THE PEOPLES GIVE THANKS UNTO THEE, ALL OF THEM.

LET THE PEOPLES GIVE THANKS UNTO THEE. The nations will also give thanks to You for Your judgments,[4] for You justify the righteous and declare the wicked guilty.[5] You give tranquility to the earth when You judge the wicked. Also for this,[6] "Let the peoples give thanks unto Thee,"

7. THE EARTH HATH YIELDED HER INCREASE; MAY GOD, OUR OWN GOD, BLESS US.

THE EARTH. The psalmists goes back and explains what he means by "and bless us."[7] It means that the earth shall give forth its produce.

8. MAY GOD BLESS US; AND LET ALL THE ENDS OF THE EARTH FEAR HIM.

MAY GOD BLESS US. In what ever we do. Then all the ends of the earth, that did not hear of God's glory and greatness, shall fear Him.

---

4. In addition to giving thanks to You for helping and blessing the weak. See Verses 3-4. Our verse repeats verse 4. Hence I.E.'s comments.

5. I.E.'s paraphrase of *For Thou wilt judge the peoples with equity* (v. 5).

6. The reference is to God's judgments. See note 4.

7. V. 2.

CHAPTER 68.

1. FOR THE LEADER. A PSALM OF DAVID, A SONG.

2. LET GOD ARISE, LET HIS ENEMIES BE SCATTERED; AND LET THEM THAT HATE HIM FLEE BEFORE HIM.

LET GOD ARISE, LET HIS ENEMIES BE SCATTERED. This is a very precious psalm. Most of the commentaries explain it to refer to the giving of the Torah. They offer proof from *as in Sinai, in holiness* (v. 18). However, they can not explain how the verses of the psalm are connected to each other, for after mentioning Israel's entrance into the Promised Land, the psalmist goes back to the splitting of the sea which occurred when our ancestor left Egypt. This is not the correct way [to construct a psalm].[1]

It appears to me that David composed this psalm regarding a war that he waged against the uncircumcised. Most of his camp consisted of Judah, Benjamin, Zebulun and Naphtali.[2] Their might in war was then revealed. He therefore mentioned these tribes.[3] The fact that David opens the psalm with, *Let God arise,* [*let His enemies be scattered; and let them that hate Him flee before Him*] is proof of this[4]. The latter is similar to *Rise up O Lord* [*and let Thine enemies be scattered; and let them that hate Thee flee before Thee*] (Num. 10:35). Its meaning is, when God rises His enemies will immediately flee. The meaning of *rise* is, show Your Might.

1. The psalmist would not list things out of chronological order. It is also possible that, "this is not the correct way" might mean, this is not the right way to explain this psalm.

2. See verse 25.

3. In verse 25.

4. That David composed this psalm regarding a war which he waged.

3. AS SMOKE IS DRIVEN AWAY, SO DRIVE THEM AWAY; AS WAX MELTETH BEFORE THE FIRE, SO LET THE WICKED PERISH AT THE PRESENCE OF GOD.

AS SMOKE IS DRIVEN AWAY. The word *ke-hindof* (as...driven away) is fully spelled.[5] Compare the word *tingosu* (exact)[6] in *And exact all your labors* (Is. 58:3).

AS WAX MELTETH. *Himmes* (melteth) is an infinite. It comes from a double root.[7]

AS WAX. The meaning of *donag,* is wax.

SO LET THE WICKED PERISH. The reference is to those who wage war against David.

4. BUT LET THE RIGHTEOUS BE GLAD, LET THEM EXULT BEFORE THE LORD; YEA LET THEM REJOICE WITH GLADNESS.

BUT LET THE RIGHTEOUS. *The righteous* refer to the people who are with David, that is, Israel. They shall be glad.

5. SING UNTO GOD, SING PRAISES TO HIS NAME; EXTOL HIM THAT RIDETH UPON THE SKIES, WHOSE NAME IS THE LORD; AND EXULT YE BEFORE HIM.

SING. Each will say to the other, "Sing unto God."

EXTOL. The word *sollu* (extol) is similar to *salseleha* (exalt her) (Prov. 4:8). It is akin to, praise.

UPON THE SKIES. *Aravo*t (skies) is a term for the sky. Rabbi Moses says that the sky is so called[8] because it is wide.[9] He also said that the word *sollu* (extol) is similar to the words *sollu* (cast up) in *Cast up, cast up the highway* (Is. 62:10). He explained that *la-*

5. In I.E.'s version of psalms the word *hindof* was spelled with a *vav*. It is usually spelled without a *vav*. Hence I.E.'s comment. It should be noted that the word is spelled without a *vav* in our editions of psalms.

6. Which is fully spelled out in I.E.'s version of Isaiah. It should be noted that the word is spelled without a *vav* in our editions of the book of Isaiah.

7. Its root is *mem, samekh, samekh*.

8. Elsewhere in Scripture. So Filwarg. However, here it refers to a plain.

9. The word *aravah* in Hebrew refers to a wide plain. See Num. 25:2; Josh 4:13.

rokhev ba-aravot (that rideth upon the skies) refers to the one who goes to celebrate in the house of God. Such a person rides[10] upon the wide places.[11]

However in my opinion *sollu le-rokhev ba-aravot* (extol Him that rideth upon the skies) refers to *To Him that rideth upon the heaven of heavens,[12] which are of old* (v. 34).[13]

[The plains are called *aravot*][14] for the following reason:[15]

There are three motions.[16] One such as fire ascends. Its counterpart is the mountain.[17] The second such as the earth descends.[18] Its counterpart is the lowland. The *aravah* is intermediary.[19] It is similar to the movement of a sphere.[20]

The *bet* of *be-Yah* (the Lord) is a preposition.[21] Its meaning is, exalt and praise God using the name *Yah*.[22] This interpretation is contrary to the opinion of many who maintain that the *bet* is an integral part of the word.[23] They go as far as to do the same with all letters.[24] The same applies to [the *bet* affixed to *Yah*) in, "*be-Yah YHVH* (in the Lord God)[25] is the conquering power" (Is. 26:4).[26]

---

10. Travels.

11. Or plains. According to Rabbi Moses *sollu la-rokhev ba-aravot* (extol Him that rideth upon the skies) should be rendered: make a road for him who rides upon the plains.

12. In other words *aravot* refers to heaven and not to a plain.

13. *La-rokhev ba-aravot* refers to God, not to the one who goes to God's house.

14. *Aravot* means the heavens. However, it also applies to plains.

15. The reason is given at the end of the paragraph.

16. Up, down and Circular. Literally, For there are three motions. The latter is I.E.'s reformulation of Aristotole. The Greek philosopher taught that there are three kinds of motion: straight lines, circular and mixed. Earth and fire move in a straight line, fire upwards and earth downward. Air and water move in a mixed motion. The heavenly bodies move in a circular motion.

17. Mountains rise up. They represent upward motion.

18. Earth is at the bottom of the world. Soil falls down. It thus represents downward motion.

19. Between up and down.

20. The heavenly sphere moves in a curcular motion. This motion is a flat motion, that is, it neither goes up or down. Neither does a plain. Hence the term *aravah* can also be applied to the plains.

21. Meaning *with*. It usually has the meaning of *in*. Hence I.E.'s comment.

22. Reading *be-shem*, rather then *ke-shem*. This interpretation reads our verse as follows: Sing unto God, sing praises to His name; extol Him that rides upon the skies, employ the name *Yah* when you exalt before him.

23. This opinion believes that the *bet* affixed to *Yah* is not a prefix but an integral part of the Divine name, *Beyah*.

24. This view maintains that new names of God are formed by prefixing various letters of the alphabet to the word *Yah*. See M. Friedlander on Is. 26:4.

25. The *bet* of *be-Yah* is a preposition.

26. Hebrew, *tokef ha-nitzu'ach*. Is. 26:4 reads: *For the Lord is God* (be-Yah YHVH), *an everlasting rock*. I.E. paraphrases the latter as, *be-Yah YHVH* (in the Lord God) is the conquering power. See I.E. and Radak on Is. 26:4.

6. A FATHER OF THE FATHERLESS, AND A JUDGE OF THE WIDOWS, IS GOD IN HIS HOLY HABITATION.

A FATHER OF THE FATHERLESS. Even though God rides upon the skies [He is a father of the fatherless and a judge of the widows]. Compare *For though the Lord be high, yet regardeth He the lowly* (Ps. 138 v. 6). The reference[27] is to the fatherless who has no one to help him and does not even possess knowledge.[28] The Torah similarly states, *for the Lord your God, he is God of Gods* (Deut. 10:17). It then afterwards reads: *He doth execute justice for the fatherless and widow* (ibid. V. 18).
The meaning of in *His holy habitation* is: [God is a father of the fatherless] even though God's glory is in a very high place[29] and orphans are in the lowliest place, namely, on the earth.

7. GOD MAKETH THE SOLITARY TO DWELL IN A HOUSE; HE BRINGETH OUT THE PRISONERS INTO PROSPERITY; THE REBELLIOUS DWELL BUT IN A PARCHED LAND.

GOD. *House* in our verse is used in the sense of *house* in *that the Lord will make thee a house* (2 Sam 7:11); *that he made them houses* (Ex. 1:21); *every man came with his house* (Ex. 1:1); and *every man…a lamb for a house* (Ex. 12:3).[30] The meaning of God *maketh the solitary to dwell in a house* is, God shall make the solitary numerous and will settle them.[31]
The word *kosharot* (prosperity) is connected to the word *asirim* (prisoners). *Asirim be kosharot* (prisoners into prosperity) is to be interpreted as if it read *asurim be-kosharot,* that is, prisoners bound in chains.[32] *Kosharot* (prosperity) means chains. For its meaning is similar to the word *Kishor* (distaff)[33] in *She layeth her hands to the distaff* (Prov. 31:19). [34]
Sorerim (rebellious) refers to those who do violence to the fatherless.
The word *tzechichah* (parched) is similar to the word *tzicheh* (parched), in *parched with thirst* (Is. 5:13). It is like the word *tzachtzachot* (drought) in, *and satisfy thy soul in drought* (Is. 58:11).

---

27. In our verse.

28. Fatherless refers to a young orphan who lacks the knowledge to fend for himself.

29. Even though God is *in His holy habitation,* He is a father of the fatherless.

30. In other words, the term "house" means a family.

31. In an inhabited place. See below.

32. The usual term for bound is, *asurim.* Hence I.E.'s comment.

33. The staff upon which the textile fibers are bound together.

34. I.E. reads our verse as follows: God maketh the solitary to dwell in a house; He bringeth out the prisoners who are bound in chains.

It[35] means parched.
The rebellious dwell but in a parched land is the reverse of *God maketh the solitary to dwell in a house*, that is, in the midst of an inhabited area.
Tzechichah means, a place of thirst.

8. O GOD, WHEN THOU WENTEST FORTH BEFORE THY PEOPLE, WHEN THOU DIDST MARCH THROUGH THE WILDERNESS. SELAH .

O GOD. All the commentaries explain that heaven and earth trembled (v. 9) at the time of the giving of the Torah.[36] Similarly, *God cometh from Teman* (Habakkuk 3:3).[37] So too, *The Lord came from Sinai* (Deut. 33:2).[38] Likewise, *Lord, when Thou didst go forth out of Seir* (Judges 5:4). Similarly, *O God, when Thou wentest forth before Thy people.*[39] However, the latter verse contradicts them.[40] This is so, because it is incorrect to say with regard to the giving of the Torah *When Thou didst march through the wilderness* (yeshimon). *Selah.* The word *yeshimon* (wilderness) is similar to the word *tishamenah* (shall be made desolate) in *and the high places shall be desolate* (Ezek. 6:6). Now when the children of Israel were at Sinai they were in an inhabited place and not in *a waste, a howling wilderness* (Deut. 32:10), that is, in that *great and dreadful wilderness* (Deut 1:19) *in a land that no man passed through* (Jer. 2:6). Israel traveled in the dreadful wilderness[41] *after* they journeyed from Mt. Sinai. Furthermore The Torah does not state that the earth and also the heaven trembled in the day that the *Torah* was given. Only Mt. Sinai trembled. [42]

The following is the interpretation of our verses:
The Torah states: *The Lord came from Sinai; [And rose from Seir unto them; He shines forth from mount Paran]* (Deut. 33:1). The meaning of the latter is that God began to come into the camp of Israel at Sinai. However, as stated in the Torah, His might was not revealed until after Israel circled Mt. Seir. Paran is close to them,[43] for the Torah clearly

35. *Tzechichah*

36. In other words, verse 9 speaks of the revelation at Sinai.

37. Habakkuk 3:3 also refers to the revelation at Sinai.

38. It too deals with the revelation at Sinai. See I.E. on Deut: 33:2.

39. It too deals with the revelation at Sinai.

40. Rather than proving that v. 9 deals with the giving of the Torah, it indicates that it does not refer to this event.

41. Lit. This occurred.

42. Ex. 19:18.

43. To Sinai and Seir. Hence Deut. 33:1 speaks of Sinai, Seir and Paran.

states, *and the Horites in their mount Seir unto El-paran* (Gen. 14:6). This[44] is the meaning of, *[Lord,] When Thou didst march out of the field of Edom* (Judges 5:4). Similarly, *God cometh from Teman* (Habakkuk (3:3);[45] for the latter [refers to Edom]. Compare, *Teman, Omar* (Gen. 36:11).[46]

When thou wentest forth before Thy people refers to the Ark going in front of the camp when Israel journeyed from Mt. Sinai.[47]

The earth trembled (v. 9) is similar to *And the hills did tremble* (Is. 5:25). Its meaning is, all the nations were afraid.[48] Can you not see that the song of David says, *Then the earth did shake and quake, The foundations [also of the mountains did tremble]* (Ps. 18:5)? The import of the latter is that the earth was almost overturned.
Scripture states *The earth trembled* as Sinai did, for the Lord [came down upon it] on the day that the Torah was given,[49] because the earth is stationary.[50]
Rabbi Moses says that the meaning of *behold this Sinai*[51] (v. 9) is: Behold, this[52] took place as long as God's glory was still upon Sinai. The meaning of *the God of Israel* (ibid.) is; God came down upon Mt. Sinai because of Israel.

10. A BOUNTEOUS RAIN DIDST THOU POUR DOWN, O GOD; WHEN THINE INHERITANCE WAS WEARY, THOU DIDST CONFIRM IT.

A BOUNTEOUS RAIN. Scripture reads, *O God, when thou wentest forth before Thy people* (v. 8) because it wants to relate the start of Israel's victories.
The word *tanif* (didst Thou pour down) means, *You saturated.* Compare, *nafti* (I have perfumed) in *I have perfumed my bed* (Prov. 7:17)

44. God's might was first revealed to Israel when they came to Edom.

45. *Teman* is another name for *Seir* (Edom).

46. *Teman* and *Omar* were the grandsons of Esau (Edom).

47. Numbers 10:38.

48. For the earth shook.

49. I.E.'s interpretation of *The earth trembled...*

50. Hence the earth's trembling is extraordinary.

51. Translated literally.

52. The trembling of Sinai.

THINE INHERITANCE. The reference is to the land of Israel. Its meaning is: God will always saturate the land of Israel with water. It is similar to *The eyes of the Lord Thy God are always upon it* (Deut. 11:12).

WAS WEARY. The meaning of *was weary*[53] is, if the land were weary[54] you would establish it.

11. THY FLOCK SETTLED THEREIN; THOU DIDST PREPARE IN THY GOODNESS FOR THE POOR, O GOD.

THY FLOCK SETTLED THEREIN. *Chayyatekha* (Thy flock) means Your congregation. Compare. *Ve-chayyat pelishtim* (and the troop of the Philistines) (2 Sam. 23:13). The verse thus relates that Israel entered its land.[55]
Thou didst prepare is addressed to God. You supported Israel in the time of their poverty. *Thou didst prepare in [Thy goodness]* means; You did do good to them.

12. THE LORD GIVETH THE WORD; THE WOMEN THAT PROCLAIM THE TIDINGS ARE A GREAT HOST.

THE LORD GIVETH THE WORD. *The Lord giveth the word* is connected to *the women that proclaim the tidings*. Its meaning is; God will fulfill the words of the women that proclaim the tidings in their songs.

A GREAT HOST. From Israel.[56] [God will answer their prayers], for their entire desire and request is that You strengthen Israel.[57]
The following is the word [proclaimed by the women:] *Kings of armies flee; they flee* (v. 13) from before you.[58] The meaning of the latter is, the kings of the armies of the nations shall flee before them.
The word *yiddodun* (flee) is written twice.[59]

53. Actually the meaning of, *When Thine inheritance was weary, Thou didst confirm it.*

54. *Ve-nilah* (when…weary) is not to be rendered "and when weary" but "if weary."

55. For *chayyatekha* (Thy flock) means, Your congregation.

56. The women that proclaim the tidings are a great host from Israel.

57. Reading *ta'avatan… she'elatan* , rather than *tavatam… she'elatam.*

58. Israel.

59. For emphasis.

13. KINGS OF ARMIES FLEE, THEY FLEE; AND SHE THAT TARRIETH AT HOME DIVIDETH THE SPOIL.

AND SHE THAT TARRIETH AT HOME. The men[60] that remain in Jerusalem and did not go out to wage war shall divide the spoil. This certainly will be the case with those who go out to war.

14. WHEN YE LIE AMONG THE SHEEPFOLDS, THE WINGS OF THE DOVE ARE COVERED WITH SILVER, AND HER PINIONS WITH THE SHIMMER OF GOLD.

WHEN YE LIE AMONG THE SHEEPFOLDS. The word *shefattayim* (sheepfolds) is similar to the word *shefot* (setting) in *the setting[61] of the pot[62]* (Ezek. 24:3; 2 Kings 4:38). The place where the pot is set is black like. The meaning of our verse is, do not fear the enemy, for even if you lie where the pot is placed[63] you will be white like a dove that is covered with silver.

AND HER PINIONS. The word *evroteha* (her pinions) is similar to the word *ever* (wings) in *Oh that I had wings like a dove* (Ps. 55:7).

WITH THE SHIMMER. *Yerakrak*[64] (shimmer) is the color of gold. Our clause is similar to, *And all faces are turned into paleness* (yerakon) (Jer. 30:6).
The meaning of our verse is, you will quickly shake off your blackness and the white [of your skin] will be seen.

15. WHEN THE ALMIGHTY SCATTERETH KINGS THEREIN, IT SNOWETH IN ZALMON.

WHEN THE ALMIGHTY SCATTERETH. The word *Shaddai* means, as the Nagid explains, Almighty.[65] The *kings* refer to the kings of the earth. The word *bah* (therein) refers to bah (therein) in *Thy flock settled therein* (v. 11).[66] *Tashleg* [*be-tzalmon*] (snoweth

60. Literally, the congregation.

61. The place where the pot is placed on the fire. *Metzudot Tzion.*

62. Translated according to I.E.

63. A soot covered place.

64. Literally, greenish. Good gold has some green in it. So *Metzudat David.*

65. The reference is probably to Rabbi Samuel Ha-Nagid.

66. *Therein* refers to the Land of Israel.

in Zalmon) means the white [67]will be seen as the snow that is always found on Tzalmon. *Zalmon* is a famous mountain on eastern side of the Jordan.
WHY?[68] The psalmist goes on to speak in praise of the land of Israel.

16. A MOUNTAIN OF GOD IS THE MOUNTAIN OF BASHAN; A MOUNTAIN OF PEAKS IS THE MOUNTAIN OF BASHAN.

A MOUNTAIN OF PEAKS. The word *gavnunnim* (peaks) is related to the word *gibben* (crooked-back)[69] in *or crooked-back, or a dwarf* (Lev. 21: 20). [70] Perhaps the mountain is really so shaped. [71]

17. WHY LOOK YE ASKANCE, YE MOUNTAINS OF PEAKS, AT THE MOUNTAIN WHICH GOD HATH DESIRED FOR HIS ABODE? YEA, THE LORD WILL DWELL THEREIN FOR EVER.

WHY LOOK YE ASKANCE. *Teratzedun* (look ye askance) means, debased. *Lammah Teratzedun harim gavnunnim* means (why look ye askance, ye mountains of peaks) means, Why are you mountains of peaks debased? This verse is connected to *When ye lie among the sheepfolds* (v. 14).[72] Its meaning is: Mount Bashan do not be debased, for you are the mountain which the angels desired for their abode. Furthermore, God's presence shall abide there.

18. THE CHARIOTS OF GOD ARE MYRIADS, EVEN THOUSANDS UPON THOUSANDS; THE LORD IS AMONG THEM, AS IN SINAI, IN HOLINESS.[73]

THE CHARIOTS OF GOD. This verse is connected to *which God hath desired for his abode* (v. 17).
The chariots of God are myriads is similar to the many myriads that surrounded Elisha.[74]

67. Of the Land of Israel. The darkness that covered the Land of Israel will be removed and its beauty revealed.

68. V. 17. The quote is probably displaced.

69. Hunchback.

70. According to this interpretation har *gavnununnim* (a mountain of peaks) means, a high mountain. Radak.

71. It is shaped liked a hunchback.

72. I.E. explains verse 14 as telling Israel not to be depressed. He interprets the verse as saying:" Even if you (Israel) lie where the pot is placed you will be white like a dove that is covered with silver." Our verse delivers a similar message to the mountains.

73. Literally, "The Lord is among them in Sinai, in holiness."

74. See 11 Kings 6:17: *and chariots of fire round about Elisha.*

EVEN THOUSANDS. *Shinan* (upon thousands) means, two in number; [75] a thousand and a thousand.[76]

The *alef* of *shinan* (upon thousands) is in place of a *yod.*[77] Compare *binyan* (building), *kinyan* (acquisition).[78]

Some say that this[79] alludes to the number of Levites in the wilderness. However, this is not in keeping with the meaning of the psalm.[80]

The meaning of *The Lord is among them* [*as in Sinai, in holines.*] is, God's presence is among them *as in Sinai,*[81] *in holiness.* The *kaf* is missing.[82] Compare, *When a wild ass' colt*[83] *is born a man* (Job.11:12).[84] Its meaning is; the holiness of the Land of Israel is like[85] that of Mt. Sinai.

19 THOU HAST ASCENDED ON HIGH, THOU HAST LED CAPTIVITY CAPTIVE; THOU HAST RECEIVED GIFTS AMONG MEN, YEA, AMONG THE REBELLIOUS ALSO, THAT THE LORD GOD MIGHT DWELL THERE.

ASCENDED. These are some one's words to David.[86] He said this under the influence of the holy spirit.[87] On the other hand it might be a prayer.[88] *On high* refers to the high forts.

75. *Shinan* is a variant of *shenayyim* (two).

76. Our verse reads: *alfe shinan* (even thousands upon thousands). I.E. interprets *alfe shinan* as, even thousands multiplied by a thousand multiplied by another thousand, that is, thousands multiplied by a thousand, multiplied by another thousand.

77. And the *nun* in place of the *mem.*

78. *Binyyan* comes from the root *bet, nun, heh. Kinyan* comes from the root *kof, nun, heh.* The *yod* takes the place of the *heh* in *banyan* and *kinyyan.* The root of *shenayim* (two) is *shin, nun, heh.* According to I.E. *shinan* is variation of *shinyan* which follows the paradigm of *binyan* and *kinyan.* However, the *alef* takes the place of the the *yod* in *shinan.*

79. *Alfe Shinan.*

80. The reference is to angels.

81. Reading *ke-sinai* rather than *be-sinai.*

82. From the word *sinai.* The latter should be read as *ke-sinai* (as at Sinai). In other words our verse should be read: *The Lord is among them in holiness as in Sinai.*

83. Heb. *Ve-ayir* (a wild ass' colt). According to I.E., this should be read *u-khe-ayir* (when like a wild ass' colt).

84. According to I.E., this verse should be rendered: "When like a wild ass' colt is born a man."

85. Reading *ke-har* rather than *be-har.*

86. In other words, this verse is directed to David.

87. The verse is to be taken as a prophecy.

88. Our verse is not a prophecy.

THOU HAST RECEIVED GIFTS AMONG MEN, YEA, AMONG THE REBELLIOUS ALSO. Slaves that are sold[89] and also the rebellious. The rebellious will establish a covenant with you. Thy will convert and dwell in the place of God's presence.

20. BLESSED IS THE LORD, DAY BY DAY HE BEARETH OUR BURDEN, EVEN THE GOD WHO IS OUR SALVATION. SELAH.

BLESSED IS THE LORD. David praises God who caused his hand to prevail.

HE BEARETH OUR BURDEN.[90] *Ya'amas lanu* (He beareth our burden) means, He heaps His blessings upon us. [91] Some say that *yeshutanu* (our salvation) is the object [of ya'amas].[92] *God [is unto us a God of deliverance]* (v. 21) means, because God is unto us a deliverance.[93]

21. GOD IS UNTO US A GOD OF DELIVERANCE; AND UNTO GOD THE LORD BELONG THE ISSUES OF DEATH.

GOD IS UNTO US. God alone is unto us for deliverance. He has the power to cause the death of our enemies.

23. THE LORD SAID: I WILL BRING BACK FROM BASHAN, I WILL BRING THEM BACK FROM THE DEPTHS OF THE SEA.

THE LORD SAID. I have seen many explanations of this verse. However, none of the interpretations connect this verse with what precedes or with what follows. According to my opinion the meaning of our verse is, the enemy who came to Bashan, to the Land Israel, shall return to his place in the following manner: He shall return, like the one who sinks in the depths of the sea returns.[94]
The meaning of *The Lord said* is, so did God decree. I have noted the latter in many places.

89. I.E.'s interpretation of gifts *among men.*

90. Literally, He heaps us.

91. This opinion renders our verse as follows: He heaps [blessings] upon us. The word blessings is not in the text but is implied in the word "heaps."

92. This opinion renders our verse as follows: Blessed is the Lord, day by day, even the God who heaps our salvation upon us.

93. In other words verse 21 is connected to verse 20.

94. They shall return as corpses, for one who sinks to the bottom of the sea drowns. Radak.

24. THAT THY FOOT MAY WADE THROUGH BLOOD, THAT THE TONGUE OF THY DOGS MAY HAVE ITS PORTION FROM THINE ENEMIES.

THAT THY FOOT MAY WADE.[95] *Thy foot* means, the sole of thy foot. The verse is directed to David. Compare,[96] *Thou haste ascended on high* (v. 19).[97] The *tav* of *timchatz raglekha* (thy foot may wade through) is a feminine prefix.[98] Compare, *ragli amedah*[99] *be-mishor* (My foot standeth in an even place) (Ps. 26:12). In this case the word *timchatz* (may wade through) is intransitive.[100] On the other hand the word *timchatz* may be directed to David.[101] This[102] was said figuratively.
Rabbi Judah says that the letters of *timchatz* have been reversed.[103] Compare *chamutz* (crimsoned)[104] in *crimsoned garments* (Is. 63:1).

THE TONGUE OF THY DOGS. This alludes to David's enemies who spoke about him.[105]

FROM THINE ENEMIES.[106] From the blood of thine enemies.

95. Hebrew, *le-ma'an timchatz raglekha*. Literally, *that thy foot may wound,* or *that thy foot may be wounded.* See below.

96. Reading *ke-mo* rather *ki.*

97. According to I.E. v. 19 is directed to David. See I.E.'s comments on verse 19.

98. In other words the *tav* of *timchatz* is a third person imperfect. It refers to *raglekha* (thy foot).

99. *Amedah* is feminine and governs *ragli.*

100. In other words *timchatz* is a third person imperfect and *timchatz raglekha* means, thy foot may be wounded, that is, your foot will appear to be wounded, for it will be red with the blood of your enemies.

101. In this case *timchatz* is a second person imperfect transitive verb and *timchatz raglekha* means, you will wound your foot, that is, you will appear to wound your foot, for it will be red with the blood of your enemies.

102. *That thy foot may wade through blood.*

103. *Timchatz* is a variant of *techematz* (you will redden).

104. From the root *chet, mem, tzadi.*

105. David's Jewish enemies, who spoke evil about him.

106. The Hebrew reads, *me-oyevim minnehu.* Hence the interpretations which follows.

FROM THINE. The word *minnehu* (from thine) is similar to *min hu* (from their beginning)[107] in *min hu va-hale'ah* (from their beginning onward*)* [108] (Is. 18:7). *Minnehu* is irregularly vocalized[109] because it comes at the end of the verse.
Some say that *thine enemies* refers to enemies in general and that the word *minnehu* is similar to the word *menhu* (of it)[110] in *a whisper of it*[111] (Job 4:12). *Minnehu* alludes to their king.[112] Others say that *minnehu* is similar to *tzivvahu* (commanded him).[113] {However, this cannot be, for] a *segol*[114] does not take the place of a *kametz gadol*, for [the *segol*] is a *pattach katan*.[115]

25. THEY SEE THY GOINGS, O GOD, EVEN THY GOINGS OF MY GOD, MY KING, IN HOLINESS.

THEY SEE. Israel saw the ways and goings that God went with Israel time after time. The meaning of *in holiness* is in heaven.[116] Compare, *The stars in their courses* (Judges 5:20).[117]

---

107. *Minnehu* is a combination of the words *min* and *hu*. *Min hu* means, from it (i.e. from that time). I.E. reads our verse as follows: That thy foot may wade through blood, the tongue of your dogs [shall lick the blood] of enemies from that time [and onwards]. In other words, David's Jewish enemies will make peace with Him and will henceforth join him when he fights against non Jewish enemies. Filwarg.

108. Lit. From then onward.

109. *Minnehu* is vocalized with a *chirik* beneath the *mem* and a *tzere* beneath the *nun*. The word is normally vocalized with a *segol* beneath the *mem* and a *sheva* beneath the *nun*. Compare, *menhu* (thereof) in Job. 4:12.

110. Or, of him.

111. Translated literally.

112. This interpretation reads our verse as follows: That thy foot may wade through blood, the tongue of your dogs [shall lick the blood] of enemies, from him. In other words, David's Jewish enemies will make peace with Him and will henceforth join him when he fights against non Jewish enemies and their king.

113. According to this interpretation *minnehu* is a combination of the word *minnah* (appoint a portion of food) and *oto* (him or it). Our verse should be interpreted as follows: That thy foot may wade through blood, the tongue of your dogs shall lick receive their portion from the enemies. See Rashi.

114. I.E.'s version of Psalms had a *segol* beneath the *nun* of *minnehu*. Our texts have a *tzere* beneath the *nun* of *minnehu*.

115. A *kamatz katan* (a segol) cannot take the place of a *kametz gadol*. If *minnehu* is like *tzivvahu* then *minnehu* should be vocalized *minnahu*. One cannot maintain that the *segol* beneath the *nun* of *minnehu* is in place of a *kametz*, for a *segol* does not take the place of a *kametz gadol*,

116. *Even Thy goings of my God, my king in holiness* means, even Thy goings of my God, my king in heaven.

117. *The stars in their courses* is another way of saying, the stars in heaven.

26. THE SINGERS GO BEFORE, THE MINSTRELS FOLLOW AFTER, IN THE MIDST OF DAMSELS PLAYING UPON TIMBRELS.

THE SINGERS GO BEFORE. The word *tofefot* (timbrels) is an adjective.[118] On the other hand *tofefot* might be a verb in the present. It based on a double root.[119] The *peh* is vocalized with a *kametz*[120] because *tofefot* comes at the end of a verse. However, the word *metofefot* (tabering) in *Tabering upon their breasts* (Nahum 2:8) comes from a stem that drops its middle root letter.[121]

27. BLESS YE GOD IN FULL ASSEMBLIES, EVEN THE LORD, YE THAT ARE FROM THE FOUNTAINS OF ISRAEL.

IN FULL ASSEMBLIES... FROM THE FOUNTAINS OF ISRAEL. Those who are descended from the fountain of Israel.[122] Compare, *And are come forth out of the fountain of Judah* (Is. 48:1).

28. THERE IS BENJAMIN, THE SMALLEST,[123] RULING THEM, THE PRINCES OF JUDAH THEIR COUNCIL, THE PRINCES OF NAPHTALI.

THERE IS BENJAMIN, THE SMALLEST.[124] The smallest tribe in number.[125] Benjamin is so described because this poem was composed close in time, to the incident of the concubine in Gibeah.[126] On the other hand the tribe might be so termed, because Benjamin was the youngest of the son's of Jacob.

118. Meaning drummers. I.E. renders the end of our verse, "in the midst of damsels [who are] drummers."

119. Its root being *taf, peh, peh.*

120. A *tzere.* A *tzere* is referred to as a *kametz katan.* Hence I .E. refers to the *tzere* as a *kametz.* (Filwarg) I.E.'s point is that *tofefot* is vocalized with a *tzere* rather than with a *sheva* because it comes at the end of a verse.

121. It comes from the root *taf, vav, peh.*

122. Our verse literary reads: *Bless ye God in full assemblies, even the Lord, from the fountains of Israel.* Hence I.E.'s comments.

123. Translated according to I.E. See next note.

124. Hebrew *tza'ir.* The word *tza'ir* means small, little or insignificant. It also means young.

125. In population.

126. Where the tribe of Benjamin was decimated. See Chapter 20 of Judges.

The meaning of *rodem* (ruling them), is their ruler.[127] The *mem* of *rodem* is a suffix. It refers to the assemblies (v. 27).[128] The *dalet* of *rodem* is vocalized with a *tzere* in place of a *kametz*.[129] Compare, *ha-ma'alem* (that brought them up)[130] in *that brought them up out of the sea* (Is. 63:11). The word *rigmatam* (their council) means [their] princes. Similarly, *and Regem-melech* (Zech. 7:2).[131]

I have taken note of this verse at the beginning of the psalm.[132]

29. THY GOD HATH COMMANDED THY STRENGTH; BE STRONG, O GOD, THOU THAT HAST WROUGHT FOR US.

THY GOD HATH COMMANDED THY STRENGTH. *Thy strength* is directed at David. The word *uzzah* (strong) means, might. The meaning of *uzzah Elohim zu pa'alta lanu* (be strong, O God, Thou hast wrought for us) is: You O God wrought this mighty thing[133] for us.[134] *Uzzah* (strong) follows the paradigm of *chukkah* (statute) (Num. 9:14).

30. OUT OF THY PALACE[135] AT JERUSALEM, WHITHER KINGS SHALL BRING PRESENTS UNTO THEE.

OUT OF THY PALACE. The *kaf* of *hekhalekha* (thy temple) is directed to David. The meaning of our verse is: The gifts brought to you shall extend from your palace to the distant places.[136]

127. For *rodem* is a combination of the words *rodeh* and *otam*.

128. The meaning *sham Binyamin rodam* (there *is Benjamin...ruling them*) is, there Benjamin is their ruler, that is, Benjamin is ruling the assemblies.

129. According to the rules of Hebrew grammar our word should have read *rodam*.

130. Here too a *tzere* has been substituted for a *kametz*, for the word should have read *ha-ma'alam*.

131. The word *regem* and *melekh* (king) are similar in meaning.

132. See I.E. on verse 2.

133. You gave David the might referred to in the first clause of this verse.

134. I.E. reads our clause, *uzzah zu Elohim pa'alta lanu.*

135. Translated according to Ibn Ezra. I.E. renders *hekhalekha* (They temple) your palace.

136. I.E. renders *Out of your palace* as, a great distance out of your palace. He interprets our verse as follows: From a great distance out of your palace at Jerusalem, shall the gifts that the kings bring to you extend.

31. REBUKE THE WILD BEASTS OF THE REEDS, THE MULTITUDE OF THE BULLS, WITH THE CALVES OF THE PEOPLES, EVERY ONE SUBMITTING HIMSELF WITH PIECES OF SILVER; HE HATH SCATTERED THE PEOPLES THAT DELIGHT IN WAR.

REBUKE THE WILD BEASTS. The word *ga'ar* (rebuke) is similar to the word *go'er* (rebuke), which does not have a *bet* following it, in *Behold, I will rebuke the seed* (Mal. 2:3) [137]

THE WILD BEASTS. The word *chayyat* (the wild beasts of) means, a group.[138] [Compare,] *Thy flock* (chayyatekha) *settled therein* (v. 11). [139]

THE REEDS. Of the group.[140] The spears are refereed to as *reeds* because they are as long as reeds. Spears are similarly called in Arabic.

WITH THE CALVES OF THE PEOPLES. This means the same *as the multitude of the bulls* (abirim).[141] *Adat abbirim* (The multitude of bulls) is similar to *abbire vashan (strong bulls of Bashan* (Ps. 22:13).[142] *Abbire vashan* means the cows[143] of Bashan. Scripture repeats itself. [The meaning of our verse is,] rebuke them until each one of them will submit to you,[144] by delivering pieces of silver as tribute. [The verse goes on to] say that all those who wanted to fight against David[145] scattered.

HE HATH SCATTERED. *Bizzar* (scattered) is similar to the word *yivzor* (he shall scatter) in *he shall scatter.... substance* (Dan.11: 24).

WAR. The word *keravot* (war) is similar to the word *kerav* (war) in *Who traineth my hands for war* (Ps. 144:1).

---

137. The word *ga'ar* or *go'er* is usually followed by a *bet*. Compare, *yigar Adonai be-kha ha-satan* (Zech. 3:2).

138. A troop.

139. See I.E. on verse 11.

140. Of the troop.

141. Scripture repeats itself in different words.

142. In other words *abbirim* means bulls.

143. Bulls. I.E. uses the term *cows* because he employs a phrase from Amos 4:1 which reads *parrot ha-bashan* (the cows of Bashan). See I.E. on Ps. 22:13.

144. To David.

145. Lit. You.

32. NOBLES SHALL COME OUT OF EGYPT; ETHIOPIA SHALL HASTEN TO STRETCH OUT HER HANDS UNTO GOD.

NOBLES SHALL COME. The word *chashmannim* (nobles) means rulers. Compare the term *chashmona'i* (Hasmoneans). Ethiopia shall hasten to stretch out her silver [filled] hands.

33. SING UNTO GOD, YE KINGDOMS OF THE EARTH; O SING PRAISES UNTO THE LORD. SELAH.

YE KINGDOMS OF THE EARTH. Who bring tribute to David.

34. TO HIM THAT RIDETH UPON THE HEAVENS OF HEAVENS, WHICH ARE OF OLD; LO, HE UTTERETH HIS VOICE, A MIGHTY VOICE.

TO HIM THAT RIDETH. When the word *rokhev* (rideth) is connected to that which follows by a *bet*[146] its meaning is, the road taken by the animal upon which I ride upon.[147]
Sheme sheme kedem refers to *the heavens of heavens.*[148] There is a secret meaning to *old.*[149]
They are *old* in contrast to those now alive.[150]
The object of *yitten* (he uttereth) is *kol oz* (a mighty voice).

35. ASCRIBE YE STRENGTH UNTO GOD; HIS MAJESTY IS OVER ISRAEL, AND HIS STRENGTH IS IN THE SKIES.

ASCRIBE. This verse explains the meaning of *[a mighty] voice* (V. 34). It explains that God said *ascribe ye strength,* that is, praise God verbally.

146. The usual form is to say *rokhev al.* Hence I.E.'s comment.

147. *La-rokhev bi-sheme sheme kedem* (to Him that rideth upon the heavens of heavens) literally means, to the one who rides in the heavens of heavens. I.E. interprets "in the" to mean on the roads of.

148. The reference is to the heaven, which is beyond the horizon. See I.E. on Gen. 1:1. According to Radak, the reference is to the highest heavenly sphere, which propels all other spheres. God propels this sphere. Hence God is said to ride upon the heaven of heavens.

149. I.E. is apparently alluding to his belief that the heavens are older than the earth. See I.E. on Gen. 1:1.

150. They are not old in with regard to God, for God preceded them. Aristotle and those who followed him believed that the heavens are eternal. Hence I.E.'s comment.

HIS MAJESTY IS OVER ISRAEL. Who are the Lord's treasure from among all those who are upon the earth.[151]

AND HIS STRENGTH IS IN THE SKIES. For from there God's strength shall come to Israel.

36. AWFUL IS GOD OUT OF THE HOLY PLACES; THE GOD OF ISRAEL, HE GIVETH STRENGTH AND POWER UNTO THE PEOPLE; BLESSED BE GOD.

AWFUL. From the place of the sanctuary shall the fear of God be upon the earth. Our verse is similar to *Blessed be the Lord out of Zion* (Ps. 135:21).[152] In reality [our verse speaks of the *holy places*][153] because the holy temple on earth is aligned with the holy temple in heaven. Compare, *and this is the gate of heaven* (Gen. 28:17). This is a concealed secret.[154]

Since Scripture states *Ascribe ye strength unto God* (v. 35) the meaning of which is, praise God and say that power is His, it goes on to say that God will in actuality give true strength and power to Israel. Give thanks to God [for this]. Therefore Scripture goes on to say *Blessed be God.*[155]

---

151. Ex. 19:5.

152. The meaning of which is, according to I.E., the blessing of the Lord shall come out of Zion.

153. The plural is employed.

154. The reference to the Holy Temple in heaven. According to Radak the reference is to the "Throne of Glory."

155. Which is the way Israel gives thanks to God.

CHAPTER 69.

1. FOR THE LEADER; UPON SHOSHANIM. [A PSALM OF] DAVID.

FOR THE LEADER; UPON SHOSHANIM. A poem, which opened with the word *shoshanim.*[1]

2. SAVE ME, O GOD; FOR THE WATERS ARE COME IN EVEN UNTO THE SOUL.

SAVE ME, O GOD; FOR THE WATERS ARE COME The psalmist compared his[2] enemies to water. Compare, *He drew me out of many waters* (Ps. 18:17).[3]

3. I AM SUNK IN DEEP MIRE, WHERE THERE IS NO STANDING; I AM INTO DEEP WATERS, AND THE FLOOD OVERWHELMETH ME.

I AM SUNK IN DEEP MIRE. The meaning of *yeven* is mire. Compare, *yaven* (miry) in *out of the miry clay* (Ps. 40:3).

WHERE THERE IS NO STANDING. The *ayin* in *mo'omad* (standing) is vocalized with a *chataf kametz.* Compare the word *mo'omad* (stayed up) in *and the king was stayed up in his chariot* (1 Kings 22:35). *Mo'omad* should have been vocalized with a *pattach*[4] for it is a noun.[5] Rabbi Moses says that *mo'omad* is a noun that follows the paradigm of

1. This psalm was to be performed to the tune of a poem, which opened with the word *shoshanim.* See I.E. on Psalm 4:1.

2. Literally, the enemies.

3. *He drew me out of many waters* means, He saved me from many enemies

4. Like the word *ma'amad* (Ta'anit 4:3).

5. *Mo'omad* appears to be a verb in the *hofal.* See Radak. Hence I.E.'s comments.

muktar (offerings) in *offerings are presented* (Mal. 1:11). The vowel[6] changes because of the guttural.[7]

AND THE FLOOD. The word *shibbolet* (flood) means, the river.
The meaning of *the flood overwhelmeth me* is, in but a little while the floods would have overwhelmed me.[8] Our verse is similar to *neither was there breath left in me* (Dan. 10:17).[9] The fact that the psalmist goes on to pray, *Let not the waterflood overwhelm me* (v. 16) is proof of this. [10]

4. I AM WEARY WITH MY CRYING; MY THROAT IS DRIED; MINE EYES FAIL WHILE I WAIT FOR MY GOD.

I AM WEARY …MY THROAT IS DRIED. The word *nichar* (dried) is related to *vecharah* (may burn) in *and the bottom thereof may burn* (Ezek. 24:11). The *nun* of *nichar* is vocalized with a *chirik* like the *nun* of *nichal* (was profaned) in *against My sanctuary, when it was profaned* (Ezek. 25:3.). It[11] is a *nifal* and comes from a double root.[12]

MINE EYES FAIL. Because I[13] wait for my God.

5. THEY THAT HATE ME WITHOUT A CAUSE ARE MORE THAN THE HAIRS OF MY HEAD; THEY THAT WOULD CUT ME OFF, BEING MINE ENEMIES WRONGFULLY, ARE MANY; SHOULD I RESTORE THAT WHICH I TOOK NOT AWAY?

THEY THAT WOULD CUT ME OFF. The psalmist speaks of what the enemy thinks.[14]

6. The vowel beneath the *mem* changes from a *shuruk* to a *kametz katan.*

7. The *ayin.*

8. In other words *the flood overwhelmeth me* is; I was almost swept away by the flood.

9. The meaning of which is, I almost died.

10. The psalmist would not have prayed *Let not the water flood overwhelm me,* if the waters had already swamped him.

11. *Nichar.*

12. Its root is *chet, resh, resh.*

13. Literally, because he.

14. Our verse literally reads: They that cut me off, being mine enemies wrongfully, are many. According to I.E., they that cut me off (*matzmitai*) speaks of what the enemies intend to do to him. Hence the translation, *they that would cut me off.*

Compare, *Then Balak the son of Zippor, king of Moab, arose and fought against Israel* (Josh. 24:9)[15] and *the men pursued after them* (Josh. 2:7).[16]

6. O GOD, THOU KNOWEST MY FOLLY; AND MY TRESPASSES ARE NOT HID FROM THEE.

O GOD.[17] You are[18] the true judge.[19]

THOU KNOWEST. If I was foolish.

AND MY TRESPASSES. Which I erroneously or deliberately committed against my[20] enemies.[21] Our verse is keeping with David's earlier statement: *mine enemies wrongfully* (v. 5). The *lamed* of *le-ivvalti* (my folly) is superfluous. It is like the *lamed* of *le-avner* (Abner) in *slew, Abner* (2 Sam. 3: 30).[22]

7. LET NOT THEM THAT WAIT FOR THEE BE ASHAMED THROUGH ME, O LORD GOD OF HOSTS; LET NOT THOSE THAT SEEK THEE BE BROUGHT TO CONFUSION THROUGH ME, O GOD OF ISRAEL.

O LORD GOD OF HOSTS. The Lord who is the God of heaven, for the hosts[23] are there.
O GOD OF ISRAEL. Who are His hosts on earth.

15. Balak did not fight against Israel. He intended to fight against Israel. Thus Scripture speaks of what was in Balak's mind.

16. The men thought that they were pursuing the spies. They did not actually pursue them.

17. Heb. *Elohim.*

18. So *Ha-Keter.*

19. *Elohim* also means a judge. Hence I.E. comment.

20. Literally, the enemies.

21. According to I.E. *and my trespasses are not hid from Thee* implies the following: You know that I did not commit any trespasses, either deliberately or unintentionally, against my enemies.

22. Both *lameds* are superfluous. *Le-ivvalti* is to be rendered "my folly" not "to my folly" and *le-avner* is to be rendered Abner not "to Abner."

23. The angels. See I.E. On Gen. 1:1.

8. BECAUSE FOR THY SAKE I HAVE BORNE REPROACH; CONFUSION HATH COVERED MY FACE.

BECAUSE FOR THY SAKE. *Ki alekha* (because for Thy sake) means, because of You. My enemies reproach me because I am your servant.

9. I AM BECOME A STRANGER UNTO MY BRETHERIN, AND AN ALIEN UNTO MY MOTHER'S CHILDREN.

I AM BECOME A STRANGER UNTO MY BRETHERIN. Its meaning is: I have so changed that my brothers do not recognize me. I appear to them like a stranger.

10. BECAUSE ZEAL FOR THY HOUSE HATH EATEN ME UP, AND THE REPROACHES OF THEM THAT REPROACH THEE ARE FALLEN UPON ME.

BECAUSE ZEAL FOR THY HOUSE. *Zeal for Thy house* indicates that the enemies[24] cursed the edifice that housed the ark. [25] This psalm most likely speaks of the time of the exile and was said under the influence of the Holy Spirit.[26] The fact that it reads *and build the cities of Judah* (v. 36) is proof of this.

11. AND I WEPT WITH MY SOUL FASTING, AND THAT BECAME UNTO ME A REPROACH.

AND I WEPT. *Nafshi* (my soul)[27] is the object of the verb *va-evkeh* (and I wept).[28] Compare, *Ve-livkotah* (and to weep for her) (Gen.23: 2).[29]

AND THAT BECAME. This verse is to be understood in accordance to what I have previously mentioned, namely, that the noun is implied in verbs[30] in the perfect or imperfect.

24. Of Israel.

25. The enemies of Israel cursed the temple.

26. For it prophesies the exile.

27. So Filwarg and *Ha-Keter.*

28. Ibn Ezra renders *va-evkeh va-tzom nafshi* (and I wept with my soul fasting): and I bewailed my soul in a fast. The point is that *evkeh* is transitive. The Hebrew word for cry is usually intransitive. Hence I.E.'s comment.

29. Here too the Hebrew word for cry is transitive, for *ve-livkotah* is to be rendered, and to bewail her. See I.E. on Gen. 23:2).

30. See I.E. on Ps 3:8. According to this note *va-evkeh va-tzom nafshi* (and I wept with fasting) is to be rendered, and I bewailed my soul with a bewailing in a fast.

Our verse is to be understood as follows: *I wept* a weeping.... It[31] was a reproach unto me.[32]

13. THEY THAT SIT IN THE GATE TALK OF ME; AND I AM A SONG OF THE DRUNKARDS.

THEY... TALK. The psalmist relates that the people who sit in the gates mock him because of his sins.

14. BUT AS FOR ME, LET MY PRAYER BE UNTO THEE, O LORD, IN AN ACCEPTABLE TIME; O GOD, IN THE ABUNDANCE OF THY MERCY, ANSWER ME WITH THE TRUTH OF THY SALVATION.

BUT AS FOR ME. But I pray, perhaps it will be[33] an acceptable time. [34]

WITH THE TRUTH OF THY SALVATION. *Be'emet yishekha* (with the truth of thy salvation)[35] is to be interpreted as if written *be-yishekha be'emet*[36] (truly with Your salvation).[37] Some say that the *bet of be-emet* (with truth) is to be rendered "because."[38] Compare *be-va' al pe'or* (In Baal peor)[39] (Deut. 4:3). However, this does not appear to me to be correct. The following is my prayer: *Deliver me out of the mire* (v. 15). The reference is to *the deep mire* (v. 3).[40]

31. The weeping.

32. My enemies laughed at my weeping. Rashi.

33. Literally, perhaps I will find.

34. That is, I pray, and I hope that it is an acceptable time. *In an acceptable time can* not be taken literally, for the psalmist has no way of knowing if the time is propitious or not.

35. Literally, in truth, your salvation.

36. Literally, with Your salvation in truth.

37. Help me in reality.

38 According to this interpretation *be'emet yishekha* means, because of Your true salvation.

39. According to I.E. this is to be rendered, because of Baal-peor. See I.E. on Deut. 4:3.

40. The reference is to the deep mire mentioned in verse 3.

15. DELIVER ME OUT OF THE MIRE, AND LET ME NOT SINK; LET ME BE DELIVERED FROM THEM THAT HATE ME, AND OUT OF THE DEEP WATERS.

THE DEEP WATERS. *The Deep waters* correspond to *the deep pit* (v. 16).[41]

16. LET NOT THE WATERFLOOD OVERWHELM ME, NEITHER LET THE DEEP SWALLOW ME UP; AND LET NOT THE PIT[42] SHUT HER MOUTH UPON ME.

AND LET NOT THE PIT[43] SHUT HER MOUTH UPON ME. For it contains living waters. [44]
The word *tetar* means, close or shut. Compare, *itter* (left-handed)[45] in *a man left handed* (Judges 3:15).

17. ANSWER ME, O LORD, FOR THY MERCY IS GOOD; ACCORDING T0 THE MULTITUDE OF THY COMPASSIONS TURN THOU UNTO ME.

ANSWER ME, O LORD, FOR THY MERCY IS GOOD. The meaning of *ki tov chasdekha* (for Thy mercy is good) is, for Your mercy does good. Or its meaning is; how good Your mercy is for me.

18. AND HIDE NOT THY FACE FROM THY SERVANT; FOR I AM IN DISTRESS; ANSWER ME SPEEDILY.

AND HIDE NOT. The psalmist said *hide not* because he was in a hidden place, that is, in the deep waters.

41. Which contains mire. See verse 3.

42. Hebrew, *be'er*. Literally, well.

43. Hebrew, *be'er*. Literally, well.

44. A well has a "mouth" through which its waters bubble up.

45. According to I.E., an *itter* is a person whose right hand is shut, that is, one who is left-handed.

19. DRAW NEIGH UNTO MY SOUL, AND REDEEM IT; RANSOM ME BECAUSE OF MINE ENEMIES.

DRAW NEIGH UNTO MY SOUL. Rabbi Moses says that *korvah* (draw neigh) is similar to the word *ve-karav* (and join them) in *and join them* (Ezek. 37:17).[46] *Ve-karav ge'alah* (and redeem it) means, its redemption.[47]

Rabbi Moses explains as follows:[48] The word *korvah* is a transitive verb in the imperative. The psalmist prays to God: "Draw neigh the redemption of my soul."[49] *Korvah* is similar to *ve-karav* (and join)[50] in *and join them*[51] (Ezek. 37:17) which is an imperative[52] like the words *balla* (destroy) and *palag* (divide)[53] in, *Destroy, O Lord, and divide their tongue* (Ps. 55:10). *Ve-karav*[54] is therefore entirely vocalized with *pattachs*.[55] *Ge'alah* is a noun vocalized with a *pattach*.[56] Compare, *zehavah* (her gold);[57] *shelalah*[58] (spoil of it) (Deut. 13:17). *Ge'alah* is similar to *ge'ullatah* (her redemption.)[59] This is the way the wise man,[60] may God grant him life,[61] explained it me.[62]

---

46. In other words *korvah* is transitive, for *korvah* is a variant of *karav*. (Filwarg) The root *kof, resh, bet* is intransitive in the *kal* and is transitive in the *piel*. According to Rabbi Moses *karav* in Ezek. 37:17 is a variant of *karev* (a piel).

47. *Ge'alah* is a variant of *ge'ullatah* (its redemption).

48. This paragraph is a gloss by a student of I.E. It relates how I.E. explained Rabbi Moses' interpretation to him. Filwarg.

49. Our verse reads: *korvah el nafshi ga'alah*. Rabbi Moses interprets this as : Draw neigh to my soul, its redemption

50. That is to *karav*. In other words *korvah* is a *piel*.

51. Literally, and cause them to come close to each other.

52. In the *piel*.

53. *Balla* and *pallag* are *piel* imperatives. Similarly, the word *karav* in *ve-karav*. However, the *kaf* in *karav* is vocalized with a *kametz* rather than a *pattach* because it comes before a guttural.

54 That is *korvah*.

55 Actually *kametz, pattach*. I.E.'s student refers to the *kametz* as a *pattach*.

56. *Ga'al. Ga'alah* is the noun *ga'al* plus the pronoun *otah*.

57. Which is the word *zahav* and the pronoun *otah*.

58. Which is the word *shalal* plus the pronoun *otah*.

59. It is the word *ge'ulah* plus the pronoun *otah*. *Ge'alah* is the masculine form of *ge'ullatah*. It consists of the word *ga'al* plus the pronoun *otah*

60. Ibn Ezra.

61. Ibn Ezra was still alive when the gloss was inserted.

62. The insertion of Ibn Ezra's student ends here.

However, in reality *korvah* is similar to *zokhrah* (remember)[63] in *Remember unto me* (Neh.5: 6). *Ge'alah* (redeem it) is an imperative similar to *lammedah* (teach thou) in *and teach thou it the children of Israel* (Deut. 31:19).[64] On the other hand the word *asher* (that) might have been omitted from our verse.[65] Our clause is to be interpreted as if written *korvah el nafshi* (Draw close to my soul) *asher ga'alah*. The meaning of *asher ga'alah* is, the one who redeemed it.[66]

The meaning of *because of mine enemies* is, *because of mine enemies* who do violence to me.

20. THOU KNOWEST MY REPROACH, AND MY SHAME, AND MY CONFUSION; MINE ADVERSARIES ARE ALL BEFORE THEE.

THOU KNOWEST. You know the curses[67] that are in their hearts[68] [and their intention] to execrate me,[69] for mine adversaries are all before Thee.

21. REPROACH HATH BROKEN MY HEART; AND I AM SORE SICK; AND I LOOKED FOR SOME TO SHOW COMPASSION, BUT THERE WAS NONE; AND FOR COMFORTERS, BUT I FOUND NONE.

REPROACH. The reproach, with which they reproached me, humbled my heart.[70]

AND I AM SORE SICK. The *alef* prefixed to *anushah* (I am sore sick) is a first person prefix.[71] The *alef* of *va-ye'anash* (and it was very sick) (2 Sam. 12:15) is missing.[72] *Anush-*

---

63. *Zohkrah* is a variant of *zekhor*. It is a *kal* imperative. *Korvah* is similarly a *kal* imperative. It is a variant of *kerav* (draw near). In this case our verse reads: *Draw neigh unto my soul.*

64. Meaning redeem. According to this interpretation the first part of our verse reads: "Draw neigh unto my soul, redeem it."

65. Our verse reads: *korvah el nafshi ga'alah.*

66. In this case *ga'alah* is the third person perfect (ga'al) plus the Hebrew pronominal suffix for it. The first part of our verse is to be interpreted: "Draw close to my soul [He who] redeemed it." In this case *ga'alah* is the third person (ga'al) plus the Hebrew pronominal suffix for it

67. The reference is to "reproach, shame, and confusion (literally, mortification)."

68. Reading *be-libbam* rather than *be-libbekha*. *Ha-Keter.*

69. Hence the psalmist speaks of *my reproach, and my shame, and my confusion.*

70. I.E.'s interpretation of *Reproach hath broken my heart*

71. It is not a root letter. The root of *anushah* is *alef, nun, shin*. Hence I.E.'s comment. .

72. *Anushah* (I am sore sick) comes from the same root as *va-ye'anash*. The *alef* in *va-ye'anash* is a root letter. I.E.'s point is that the root *alef* is missing in *anushah*. However, it is present in *va-ye'anesh.*

ah is vocalized with a *shuruk* rather than a *cholam*. Compare *yishputu hem* (they judged themselves) (Ex.18: 26).[73]

FOR SOME TO SHOW COMPASSION. The word *la-nud* (to show compassion) is similar to the word *la-nud* (to bemoan) in *to bemoan him*[74] (Job 2:11).[75]

22. YEA, THEY PUT POISON INTO MY FOOD; AND IN MY THIRST THEY GAVE ME VINEGAR TO DRINK.

INTO MY FOOD.[76] The psalmist, as earlier mentioned, fasted.[77] Compare, *And I wept with my soul fasting* (v. 11). [The fact that our verse speaks of] hunger and thirst[78] is proof of this.[79] The word *be-varuti* (into my food) is related to the word *ha-biryah* (the food) (2 Sam. 13:5).

23. LET THEIR TABLE BEFORE THEM BECOME A SNARE; AND WHEN THEY ARE IN PEACE, LET IT BECOME A TRAP.

LET THEIR TABLE BEFORE THEM BECOME A SNARE. For, *they put poison into my food.*

AND WHEN THEY ARE IN PEACE. *Ve-lishlomim* (and when they are in peace) should be rendered, and in place of their peace. The *lamed* of *ve-lishlomim* is similar to the *lamed* prefixed to *le-aven* (for stone) in *And they had brick for stone* (Gen. 11:3). [80]

73. Rather than *yishpotu.*

74. To mourn with Job.

75. One who bemoans his friend shows compassion.

76. Hebrew, *be-varuti.*

77. According to I.E. the term *biryah* refers to the first meal in the morning or the first meal after a fast. (Filwarg). When the psalmist concluded his fast, his enemies put poison into his food. I.E. renders our verse: They put poison into the food that I ate to break my fast.

78. Fasting (verse 1) refers to abstaining from food and drink.

79. That David was fasting.

80. I.E. renders *ve-lishlomim le-mokesh* (and when they are in peace, let it become a trap) as, let their peace turn into a trap.

24. LET THEIR EYES BE DARKENED, SO THAT THEY SEE NOT; AND MAKE THEIR LOINS CONTINUALLY TO TOTTER.

LET THEIR EYES BE DARKENED. When they will not be able to see, they will totter and fall.

25. POUR OUT THINE INDIGNATION UPON THEM, AND LET THE FIERCENESS OF THINE ANGER OVERTAKE THEM.

POUR. This is tied to what comes before it. [The meaning of our verse is:] When they fall, pour Your indignation on top of them,[81] so that if they flee, the fierceness of Your anger shall overtake them. When they will not be able to escape, their palaces shall be desolate (v. 26).

26. LET THEIR ENCAMPMENT [82] BE DESOLATE; LET NONE DWELL IN THEIR TENTS.

27. FOR THEY PERSECUTE HIM WHOM THOU HAST SMITTEN; AND THEY TELL OF THE PAIN OF THOSE WHOM THOU HAST WOUNDED.

FOR. Rabbi Moses says that the meaning of *and they tell of the pain of those whom thou hast wounded*[83] is, they tell each other to pain Your wounded,[84] for we are smitten and wounded.

28. ADD INIQUITY UNTO THEIR INIQUITY; AND LET THEM NOT COME INTO THY RIGHTEOUSNESS.

ADD INIQUITY. Place this sin - their telling [of the pain of Your wounded][85] and praising themselves- among their sins.

---

81. Hebrew *le-ma'alah*. Perhaps we should emend to *mi-le-ma'alah*. In this case I.E. reads: When they fall, pour from above, Your indignation upon them.

82. Hebrew, *tiratam*. I.E. renders *tiratam*, their palaces. See Radak.

83. The psalmist attributes his wounds to God, for God permitted him to be wounded. Radak.

84. There does not seem to be anything wrong with speaking of the pain of the wounded. Hence Rabbi Moshe's interpretation. According to Rabbi Moses, *ve-el makhov...yesapperu* (and they tell of the pain) is to be rendered: they tell [each other] to pain Your wounded. See Radak.

85. Their telling each other to injure Your wounded.

AND LET THEM NOT COME INTO THY RIGHTEOUSNESS. Rabbi Moses says that the meaning of *Thy righteousness* is in the righteous manner in which You act towards them. However, in my opinion the reference is to that which follows in the next verse namely, *And not be written with the righteous.* [86]

29. LET THEM BE BLOTTED OUT OF THE BOOK OF THE LIVING, AND NOT BE WRITTEN WITH THE RIGHTEOUS.

LET THEM BE BLOTTED OUT. I have already explained in my book that the Book of the Living refers to the heavens.[87] All the decrees that are destined to come are there written. They were there inscribed on the day that they were created.

30. BUT I AM AFFLICTED AND IN PAIN; LET THY SALVATION, O GOD, SET ME UP ON HIGH.

BUT I AM AFFLICTED. *Set me up on high* is in contrast to [*but I am*] *afflicted.*

31. I WILL PRAISE THE NAME OF GOD WITH A SONG, AND WILL MAGNIFY HIM WITH THANKSGIVING.

I WILL PRAISE. The meaning of *with thanksgiving* is; I will thank God for the loving kindness that He showed me.

32. AND IT SHALL PLEASE THE LORD BETTER THAN A BULLOCK THAT HATH HORNS AND HOOFS.

AND IT SHALL PLEASE THE LORD BETTER THAN A BULLOCK. The *mem* prefixed to *shor* (bullock) also serves as a prefix for *par.*[88] *Mi-shor par* (than a bullock)[89] should be read as if written *mi-shor, mi-par* (better than an ox, better than a bullock).[90] It is similar to *ke-keves alluf* (like a docile lamb) [91](Jer. 11:19), which is to be read as if

86. The meaning of *And let them not come into Thy righteousness* is, And let them not be written with the righteous.

87. See I.E.'s Long and Short commentaries on Ex. 32:32.

88. Literally, for another word.

89. *Mi-shor par* (than a bullock) literally means, than an ox bullock. Hence I.E.'s comment.

90. According to I.E. our verse reads, And it shall please the lord better than a bullock, better than an ox.

91. Literally like a lamb, cattle.

written *ke-keves ke-alluf* (like a lamb, like cattle). *Mi-shor par* is to be so interpreted for an ox is bigger than a bullock. How can the word *shor* (ox) be connected to *par* (bullock) when they do not refer to animals of the same size? *Mi-shor par* is similar to *par ha-shor* (bullock) in *Take thy father's bullock* (par ha-shor) (Judges 6:25).[92]

THAT HATH HORNS AND HOOFS. This refers back to the bullock alone.[93] It indicates that the bullock is not very small. It is a bullock whose horns and hoofs are visible.[94]

33. THE HUMBLE SHALL SEE IT, AND BE GLAD; YE THAT SEEK AFTER GOD, LET YOUR HEART REVIVE.

SHALL SEE. The *vav* prefaced to *vi-yechi* (let...revive) in *Let your heart revive*[95] is similar to the aspirated *fah* in Arabic.[96] Compare, *Va-yissa* (lifted) in, *On the third day Abraham lifted up his eyes* (Gen. 22:4);[97] *va-ya'azov* (left) in *left his servants* (Ex. 9:21)[98]; [The meaning of our verse is,] You who seek the Lord see this,[99] let your heart revive.

34. FOR THE LORD HEARKENETH UNTO THE NEEDY, AND DESPISETH NOT HIS PRISONERS.

FOR ...THE NEEDY. The psalmist speaks of the needy because he earlier said, *But I am afflicted and in pain* (v. 30).

HIS PRISONERS. The palmist speaks of that which is in the mind of David's enemies.[100] They intend to take him prisoner. However, it is better to interpret our verse as speaking of the exiles.[101]

---

92. In Judges 6:25 the word *par* is not connected to *shor*. See Radak on Judges 6:25 who explains *par ha-shor* as meaning a bullock as large as an ox.

93. It does not refer to the ox.

94. Scripture would have no need to describe the ox in this way, for it is normal for an ox to have hoofs and horns.

95. *Vi-yechi* (let...revive) may be translated, and let revive. Hence I.E. comments.

96. Which does not necessarily open a new clause. The *vav* similarly does not always have the meaning of *and.*

97. Here too the *vav* does not have the meaning of "and," for the meaning of Gen. 22:4 is *On the third day Abraham lifted (va-yissa) up his eyes,* not "and on third day Abraham lifted (*va-yissa*) up his eyes. "

98. Here too the *vav* does not have the meaning of "and," for the meaning of Ex. 9:21 is, left *(va-ya'azov) his servants* not *and left* (va-ya'azov) *his servants.*

99. God's salvation.

100. Literally, the enemies.

101. According to this interpretation our psalm speaks of the Babylonian exile. See Radak on verse 1.

35. LET THE HEAVEN AND EARTH PRAISE HIM, THE SEAS, AND EVERYTHING THAT MOVETH THEREIN.

PRAISE HIM. *Heaven and earth* refer to those who dwell in heaven and earth. *The seas* refer to those who cross the seas. On the other hand our verse might be metaphorical, as in *The mountains and the hills shall break forth before you into singing* (Is. 55:12).

36. FOR GOD WILL SAVE ZION, AND BUILD THE CITIES OF JUDAH; AND THEY SHALL ABIDE THERE, AND HAVE IT IN POSSESSION.

FOR GOD. Some say that its meaning[102] is as follows: When I shall praise God[103] then the heavens and earth shall praise Him.[104] If this psalm speaks of the exile then its meaning is; the heaven and earth will praise God when He helps Zion. The psalmist mentions *the cities of Judah* because they have a share in Jerusalem.

37. THE SEED ALSO OF HIS SERVANTS SHALL INHERIT IT; AND THEY THAT LOVE HIS NAME SHALL DWELL THEREIN.

THE SEED. They and their children in the days of David *shall inherit it.* Or they and their children in the days of the messiah *shall inherit it.*

102. The meaning of verse 35. It is possible that this comment belongs at the end of the previous verse and has been misplaced.

103. For saving Zion and building the cities of Judah.

104. Verse 35.

CHAPTER 70

1. FOR THE LEADER. [A PSALM] OF DAVID; TO MAKE MEMORIAL.

[TO MAKE MEMORIAL] A psalm to be performed to the tune of a song that opened with the word *le-hazkir* (to make memorial).[1]

2. O GOD DELIVER ME,[2] O LORD, TO HELP ME, MAKE HASTE.

MAKE HASTE. The word *haste* applies to an earlier mentioned word.[3] Our clause should be interpreted as if written *to deliver me make haste.* It is similar to; *The lamp of the Lord the spirit of man*[4] (Prov. 20:27).[5] There are many such instances.

3. LET THEM BE ASHAMED AND ABASHED THAT SEEK AFTER MY SOUL; LET THEM BE TURNED BACKWARD AND BROUGHT TO CONFUSION THAT DELIGHT IN MY HURT.

LET THEM BE ASHAMED. When You help me they will immediately be ashamed.

1. See I.E. on Ps. 4:1.

2. Hebrew, *le-hatzileni.* Literally, to deliver me.

3. In other words, *chushah* does not only refer to *le-ezrati* (*to help me)* but also to *le-hatzileni* (*to deliver me).* Our verse is to be read as follows: O God make haste to deliver me, O Lord, make haste to help me. See Radak.

4. Translated lit.

5. Prov. 20:27 literally reads, The *lamp of the Lord the spirit of man; searches all the inward parts.* According to I.E. the word *searches* also applies to *the lamp of the Lord.* The verse should be read as follows: *The lamp of the Lord searches the spirit of man; it* [similarly] *searches all the inward parts..*

LET THEM BE TURNED BACKWARD. The word *yissogu* (let them be turned backward) is a *nifal*. It is like the word *yikkonu* (let them be established)[6] in *let them be established altogether* (Prov. 22:18). *Yissogu* is related to the word *sig* (dross). Its meaning is, let their dross be seen.

4. LET THEM BE TURNED BACK[7] BY REASON OF THEIR SHAME THAT SAY: AHA, AHA.

LET THEM BE TURNED BACK The word *ekev* (by reason) is related to the word *ikve* (footsteps of) in *by the footsteps of the flock* (Cant. 1:8).[8] Others say that the meaning of *ekev* is because of, that is, in punishment and in recompense for their putting me to shame.[9] Compare *ekev* (reward) in, *In keeping them there is great reward* (Ps. 19:12). The word *ekev* means, recompense and payment.

5. LET ALL THOSE THAT SEEK THEE REJOICE AND BE GLAD IN THEE; AND LET SUCH AS LOVE THY SALVATION SAY CONTINUALLY; 'LET THE LORD BE MAGNIFIED.'

REJOICE. When the wicked will be put to shame, then those that seek You will rejoice and lift up their voices.[10]

6. BUT I AM POOR AND NEEDY; O GOD MAKE HASTE UNTO ME; THOU ART MY HELP AND MY DELIVERER; O LORD TARRY NOT.

BUT I AM POOR. *But I am poor and needy* is to be taken according to its plain meaning. Or, it is to be interpreted *But I am like the poor and needy.* On the other hand, the psalmist might be speaking of what is in the mind of the enemies. [11]

6. Which is a *nifal.*

7. Or, let them return.

8. So Rashi. According to this interpretation our verse reads: Let them turn back in the footsteps of their shame, that is, what they did to me should be done to them.

9. According to this interpretation *their shame* means, the shame they employed to degrade me.

10. So *Ha-Keter.* The commonly printed editions of I.E. have this note concluding I.E.'s comments on verse 4. However, they belong in verse 5.

11. The enemies of the psalmist consider him poor and needy.

The word *li* (unto me) in our verse is like the word *li* (of me) in *Say, of me He is my brother* (Gen. 20:13). [12]

TARRY NOT. My help. *Te'achar* (tarry) is transitive.[13] On the other hand *te'achar* might be intransitive. In this case *te'achar* (tarry) in *tarry not* is similar to *echeru* (tarry) in *Why tarry?* (Judges 5:28). Its meaning is, *Tarry not* from acting as my deliverer.

---

12. The word *li* (unto me) in our verse is to be rendered, because *of me*. Thus according to I.E. our verse is to be translated, *O God make haste for me*, that is, make haste on my behalf.

13. According to this interpretation *al te'achar* (do not tarry) is to be interpreted, "do not tarry my help," that is, do not delay my help.

CHAPTER 71.

1. IN THEE, O LORD, HAVE I TAKEN REFUGE; LET ME NEVER BE ASHAMED.

HAVE I TAKEN REFUGE. I believe that David composed this psalm, for it is connected to the previous psalm.[1] It is similar to the Psalm which opens with, *Bless the Lord, O my soul, O Lord my God, Thou art very great* (Ps. 104:1).[2]

IN THEE. You God exist forever. I shall therefore never be ashamed.

2. DELIVER ME IN THY RIGHTEOUSNESS, AND RESCUE ME; INCLINE THINE EAR UNTO ME, AND SAVE ME.

IN THY RIGHTEOUSNESS. Its meaning is, Judge righteously,[3] for my enemies do evil to me.

3. BE THOU TO ME A SHELTERING ROCK, WHEREUNTO I MAY CONTINUALLY RESORT, WHICH THOU HAST APPOINTED TO SAVE ME; FOR THOU ART MY ROCK AND MY FORTRESS.

BE THOU TO ME. *Ma'on* (sheltering) means, a dwelling place to hide in.[4] *Whereunto I may continually resort* therefore follows.

---

1. Which was written by King David.

2. Ps. 104 has no title identifying its author, because it is connected to the Psalm that precedes it. The latter was composed by King David. Hence it too was composed by King David. The same is the case with our psalm.

3. Literally, So that You will judge righteously.

4. It does not refer to an ordinary dwelling.

It is for this reason that every *ma'on* (shelter) is [high and] above.[5]
Which thou hast appointed[6] refers to what Samuel promised David.[7] On the other hand it might be interpreted like *He commanded, and it stood* (Ps. 33:9). It refers to God's word, that is, to the decrees executed via the angels.

4. O MY GOD, RESCUE ME OUT OF THE HAND OF THE WICKED ONE, OUT OF THE GRASP OF THE UNRIGHTEOUSNESS AND RUTHLESS MAN.

O MY GOD. This verse explains *in Thy righteousness* (v. 2).[8]

AND RUTHLESS MAN. The word *chometz* (ruthless man) is similar to *chamotz* (oppressed) in *relieve the oppressed* (Is. 1:17).[9]

5. FOR THOU ART MY HOPE; O LORD GOD, MY TRUST FROM MY YOUTH.

FOR THOU ART MY HOPE. I have no hope but You. Scripture similarly states *For Thee do I wait* (Ps. 25:5).[10] [I have no hope but You…] from the day that I was upon the earth.[11] This is the meaning of; You have been my trust from my youth.

6. UPON THEE HAVE I STAYED MYSELF FROM BIRTH; THOU ART HE THAT TOOK ME OUT OF MY MOTHER'S WOMB; MY PRAISE IS CONTINUALLY OF THEE.

UPON THEE … THAT TOOK ME OUT The word *gozi* (took me out) is similar to the word *va-yagaz* (and brought across) in *and brought across quails* (Num. 11:31).

5. A high place which the enemy can not reach.

6. The word *which* is not in the text. Our verse literally reads, *Thou hast commanded.* I.E. interprets our verse as follows: You have commanded via the word of Samuel that I be saved.

7. Samuel's prophecy that David would be king. See 1 Sam.16: 13.

8. V. 2 reads: *Deliver me in Thy righteousness, and rescue me.* It does not say from whom David prayed to be delivered and rescued. Our verse explains that David prayed that God deliver him *out of the hand of the wicked one, out of the grasp of the unrighteousness and ruthless man.*

9. I.E. renders *chometz* (ruthless) oppressor.

10. Or hope. According to I.E. "for Thee do I hope" means, I have no hope but You. See I.E. on Ps. 25:5.

11. Verse 6 continues the thought expressed at the end of verse 5.

[UPON THEE HAVE I STAYED MYSELF FROM BIRTH; THOU ART HE THAT TOOK ME OUT OF MY MOTHER'S WOMB.] Hence, *my praise is continually of Thee.*

7. I AM AS A WONDER UNTO MANY; BUT THOU ART MY REFUGE.

I AM AS A WONDER. Its meaning is, I relied on You and You supported me. I am thereby become as a sign[12] to many who did not believe in You. Our verse is similar to *Thus shall Ezekiel be unto you a sign* (Ezek. 24:24).[13]

8. MY MOUTH SHALL BE FILLED WITH THY PRAISE, AND WITH THY GLORY ALL THE DAY.

SHALL BE FILLED. Our verse is parallel to *My praise is continually of Thee* (v. 6). *My praise is continually of Thee* to the point that my mouth is filled with Your praise. The meaning of *all the day* is, all my days.

9. CAST ME NOT OFF IN THE TIME OF OLD AGE; WHEN MY STRENGTH FAILETH, FORSAKE ME NOT.

CAST ME NOT. The meaning of our verse is, help me in my old age as you did from my youth and onwards.

10. FOR MINE ENEMIES SPEAK CONCERNING ME, AND THEY THAT WATCH FOR MY SOUL TAKE COUNSEL TOGETHER.

FOR MINE ENEMIES SPEAK CONCERNING ME. The word *li* means concerning me.[14] It is similar to the word *li* (of me) in "that my enemies say not of me" (Judges 9:54).[15]

AND THEY THAT WATCH FOR MY SOUL. They whom I considered to be my helpers[16] took counsel with my enemies. [17]

---

12. That God supports those who trust in Him.

13. I.E. renders *mofet* (wonder) as, a sign. He translates our verse as follows: *I am as a sign unto many, for Thou art my refuge.*

14. *The word li* literally *means to me. Hence I.E.'s comment.*

15. I.E. is probably paraphrasing. The verse literally reads: "Lest they of me."

16. I.E.'s interpretation of *they that watch for my soul.* The word *nefesh* (soul) also means life or body. According to I.E., *they that watch for my soul* means those who were supposed to protect me or I thought would protect me.

17. I.E.'s interpretation of *take counsel together.*

11. SAYING; GOD HATH FORSAKEN HIM; PURSUE AND TAKE HIM; FOR THERE IS NON TO DELIVER.

SAYING. They say this.[18] They say this, one to another.

12. O GOD, BE NOT FAR FROM ME; O MY GOD, MAKE HASTE TO HELP ME.

O GOD, BE NOT FAR FROM ME. If the day of my salvation will be far off, then my enemies shall think that You distanced Yourself from me.

13. LET THEM BE ASHAMED AND CONSUMED THAT ARE ADVERSARIES TO MY SOUL; LET THEM BE COVERED WITH REPROACH AND CONFUSION THAT SEEK MY HURT.

LET THEM BE ASHAMED... THAT ARE ADVERSARIES TO MY SOUL. Those who were his friends are now adversaries of his soul. [19]

THAT SEEK MY HURT. They are my enemies.[20]

14. BUT AS FOR ME, I WILL HOPE CONTINUALLY, AND WILL PRAISE THEE YET MORE AND MORE.

BUT AS FOR ME. Its meaning is: If the day of my salvation is far off, I will persist in my hope and will continue to praise You.

15. MY MOUTH SHALL TELL OF THY RIGHTEOUSNESS, AND OF THY SALVATION ALL THE DAY; FOR I KNOW NOT THE NUMBERS THEREOF.

MY MOUTH SHALL TELL OF THY RIGHTEOUSNESS. My mouth shall tell of the righteous acts You did for me and for others in the early days. It shall also relate the acts of salvation that You performed.

18. *God hath forsaken him...*

19. That is, Those who were my friends are now adversaries of my soul. I.E. speaks of the psalmist in the third person.

20. So *Ha-Keter.*

FOR I KNOW NOT THE NUMBERS THEREOF. This similar to, *for it is a stiff-necked people* (Ex. 34:4).[21] *For I know not the numbers thereof* is to be rendered, even though I do not know the numbers thereof. The *cholam* in *seforot* (numbers) is in place of a *shuruk*. *Seforot* follows the form of *gevurot* (might).[22]

16. I WILL COME WITH THY MIGHTY ACTS, O LORD GOD; I WILL MAKE MENTION OF THY RIGHTEOUSNESS, EVEN OF THINE ONLY.

I WILL COME. *I will come* to tell of *Thy mighty acts*.[23] The Psalmist says; I will tell of *Thy righteousness, even of Thine only* because it is the nature of the mighty to extol themselves.[24]

17. O GOD, THOU HAST TAUGHT ME FROM MY YOUTH; AND UNTIL NOW DO I DECLARE THY WONDROUS WORKS.

O GOD. The word *limmadtanni* (Thou hast taught me) means trained me. *Limmadtanni* is similar to *limmud* (trained) in A *wild ass trained in the wilderness* (Jer. 2:24).[25]
I am very greatly obligated[26] to praise you, for You trained me and You also helped me to walk my customary way. [27]

18. AND EVEN UNTO OLD AGE AND HOARY HAIRS, O GOD, FORSAKE ME NOT; UNTIL I HAVE DECLARED THY STRENGTH UNTO THE NEXT GENERATION, THY MIGHT TO EVERY ONE THAT IS TO COME.

THY STRENGTH. *Zero'akha* (Thy strength)[28] means, the might of your arm.

---

21. Ex. 34:9 reads: *I pray Thee, go in the midst of us; for* (ki) *it is a stiff-necked people*. This makes no sense. Why should God go in the midst of Israel *because* it is stiff-necked? Hence I.E. comments that the word *ki* is to be rendered **even though** (I.E. on Ex.34:9). Ex. 34:9 is to be read as follows: *I pray Thee, go in the midst of us;* ***even though*** (ki) *it is a stiff-necked people*. Similarly, *My mouth shall tell of Thy righteousness…*; *for* (ki) *I know not the numbers thereof* is to be rendered: *My mouth shall tell of Thy righteousness…*; **even though** (ki) *I know not the numbers thereof.*

22. With a *cholam* in place of a *shuruk*. Hence the reading *seforot* and not *sefurot*.

23. *I will come with Thy mighty acts* means; I will come to tell of Thy mighty acts.

24. I will speak only of Your righteousness, even though it is the nature of the mighty to extol themselves.

25. Translated according to I.E.

26. Literally, how much was I obligated.

27. You trained me to be the person that I am.

28. Literally, Your arm. Hence I.E.'s comment.

UNTO THE NEXT GENERATION. *Le-dor*[29] *is* to be interpreted unto the next generation.

TO EVERY ONE THAT IS TO COME. *Le-khol yavo*[30] is to be rendered, to every one that is to come.[31] The meaning of *to come* is, to be born. Compare, *One generation passeth away, and another generation cometh* (Ecc. 1:4).

19. THY RIGHTEOUSNESS ALSO, O GOD, WHICH REACHETH UNTO HIGH HEAVEN; THOU WHO HAST DONE GREAT THINGS, O GOD, WHO IS LIKE UNTO THEE?

THY RIGHTEOUSNESS. Your righteousness is higher than the righteousness of any of the righteous. Our verse is similar to, [*Thy glorious Name...is] exalted above all blessings and praise* (Neh. 9:5). Yefet[32] says [that the meaning of our verse is:] I can not describe Your righteousness, for it reaches unto the high heaven. The great things that You have done are proof that there is no god like You.

20. THOU, WHO HAST MADE ME TO SEE MANY AND SORE TROUBLES, WILT QUICKEN ME AGAIN, AND BRING ME UP AGAIN FROM THE DEPTHS OF THE EARTH.

THOU, WHO HAST MADE ME [The psalmist goes on] to tell of the great things that God did.[33] The poet compares his troubles to being in the depths of the earth.[34]

21. THOU WILT INCREASE MY GREATNESS, AND TURN AND COMFORT ME.

THOU WILT INCREASE .The word *terev* (thou wilt increase) is in the heavy conjugation.[35] It is similar to the word *va-yefen* (and turned)[36] in *and turned tail to tail* (Judges 15:4). The

29. Literally, to generation.

30. Literally, to all he will come.

31. In other words *le-khol yavo* (literally, to all he will come) is to be interpreted as if written *le-khol asher yavo.*

32. **Yefet** ben Ali, a tenth century Karaite Bible commentator.

33. That God saved the psalmist from immense troubles.

34. So great were his troubles.

35. It is a *hifil.*

36. *Terev* is similar to *yefen*. They are both *hifils* in the shortened form.

statement *(Thou wilt increase) my greatness* is parallel to *Thou who hast done great things* (v. 19). The meaning of *comfort me* is, comfort me because of the troubles that passed over me.[37]

22. I ALSO WILL GIVE THANKS UNTO THEE WITH THE PSALTERY, EVEN UNTO THY TRUTH, O MY GOD; I WILL SING PRAISES UNTO THEE WITH THE HARP, O THOU HOLY ONE OF ISRAEL.

I ALSO… THY TRUTH. This[38] is Thy truth for which I am [39] obligated to give thanks.

23. MY LIPS SHALL GREATLY REJOICE WHEN I SING PRAISES UNTO THEE; AND MY SOUL, WHICH THOU HAST REDEEMED.

MY LIPS SHALL GREATLY REJOICE. The *dagesh* in the *nun* of *terannennah* (shall greatly rejoice) compensates for the missing third nun,[40] for *terannennah* comes from a double root.[41] The meaning of our verse is: When I sing praises to You with the harp, my lips and also my soul shall greatly rejoice. The psalmist mentions redeem in relation to the soul, because the soul rules the body.[42]

24. MY TONGUE ALSO SHALL TELL OF THY RIGHTEOUSNESS ALL THE DAY; FOR THEY ARE ASHAMED, FOR THEY ARE ABASHED, THAT SEEK MY HURT.

ALSO. I shall now sing with the harp. However, my tongue shall always tell of Your righteousness without employing a harp. Scripture therefore reads *also*. The psalmist says, *for they are ashamed, for*[43] *they are abashed.* The meaning of the aforementioned is; I shall rejoice because I do not fear.[44]

37. Lit. Over him.

38. What precedes.

39. Literally, the psalmist.

40. *Terannennah* is spelled with two *nuns*. The first *nun* is a root letter. The second *nun* is part of the pronominal suffix.

41. Its root is *resh, nun, nun.*

42. Thus if the soul is redeemed, so is the body.

43. Reading *ki* rather than *o*. Filwarg.

44. I will not fear my enemies because for they are ashamed and abashed. The meaning of our verse is, I will rejoice (*My tongue also shall tell of Thy righteousness all the day*) because I do not fear my enemies (*for they are ashamed, for they are abashed*).

CHAPTER 72

1. [A PSALM] OF SOLOMON. GIVE THE KING THY JUDGMENTS, O GOD, AND THY RIGHTEOUSNESS UNTO THE KINGS SON.

[A PSALM] OF SOLOMON. GIVE THE KING THY JUDGMENTS. This psalm is a prophecy by David[1] or one of the poets[2] regarding Solomon or the messiah. The letter *lamed*[3] [in li-shelomoh (of Solomon)] has the meaning of "because.[4]" It is like the *lamed* of *u-le-levi* (and of Levi) in *and of Levi he said* (Deut. 33:8),[5] for *Thy Thummim and Thy Urim* (ibid)[6] is directed to God.[7]
The psalmist begins his charge with "*Elohim* (God)"[8] because he next states *Thy judgments.*[9] *Give the king Thy judgments, O God* indicates that God gave the king[10] permission to execute God's judgments. *Thy righteousness* has a similar meaning. He[11] shall also be a righteous judge.[12] This is the meaning of *That he may judge* [*Thy people with righteous*] (v. 2). [13]

1. According to this opinion, King David composed this psalm.

2. According to this opinion, an anonymous poet composed this psalm.

3. Which usually has the meaning of "to."

4. Or regarding. According to this interpretation our psalm reads: [A psalm] regarding Solomon.

5. *U-le-levi* is to be rendered *and of Levi* not "and to Levi."

6. Which follows *u-le-levi* (and of Levi).

7. The *lamed* of *u-le-levi* (and of Levi) cannot be rendered as "to" for then the verse would open "And to Levi he said" and then go on to address God with *Thy Thummim and Thy Urim* etc. The latter is an impossible reading, for it does not tell us what Moses said to Levi.

8. Heb. *Elohim*. Our Psalm literally reads: *O God give the king Thy judgments.*

9. *Elohim* also means, judge. See I.E. on Gen. 1:1. Hence Scripture employs this name for the Lord here.

10. Solomon or the messiah.

11. Solomon or the messiah.

12. Reading *ve-she-yiheyeh* as in the standard printed texts, rather *she-yiyeh* as in the *Ha-Keter* edition.

13. In the printed texts "That he may judge (v. 2) has a similar meaning" opens I.E. comments on verse 2. It has been misplaced and belongs at the end of I.E.'s comments on verse 1.

2. [THAT HE MAY JUDGE THY PEOPLE WITH RIGHTEOUSNESS, AND THY POOR WITH JUSTICE.]

The princes and the wealthy overpower the poor. Scripture therefore reads: *And Thy poor with justice.*

3. LET THE MOUNTAINS BEAR PEACE TO THE PEOPLE, AND THE HILLS, THROUGH RIGHTEOUSNESS.

LET THE MOUNTAINS BEAR PEACE. The following is the meaning of our verse: When the king is a righteous judge then peace is multiplied in the land. *Mountains* refer to an uninhabited place. The meaning of *bi-tzedakah* (through righteousness) is, because of the righteousness, that is, because of the righteousness [of the king] the mountains and the hills shall bear peace. *Bi-tzedakah* is similar to *be-va'al pe'or* (because of Baal-peor)[14] (Deut. 4: 3).[15] Some say that *bi-tzedakah* is similar to *shalom* (peace).[16]

4. MAY HE JUDGE THE POOR OF THE PEOPLE, AND SAVE THE CHILDREN OF THE NEEDY, AND CRUSH THE OPPRESSOR.

MAY HE JUDGE? Our verse is similar to *Be Thou my judge, O God* (Ps. 43: 1).[17] [Its meaning is,] May God judge on behalf of the poor.[18] *The oppressor* refers to the one who takes his neighbor's wealth employing guile, seduction, and secrecy. Solomon in his great wisdom will recognize the oppressor.

5. THEY SHALL FEAR THEE WHILE THE SUN ENDURETH, AND SO LONG AS THE MOON, THROUGHOUT ALL GENERATIONS.

THEY SHALL FEAR THEE. When You[19] crush the oppressor, all oppressors will fear You.

14. Translated according to I.E.

15. *Bi-tzedakah* is similar to *be-va'al pe'or* (in Baal-peor) in that the *bet* prefixed to both words has the meaning of because.

16. The word *shalom* does not have a *bet* preceding it. *Bi-tzedakah* does. Now *Shalom* is parallel to *bi-tzedakah.* The *bet* of *bi-tzedakah* thus seems to be superfluous. Hence this interpretation believes that *bi-tzedakah* is to be read as *tzedakah.* This interpretation reads our verse as follows*: Let the mountains bear peace to the people, and the hills righteousness.*

17. The meaning of which is, execute judgment on my behalf. See I.E. on 43:1.

18. Literally, for them.

19. Lit. He.

The meaning of *im ha-shemesh*[20] (while the sun endureth) is all the days that the sun endures. The same is the case with *ve-lifne yare'ach*[21] (and so long as the moon). It is similar to *Who are crushed so long as Hyades endures* (lifne ash)[22] (Job 5:19).

6. MAY HE COME DOWN LIKE RAIN UPON THE MOWN GRASS, AS SHOWERS THAT WATER THE EARTH.

MAY HE COME DOWN LIKE RAIN. *May he come down* from his palace to the place of judgment. Or, may the judgment that the psalmist mentions in *May he judge the poor* (v. 4), come down.[23] Our verse is similar to *My doctrine shall drop as rain* (Deut. 32:2).[24] The word *gez* (mown grass) comes from a double root.[25] It is related to *li-gezoz* (to shear) (Gen. 31: 19) and *gizze (*mowing) in *the kings mowing* (Amos 7:1).

THAT WATER. The word *zarzif* (water) comes from a four-letter root.[26] It has no neighbor.[27] The meaning of *zarzif* is, saturate or satiate.

7. IN HIS DAYS LET THE RIGHTEOUS FLOURISH, AND ABUNDANCE OF PEACE, TILL THE MOON BE NO MORE.

FLOURISH. The rain[28] induces growth. Scripture therefore reads *let [the righteous] flourish*. Its meaning is, may the righteous multiply and abundance of peace flourish.[29] Or, may abundance of peace be in his days[30] till the moon be no more, that is, always.[31]

20. Lit. With the sun.

21. Lit. And before the moon. The meaning of *ve-lifne yare'ach* is, and so long as the moon endures.

22. Translated according to I.E.

23.This interpretation renders *yered* (may he come down) as, May it come down.

24. Both verses employ similar metaphors.

25. Its root is *gimel, zayin, zayin.*

26. Its root is *zayin, resh, zayin, peh.*

27. It is not found again in Scripture.

28. Mentioned in the previous verse.

29. This interpretation reads our verse as follows: In his days let the righteous flourish; and let abundance of peace [flourish] till the moon be no more. In other words the word *yifrach* (flourish) governs both *tzadik* (the righteous) and *rov shalom* (abundance of peace).

30. This interpretation reads our verse as follows: In his days let the righteous flourish and abundance of peace [be in his days] till the moon be no more.

31. *Till the moon be no more* means, always.

8. MAY HE HAVE DOMINION ALSO FROM SEA TO SEA, AND FROM THE RIVER UNTO THE ENDS OF THE EARTH.

MAY HE HAVE DOMINION. If the psalm speaks of Solomon then the meaning of *from sea to sea* is, from the Sea of Reeds to the Sea of the Philistines.[32] *The river* refers to the Euphrates and *the ends of the earth* to the wilderness.[33] Scripture mentions the width and breadth of the Land of Israel.[34] If the psalm speaks of the messiah then the "sea" refers to the Southern Sea that is known as the Red Sea. [*From sea to sea* means, from the Red Sea] to the North Sea, that is, the ocean.[35] *And from the river* refers to the river that comes out of Eden. This river is located where east begins.[36] *The ends of the world*[37] are located at the end of the west.[38]

9. LET THEM THAT DWELL IN THE WILDERNESS BOW BEFORE HIM; AND HIS ENEMIES LICK THE DUST.

LET THEM THAT DWELL IN THE WILDERNESS BOW BEFORE HIM. *Tziyyim* (wilderness) means, *them that dwell in the wilderness.*[39] However, in my opinion *tziyyim* means the owners of vessels,[40] for Scripture afterwards reads *tarshish ve-iyyim* (Tarshish and of the isles) (v. 10). The meaning of *iyyim* is the isles of the sea.[41] Rabbi Moses says that *iyyim* means those who dwell with the falcon (ayyah) in the wilderness. However, this is incorrect.[42]

32. The Mediterranean.

33. The boundaries of the land of Israel are given in Ex. 23:31. Scripture there states: "And I will set thy border from the Sea of Reeds even unto the sea of the Philistines, and from the wilderness unto the river."

34. In our verse.

35. The Atlantic.

36. The most eastern part of the earth's land mass.

37. Literally, *Unto the ends of the world.*

38. The most western part of the earth's land mass. According to this interpretation, our verse predicts that the messiah will rule over the entire world.

39. *Tziyyah* is a wilderness. *Tziyyim* thus could conceivably be translated as, those who dwell in the wilderness. Hence I.E.'s comment.

40. Compare, *tziy* (ship) in Is. 33:21. The word *tziyyim* means ships. However, ships do not bow. Hence I.E. renders *tziyyim*, the owners of ships.

41. Ships travel to isles.

42. The psalmist would not say, "The king of those who dwell with the falcon in wilderness shall render tribute," for what tribute can such a king offer?

The meaning of *yashivu* (shall render) is, they shall always render.[43] Compare, *and he rendered* (ve-heshiv) *unto the king of Israel* (2 Kings 3:4).[44] Others say that the meaning of *minchah yashivu* (shall render tribute) is; they shall render tribute at the turn[45] of each year.

10. THE KINGS OF TARHISH AND OF THE ISLES SHALL RENDER TRIBUTE; THE KINGS OF SHEBA AND SEBA SHALL OFFER GIFTS.

TRIBUTE. *Eshkar* means gifts.

11. YEA, ALL KINGS SHALL PROSTRATE THEMSELVES BEFORE HIM; ALL NATIONS SHALL SERVE HIM.

SHALL PROSTRATE. The psalmist first specifies the kings of Tarshish and Sheba. He then generalizes and states that all kings that are subservient to Tarshish and Sheba shall prostrate themselves before him.

12. FOR HE WILL DELIVER THE NEEDY WHEN HE CRIETH; THE POOR ALSO, AND HIM THAT HATH NO HELPER.

FOR. The following is its meaning: He shall judge the kings (v. 11). He shall also judge the nations (ibid). He will save the king who is poor with regard to another king.

13. HE WILL HAVE PITY ON THE POOR AND THE NEEDY, AND THE SOULS OF THE NEEDY HE WILL SAVE.

HE WILL HAVE PITY. He will have pity on the poor and the needy of the nations.

14. HE WILL REDEEM THEIR SOUL FROM OPPRESSION AND VIOLENCE, AND PRECIOUS WILL THEIR BLOOD BE IN HIS SIGHT.

FROM OPPRESSION. The work *tokh* (oppression) refers to oppression done in secret. *Chamas* (violence) is done in public. The word *chamas* is related to *nechmesu* (suffer vio-

43. *Yashivu* comes from the root *shin, vav, bet* which means to return, to repeat. Hence I.E.'s interpretation.

44. The verse does not speak of a one-time gift. It speaks of tribute that is given time after time.

45. The beginning.

lence) in *thy heels suffer violence* (Jer. 13:22). [The wicked oppress and injure them] even though they are needy.

AND PRECIOUS WILL THEIR BLOOD BE IN HIS SIGHT. The word *damam* (their blood) is similar to the word *damim* (blood) in *there shall be blood for him* (Ex. 22:2).[46] Its meaning is; they are precious in his eyes. He does not want them to be killed. Therefore Scripture goes on to say, *[That they may live ...]*

15. THAT THEY[47] MAY LIVE, AND THAT HE MAY GIVE THEM[48] OF THE GOLD OF SHEBA, THAT THEY[49] MAY PRAY FOR HIM CONTINUALLY, YEA, BLESS HIM ALL THE DAY.

THAT THEY[50] MAY LIVE.[51] That each one of them[52] may live. He will not only sustain him[53] but he will also enrich him.[54] The latter is the meaning of that *he may give them of the gold of Sheba*. All the poor will continually pray for him.[55]

16. MAY HE BE AS A RICH CORNFIELD IN THE LAND UPON THE TOP OF THE MOUNTAINS; MAY HIS FRUIT RUSTLE LIKE LEBANON; AND MAY THEY BLOSSOM OUT OF THE CITY LIKE GRASS OF THE EARTH.

MAY HE BE. *May he be* means may the poor be. The word *pissat* (rich) in *pissat bar* (a rich cornfield) is similar to the word *pas* (palm) in *palm of the hand* (Dan. 5:5). [The meaning of our verse is: May the poor be] as the palm of a hand sowing corn in the land

46. Translated literally. The word blood in Ex. 22:2 means bloodshed. So too here.

47. Lit., he.

48. Lit., him.

49. Lit. He.

50. Lit. He.

51. Hebrew, *vi-yechi*. I.E. renders *vi-yechi* as, he will sustain.

52. Each one of the poor and oppressed.

53. Each one of the poor and the oppressed.

54. Each one of the poor and the oppressed.

55. I.E. renders the first part of our verse as follows: He will sustain him (each one of the poor and oppressed) and give him (each one of the poor and oppressed) of the gold of Sheba. He (each one of the poor and oppressed) shall always pray for him.

or upon the top of the mountains. [*May his fruit rustle like Lebanon* means], the corn shall be huge and shall rustle like the trees of Lebanon.[56]

AND MAY THEY BLOSSOM OUT OF THE CITY. The word *me-ir* (out of the city) is to be rendered, in the city.[57] *Me-ir* is the reverse of *ba-basar u-va-lachem* (of the flesh and of the bread) (Lev. 8:32).[58]
Some say that the word *bar* (cornfield) is similar to the word *bor* (cleanness) in *according to the cleanness of my hands* (Ps. 18:21). This interpretation does not make sense. [59]

17. MAY HIS NAME ENDURE FOR EVER; MAY HIS NAME BE CONTINUED AS LONG AS THE SUN; MAY MEN BLESS THEMSELVES BY HIM; MAY ALL NATIONS CALL HIM HAPPY.

MAY HIS NAME ENDURE. The reference is to the name of Solomon or to the name of the messiah.[60]

BE CONTINUED. *Yinnon* (be continued)[61] is a *nifal.* It is similar to *yibbol* (shall fall down) (Is. 34: 4).[62] It is related to the word *nin* (posterity) (Is. 14:22). *Yinnon* means, he will bear fruit and multiply.

18. BLESSED BE THE LORD GOD, THE GOD OF ISRAEL, WHO ONLY DOETH WONDROUS THINGS.

BLESSED. Then all nations shall say: *Blessed be the Lord the God of Israel.* The meaning of *who only doeth wondrous things* is, who continually does [wondrous things] for Israel.[63]

---

56. I.E. explains our verse as follows: May the poor be as successful as a hand that sows and produces corn that is so large, that it rustles like the trees in Lebanon.

57. The letter *mem* prefixed to a word usually means *from.* Hence I.E. points out that here it means, *in.*

58. The *bet* prefixed to a letter usually has the meaning of "in." However, here it means "of" or "from." Thus Ps. 72:16 is the reverse of Lev. 8:32, for in our verse the *mem* has the meaning of the *bet,* while in Lev. 8:32 the *bet* has the meaning a *mem.*

59. It does not fit into the context of our verse.

60. *His name* refers to the name of Solomon or to the name of the messiah.

61. From the root *nun, vav, nun.*

62. A *nifal,* from the root *nun, bet, lamed.*

63. In other word, *doeth wondrous things* means, doeth wondrous things for Israel.

19. AND BLESSED BE HIS GLORIOUS NAME FOREVER; AND LET THE WHOLE EARTH BE FILLED WITH HIS GLORY. AMEN AND AMEN.

AND BLESSED. *His glorious name* refers to the glorious name [YHVH], which is God's proper name.[64] There is no proper name for the Lord in any of the languages. There are only adjectives such as the Lord, God and Almighty. Scripture states *this*[65] *is My name for ever* (Ex. 3:15) because it[66] alone is the name of God. Similarly, *and His name one* (Zech. 14:9).[67] The meaning of and *let the whole earth be filled with His glory* is, and let the whole earth be filled with His praise.[68]

AMEN AND AMEN. The word *amen* is related to the word *emunah* (faithfulness).

20. THE PRAYERS OF DAVID THE SON OF JESSE ARE ENDED.

ENDED. Some say that its meaning is, then[69] the prayers of the son of Jesse will be fulfilled.

Others say that the word *kallu* (ended) is related to the word *kalellu* (perfected) in *they have perfected thy beauty* (Ezek. 27:11). However, this is incorrect.

Rabbi Judah Ha-Levi says that the first author[70] wrote this,[71] because it is the end of the book. It similar to our practice of writing, "Blessed is He who gives strength to the weary." [72]

---

64. It refers to the grammaton.

65. *YHVH.*

66. *YHVH.*

67. In the future God will only be known by the name *YHVH.* Radak.

68. The world is also presently filled with God's glory. Hence what the psalmist means by, *And let the whole earth be filled by God's glory* is, a time will come when people will acknowledge that God's glory fills the world.

69. When the whole earth is filled with God's glory.

70. King David. Rabbi Judah Ha-Levi may be referring to King David as the first author because he believed that there are post Davidic psalms in this book. Indeed, very few of the psalms that follow have David's name attached to them.

71. The prayers of David the son of Jesse are ended.

72. See Is. 40:29.

BIBLIOGRAPHY

Ben-Menahem, N. *Ibn Ezra Studies* (Hebrew). Jerusalem: 1978

Cohen, Joseph. *Haguto Ha-Filosofit Shel Rabbenu Avraham ibn Ezra.* Israel: 1996.

Goldstein, David. *The Jewish Poets of Spain.* London:1965.

Filwarg, J. *Bene Reshef* [Supercommentary on Ibn Ezra's Commentaries on Scripture.] Piotrekow: 1900.

Fine Harry H., *Gems of Hebrew Verse.* Boston: 1940.

Fleisher J. L. *Avraham ibn Ezra, Kovetz Ma'amarim Al Toledotav Vi-Yitzirotav.* Tel Aviv: 1970.

Friedlander, M. *Essays on the Writings of Abraham Ibn Ezra.* London: 1877.

Friedlander, M. *The Commentary of Ibn Ezra on Isaiah.* London: 1873.

Golb, Norman. *History and Culture of the Jews of Rouen in the Middle Ages (Hebrew).* Tel Aviv: 1976

Goldstein, D. *The Jewish Poets of Spain.* Middlesex: 1965.

Gratz, Heinrich. *Divre Yeme Yisrael.* Translated by J.P. Rabinowitz. 1916.

Husik, I. *A History of Mediaeval Jewish Philosophy.* Phila: 1940.

Ibn Ezra, Abraham. *Commentary on Psalms.* Mikra'ot Gedolot.

Ibn Ezra, Abraham. *Commentary on Psalms.* Mikra'ot Gedolot; Ha-Keter. Israel: 2003.

Kahana David. *Rabbi Avraham ibn Ezra.* Warsaw: 1922.

Katz, Sarah. *Fair Verses of the Jewish Adalusian Poets (Hebrew).* Jerusalem: 1997.

Klatzkin, Jacob. *Otzar Ha-Munachim Ha-Filosofiyim.* Berlin: 1928.

Kook, Abraham Yitzchak . *Orot Ha-Kodesh, Musar Ha-Kodesh Vol. 11.* Jerusalem: 1990

Krinsky, J.L. *Chumash Me-Chokeke Yehudah.* New York: 1975.

Levin, I. *Abraham Ibn Ezra Reader (Hebrew).* New York-Tel Aviv: 1985

Melammed E.Z. *Mefareshe Ha- Mikra.* Jerusalem: 1978.

Sela, Shlomo. *Abraham Ibn Ezra And the Rise of Medieval Hebrew Science.* Boston: 2003.

Schmelzer, Menahem H. *Yitzhak ibn Ezra Shirim.* New York: 1979.

Shirman, Chaim. *Ha-Shirah Ha-Ivrit Bi-Sefarad U-Ve-Provance.* Jerusalem -Tel Aviv: 1956.

Simon Uriel, *Four Approaches to the Book of Psalms: From Saadiah Gaon to Abraham ibn Ezra.*

Translated By Lenn J. Schramm. New York: Press, 1991

Strickman, H. Norman. *The Secret of the Torah: A Translation of Ibn Ezra's Yesod Mora Ve-Sod Ha-Torah.*

New Jersey, 1995.

Ibn Ezra's Commentary on the Pentateuch (Genesis).

Translated & Annotated by H. Norman Strickman and Arthur Silver. New York : 1988

Ibn Ezra's Commentary on the Pentateuch (Exodus).

Translated & Annotated by H. Norman Strickman and Arthur Silver. New York:1996 -

Ibn Ezra's Commentary on the Pentateuch (Leviticus)

Translated & Annotated by H. Norman Strickman and Arthur Silver. New York: 2004.

Ibn Ezra's Commentary on the Pentateuch (Numbers)

Translated & Annotated by H. Norman Strickman and Arthur Silver. New York: 1999.

Ibn Ezra's Commentary on the Pentateuch (Deuteronomy)

Translated & Annotated by H. Norman Strickman and Arthur Silver. New York: 2001

Menorah Press, New York. 1999.

Ibn Ezra's Commentary on the Pentateuch (Exodus) Translated & Annotated

Menorah Press, New York. 1996 -

Ibn Ezra's Commentary on the Pentateuch (Genesis) *Translated & Annotated*

Menorah Press, *New York* - 1988

Waxman Meyer, *A History of Jewish Literature, Vol. 1,* (New Jersey, 1960)

Wilinsky, M. *Sefer Ha-Rikmah Le-Rabbenu Yoneh ibn Janah, Be-Targumo Shel Rabbenu Yehudah ibn Tibbon.*

Jerusalem: 1964.

INDEX OF NAMES

INDEX OF BIBLICAL SOURCES

2 Samuel

1 Kings

2 Kings

Isaiah

Psalms

Proverbs